BENEATH THE SURFACE

MY STORY

MICHAEL PHELPS

WITH BRIAN CAZENEUVE

FOREWORD BY BOB COSTAS

SPORTS
PUBLISHING

D0776015

Sports Publishing books may be purchased in bulk at special discounts for sales promotion, corporate gifts, fund-raising, or educational purposes. Special editions can also be created to specifications. For details, contact the Special Sales Department, Sports Publishing, 307 West 36th Street, 11th Floor, New York, NY 10018 or sportspubbooks@skyhorsepublishing.com.

Sports Publishing® is a registered trademark of Skyhorse Publishing, Inc.®, a Delaware corporation.

Visit our website at www.sportspubbooks.com

10 9 8 7 6

Library of Congress Cataloging-in-Publication Data is available on file.

Cover design by Brian Peterson
Cover photos courtesy of AP Images

ISBN: 978-1-68358-087-4
Ebook ISBN: 978-1-68358-088-1

Printed in the United States of America

C O N T E N T S

EDITOR'S NOTE

Few can imagine what it's like to set foot in an Olympic stadium, compete against the best of the best, win a medal, and break a record, much less win many medals and break countless records. Michael Phelps was on top of his game when *Beneath the Surface* was first published in 2004, just after he won a record-breaking eight medals (six golds and two bronzes) at the 2004 Olympics in Athens, and he admitted that he couldn't envision the coming years being more rewarding than those leading up to that moment. If the 2004 games had been the highlight of his career and he never competed again, he'd still be revered, honored, and remembered; yet now it's clear that he was just getting started, and that the medals, honors, and accolades would keep coming in.

All eyes were on the fresh-faced twenty-three-year-old swimmer from Baltimore when he made a grand return to the 2008 Olympics, ready to keep winning, this time in Beijing, China. Phelps had already made history at the U.S. Olympic Team Trials, where he competed in six individual events, broke two records, and put himself in the running to win eight gold medals in a single Olympics. Speedo, one of his sponsors, increased the stakes by promising their spokesman $1 million if he accomplished the feat.

As the events were underway, it became clear he could do it—win eight gold medals in a single Olympic Games, beating U.S. Olympian swimmer Mark Spitz's seven gold medal record set in 1972. When Phelps won his seventh gold medal by a hair, Spitz raved to the Associated Press: "Epic. It goes to show you that not only is this guy the greatest swimmer of all time and the greatest Olympian of all time, he's maybe the greatest athlete of all time.

He's the greatest racer who ever walked the planet." That seventh medal didn't come without a fight; Serbian rival Milorad Čavić, who contested the result, claimed he was the first one to touch the wall. Although Phelps was awarded first place, officials revealed a year later that though Čavić had actually finished first, Phelps had touched the wall with such great force that he registered a faster time. This controversy drew even more attention to the sport, and all eyes were on Phelps as he got ready for his final race. Čavić didn't hold a grudge; like all of Phelps' competitors, he was happy that he got to square off against the greatest swimmer, perhaps of all time, and was ecstatic to come so close to catching him in the water.

Many remember tuning in to watch Phelps' eighth race, the 4x100-meter medley relay with teammates Brendan Hansen, Aaron Peirsol, and Jason Lezak, and the electric excitement in the air that could be felt right through the television screen. At this point, coverage of the Beijing Games centered on Phelps; his name was familiar not only in the United States, but around the globe. In his usual pre-race routine, Phelps was listening to music on his headphones while focusing on the upcoming racing, and helping his relay team to secure a victory. The stakes were higher than ever before and the moments leading up to the event and the Americans' surprising victory would be talked about for weeks to come. It was Phelps who secured the win, as the team was in third place behind Australia and Japan when he jumped in to complete the third leg. Everyone watched as he finished the fastest butterfly split ever for that event (50.58 seconds), passing his opponents and giving Lezak a lead in the final leg that he was able to hold on to until the finish.

The Olympics brought in almost 1 billion more viewers that year than the Athens Games had. Undoubtedly, Phelps and athletes like him were the reason for this high surge of interest. People become fascinated with fierce competitors like Phelps who display good showmanship while obliterating their opponents. Since Phelps' debut in the 2000 Sydney Olympics until 2010, the USA Swimming governing body saw a twenty-four-percent increase in membership of year-round swimmers; many were no doubt inspired by Phelps' dedication and competitiveness. Perhaps due to his incredible, almost superhuman successes at the 2008 Games at Beijing, Phelps did come under suspicion, with skeptics claiming he had illegal substances in his system. Phelps, who had already signed up for Project Belief, in which U.S. Olympians choose to be tested for substances in their system, proved them all wrong by passing every test with a clean slate. Some might not want to believe that a man can achieve his level of athleticism by simply training, but Phelps owes his success to his resilient coach, an intense training schedule, a supportive family, and some beneficial physical attributes that give him the edge over his competition. His arm span is slightly longer than the length of his body, which helps propel his large torso and lean legs, while his oversized feet help him to accelerate. With these features, Phelps was meant to be a fish in the water, and his mental stamina has never failed him.

***

After the 2008 Olympics, Phelps once again was in a whirl-wind, doing interviews, attracting more sponsors, and touring the world. Using his $1 million bonus from Speedo, he started the Michael Phelps Foundation, with programs to teach children the importance of a healthy and active lifestyle. The foundation also strives to expand swimming as a sport and shows kids how to set goals for themselves.

At the same time, and unbeknownst to many, Phelps did contemplate retirement. He started missing some practices, many thought he didn't take his training as seriously as before, and he gained twenty-five pounds. In an interview in the August 2012 issue with *Details* magazine, he admitted that "At that point, I just didn't have anything. It was weird going from the highest of the high, the biggest point of your life—winning eight gold medals—and then saying, 'All right, where do I go from here?' I wasn't motivated. I did nothing, literally *nothing*, for a long time."

Having accomplished so much in such a short period of time and at such a young age, Phelps wasn't sure how to move forward after hitting the glass ceiling and seemingly achieving all he could in the sport; how many more records could he possibly break? What could elevate his career past a peak that he thought he already reached? If he lost belief in himself for a bit, his fans stayed supportive, admiring his resilience and not wanting to see him quit.

Phelps found himself in the middle of more controversy when photos surfaced of the athlete smoking marijuana several months after his return from Beijing. USA Swimming, the governing body for swimming in the United States, suspended Phelps from competitive swimming for three months, and the media speculated that many of his sponsors would not renew their contracts with him. The incident could have been the first of many—a result of his fame getting to his head or too much pressure resting on his shoulders—but he chose not to go down that path. While Kellogg's did cancel his endorsement deal, most of his sponsors stuck by him. Once again he proved that he could learn from his mistakes, recover, and continue competing at an even higher level.

At the 2009 National Championships he competed in only three events, yet won them all. Later that year, he won six medals (five golds, one silver) at the World Aquatics Championships in Rome, Italy. The following year, he once again beat many competitors at the National Championships, but lost to twenty-six-year-old Ryan Lochte in the 200-meter individual medley. This was the first time he had lost to Lochte, and it served to ratchet up their competitive rivalry.

In 2011, Phelps collected four golds, two silvers, and one bronze at the World Aquatics Championships, and seemed to be back in top form. When he went into the 2012 Olympic trials in Omaha, Nebraska, he initially wanted to try swimming in some different

Phelps swims the 200-meter butterfly at the 2012 Olympic trials in Omaha. (AP Photo/Mark Humphrey)

events, like swimming sprints, and didn't want to compete in eight events, as he had four years before. However, Coach Bob Bowman wanted him to enter his signature events, and he ended up qualifying for the same eight he did in Beijing. Headed to the London Olympics in July–August 2012, Phelps felt relaxed—"I just want to have fun," he told a reporter—and calmly confident. He also let on that these would be his last Olympics.

Since Phelps had already beaten the record for most medals won in a single Olympics, his next goal was to surpass Ukranian gymnast Larisa Latynina's record for most Olympic medals won ever. Latynina set the record during the 1950s and 1960s, winning eighteen medals. But things got off to a shaky start when Phelps placed fourth in the first race of the London Games, the 400-meter individual medley. This marked the first time he didn't win a medal for an event since the 2000 Olympics in Sydney. U.S. teammate and rival Ryan Lochte claimed the first gold medal for men's swimming, while Thiago Pereira of Brazil and Kosuke Hagino of Japan finished second and third respectively. Losing right out of the gate served as a wakeup call, as Phelps came back with a vengeance for the next race.

Those who started doubting that he'd be able to pull off the record-breaking feat were quickly proven wrong when he won silver with his teammates, Nathan Adrian, Cullen Jones, and Lochte, in the 4x100-meter freestyle relay the following day. This time Team USA lost the lead to the French in the last leg, despite a 47.15 leg from Phelps, the team's fastest. Now Phelps needed to win just one more medal to tie Latynina's all-time record.

On July 31, Phelps entered his signature event, the 200-meter butterfly. Many speculated he would get his first gold medal in this race, and they were almost correct. He dominated from the start, leading the pack for almost the entire race—almost. In the last three meters his strokes became inconsistent; he lost his advantage and was defeated by Chad le Clos of South Africa by two-tenths of a second. However, his silver medal put him on the podium for the eighteenth time, tying him for the most Olympic medals won ever, with four more events still to go.

That same day, Phelps managed to break the all-time record for total number of medals with the help of his teammates in the 4x200-meter freestyle relay. Ryan Lochte really delivered in the first leg, putting the team in first place. When Conor Dwyer was handed the lead he started to fall behind but was able to recapture the lead at the end of his leg, handing it off to Ricky Berens, who continued the charge. When Phelps hit the water, he was already at a huge advantage. He beat the French and Chinese, sporting a smile in the last few meters before he even finished the race, knowing that he had made history.

Latynina was gracious about Phelps' accomplishment, saying she was happy to see the American win, and describing Phelps as "the world's greatest Olympian."

"I have a normal human attitude towards the fact that finally a strong and talented athlete has emerged who overcame this record," said Latynina, who attended the Games as a guest of the International Gymnastics Federation.

"I would like him to keep this record for as long a period as possible," she said.

In the 200-meter individual medley, Phelps once again squared off against his teammate, Ryan Lochte. In true Michael Phelps fashion, he led every leg of the race, smoking the competition, and not only winning an unprecedented twentieth medal with a time of 1:54.27, but also becoming the first male swimmer to win the same individual event three consecutive times. His mom, Debbie, and sisters, Whitney and Hilary, were in the stands, cheering and crying tears of joy. Phelps, standing on the podium, uncharacteristically had teary eyes as well, while the U.S. national anthem was played.

The next day, on August 3, he competed in what at the time was

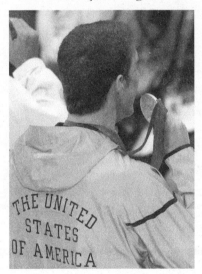

expected to be the last individual race of his career, the 100-meter butterfly. This time, he was in the back of the pack until the last 50 meters of the race, when he used his power to surge ahead of Clos and Evgeny Korotyshkin of Russia, who tied for silver. Having astounded spectators the day before by winning a "three-peat" of the 200-meter individual medley, he did it again with the 100-meter butterfly, while getting his seventeenth gold medal, hopping from one unprecedented feat to another like only he could. He won with a time of 51.21 seconds. Phelps still wasn't finished, though, with only the 4x100 meter medley relay remaining on the fol-

Phelps poses with his gold medal from the 100-meter butterfly race in London. At the time, it was expected to have been his last Olympic gold medal from an individual event, but he subsequently decided to come out of retirement for the 2016 Games in Rio. (AP Photo/ Julio Cortez) lowing day, which was expected to be the last race of his Olympic career. With Matt Grevers on backstroke, Brendan Hansen on breaststroke, Phelps in the butterfly, and Nathan Adrian in free-style, the American team had to win this for Phelps. As was the case many times before, they were behind until Phelps jumped in the pool and pulled out ahead on his second leg, giving the team a quarter second lead that they held onto to win gold—Phelps' eigh-teenth gold medal, and twenty-second medal overall. With a time of 3:29.35, they beat second-place Japan and third-place Australia by two seconds.

Phelps had not only made history for swimming in these Olympics, but for the Games as a whole. It's a tough feat to become the greatest competitor in one sport, but Phelps has earned legendary status; he's now often called the greatest athlete that has ever lived. Even with all eyes on him and the pressure on his shoulders in the 2012 Olympics, he seemed to be enjoying the events more than ever. Having started in his first Olympic event as a fifteen-year-old in 2000, the now more mature and calm twenty-seven-year-old Phelps took the time to soak in the Olympic experiences in London.

When the Games were over, Phelps planned to focus more on his foundation, his other philanthropic projects, and maybe a little bit of golf, but staying away from the thrill of competition would prove hard for the pro. In a July 2012 interview with the Associated Press, he contemplated, "It's been a part of my life for so long, so walking away will be weird, but it's something that I'm ready for. Eventually it will hit me and it will strike me that it is all over. Who knows what will happen then? I'll just take it all in steps and deal with it along the way."

Just after the London Olympics, he did indeed announce his retirement. Yet there are those who speculated that Phelps really wouldn't retire, that his intense competitive nature would draw him back in 2016. Their suspicions would prove correct when, in April 2014, Phelps announced that he would be coming out of retirement. Shortly after his announcement, Phelps told the

Charlotte Observer more about the reasoning behind his decision to return, "I'm doing it to have fun and because I love it. In Mesa [Arizona, where Phelps first un-retired in April], I felt like a kid down there swimming in a summer league meet. That's something I haven't had in awhile." The Mesa event marked the first time that he had competed in 18 months. Three weeks later, he captured first place in the 100-meter butterfly at the Charlotte Grand Prix with a time of 52.13. Highlights of that summer included his appearances at the 2014 U.S. Nationals and the Pan Pacific Championships. Though he faced tough competition from Tom Shields and Ryan Lochte, he nevertheless exerted his dominance in the pool. At the Pan Pac games, he was part of the winning 200-meter freestyle relay and 100-meter medley relay teams, and he also captured the 100-meter butterfly in 51.29. He left the Land Down Under with five medals in tow—including three gold and two silver—from six events. Phelps also ended up finishing the season with the world's fastest time in the 100-meter butterfly—51.17, which he achieved at the Nationals preliminaries.

However, what had initially been cause for celebration for Phelps' fans in seeing him return to the pool soon turned to concern when reports surfaced that he was arrested on the morning of September 30 for speeding, crossing the double yellow lines, and drunken driving. The events caused him to seek help from a rehab facility in Arizona. Phelps and others close to him have cited the positive effects that the 45 days in rehab had on him. "I wound up uncovering a lot of things about myself that I probably knew, but I didn't want to approach," he told *Sports Illustrated*, in a November 2015 profile.

That December, he was placed on 18 months' probation and received a one-year suspended sentence after pleading guilty to DUI. He also ultimately served a six-month suspension from USA Swimming events and was not able to compete in the 2015 World Championships either.

The year 2015 got off to a more promising start for Phelps, on both a personal and professional level. He and girlfriend Nicole Johnson, known by many as Miss California USA 2010, got engaged just a few months in.

"Her and I have been on and off for eight years," Phelps said. "It's been a long time. We've been through a lot. But I love her to death. We've been able to grow as a couple through everything we've been through, the positive changes I've made in my life."

He also completed his suspension from competitive swimming in April and publicly declared his intentions to compete for Team USA in the 2016 Summer Olympics in Brazil. "I am looking forward to next year. I don't think it's too hard to really realize why I came back," Phelps told the media. The return began with the Arena Pro Swim Series in Mesa, Arizona, where he won both the 100-meter butterfly and 100-meter freestyle events.

That summer, Phelps told the media of his intentions to stay sober through at least the 2016 Olympics and possibly beyond, "Before I even went to court, I said to myself that I'm not going to drink until after Rio—if I ever drink again. That was a decision I made for myself."

Perhaps the highlight of Phelps' 2015 swimming schedule took place in August at the U.S. National Championships held in San Antonio, Texas, where he placed first in three events—the 100-meter butterfly (50.45), the 200-meter butterfly (1:52.94), and the 200-meter individual medley (1:54.75). He posted 2015 world-best times in all three events.

"Maybe since 2008, I haven't felt this good swimming races back to back to back," Phelps said.

He continued his strong comeback through the end of the year, culminating in his performance at the Winter Nationals in Washington, where he once again won the 100- and 200-meter butterfly races, as well as the 200-meter individual medley.

The 2016 season began with the Arena Pro Swim Series in Austin, Texas, though most Phelps fans at this point were focused on the U.S. Olympic team trials at the end of June. In the interim,

Phelps and Johnson also welcomed a son, Boomer Robert Phelps, to the world in May.

"It's been an awesome, awesome, awesome few days. Probably—actually, not probably—100 percent probably the coolest experience that I've ever had, being able to welcome Boomer into the world with Nicole," Phelps said in a Facebook Live video.

Boomer was three months old when it came time to watch his dad on the biggest stage of all in Michael's return to the Olympics for his fourth showing. This time, Phelps, the most decorated athlete in the history of the Games, received the honor of carrying the U.S. flag during the opening ceremony in Rio. Two days later, on August 7, he returned to the pool as part of the U.S. 4x100-meter freestyle relay team that also included Caeleb Dressel, Ryan Held, and Adrian. Phelps, who swam the second leg, did so by posting the quickest 100-meter freestyle split of his storied career—47.12 seconds. Adrian finished the race with the fastest leg of the night—46.97 seconds of the U.S. team's 3:09.92 total time. France (3:10.53) and Australia (3:11.37) finished in second and third, respectively.

Despite the excitement that came with winning his nineteenth gold medal and twenty-third medal overall, Phelps did not have too much time to bask in the glory that accompanied the 4x100 race. Just two days later, he competed in two more events—the 200-meter butterfly and the 4x200-meter freestyle relay. In his first individual event of the Games, Phelps won by four one-hundredths of a second over Japan's Masato Sakai, the second-place finisher, in rather dramatic fashion.

Phelps had placed second in the event at the London Games and had been looking to redeem himself this time around.

"This is the race I really wanted back," he said.

Those watching will likely remember a number of post-race images, including that of Phelps holding up his finger once the scoreboard confirmed that he had indeed finished first. He then beckoned to the crowd with his hands and subsequently pumped his fist. Once out of the pool, he approached the stands to kiss

Phelps celebrates after his narrow victory in the 200-meter butterfly. (AP Photo/Michael Sohn)

Boomer and celebrate with his fiancée and his mother.

With his twentieth first-place Olympic finish in the books, Phelps set his sights on capturing the next race. He didn't have to wait long, as he ended up anchoring the winning 4x200-meter freestyle relay that same day. Teammates Conor Dwyer, Townley Haas, and Lochte built a lead for Phelps that he never relinquished, and the U.S. completed the race in 7:00.66. Britain and Japan followed in 7:03.13 and 7:03.50, respectively.

With three events complete and three more scheduled, the next event that Phelps set out to win was the 200-meter individual medley on August 11. The anticipation before this one was heightened due to the matchup between Phelps and his longtime rival Lochte. Though Lochte led after the first 100 meters of the race, Phelps ultimately gained the lead and finished in first place, nearly two seconds before Kosuke Hagino of Japan, who had won the 400-meter IM but took the silver in the 200-meter race. Lochte finished fifth in the event, and Phelps became the first Olympic swimmer ever to win his first four races at the same Games. It was his thirteenth individual Olympic gold, surpassing a record dating back to ancient Greece (152 B.C.), when Leonidas of Rhodes won twelve Olympic gold medals over the course of his career. In a gesture that indicates just how much Phelps' career transcended swimming, a replay of the 200 IM victory was shown on the screen in Baltimore, Phelps' hometown, at the Ravens-Carolina Panthers preseason football game.

Phelps' gold-medal streak would come to an end the next day though, with the 100-meter butterfly. Singapore's Joseph Schooling, who posted a remarkable time of 50.39, faster than all of Phelps' first-place finishes in the event at the previous three Olympic Games, would prove to be the spoiler. Phelps finished in a three-way tie for second with Hungary's Laszlo Cseh and South Africa's Chad le Clos, with a time of 51.14.

Phelps reaches up to kiss 3-month-old Boomer after his victory in the 200-meter butterfly event. (AP Photo/ Matt Slocum)

The next day, in what is expected to be the last race of Phelps' Olympic career, Ryan Murphy began the 4x100-meter medley relay for Team USA with a record-breaking 100-meter backstroke. Cody Miller followed with the breaststroke before Phelps joined for his butterfly leg. He regained the lead for the U.S., and Adrian sealed the deal with the freestyle leg. The group completed the race in 3:27.95, ahead of Great Britain (3:29.24) and Australia (3:29.93).

"It's just a perfect way to finish," Phelps said.

Now with twenty-eight Olympic medals in tow, including twenty-three gold medals, Phelps' tears after his last race seemed to represent the emotional, yet absolutely dominant, career that it's been.

"I'm just ready for something different," he told NBC after his final race. "My swimming career might be over, but I have the future ahead of me to turn the page and start whenever I want. It's not the end of a career. It's the beginning of a new journey."

Reports have speculated that a focus on his family and perhaps some time mentoring younger swimmers—amongst other duties—will take the place of the hours he spends training in the pool. Yet others argue that he came out of retirement once and just may do so again for the Tokyo Games in 2020. Regardless of what the future holds for Michael Phelps, though, his twelve-year dominance in the Olympic pool will serve as an era in its own right and one that will be extremely difficult to surpass for swimmers and athletes around the world.

—August 2016

MICHAEL PHELPS
MEDAL COUNT

2004 ATHENS OLYMPICS– six gold medals, two bronze medals

Aug. 14 – 400-meter individual medley
Gold – Phelps (4:08.26)
Silver – Erik Vendt (USA/4:11.21)
Bronze – László Cseh
 (Hungary/4:12.15)

Aug. 15 – 4x100-meter freestyle relay
Gold – South Africa (3:13.17)
Silver – Netherlands (3:14.36)
Bronze – USA (3:14.62)

Aug. 16 – 200-meter freestyle
Gold – Ian Thorpe (Australia/1:44.71)
Silver – Pieter van den Hoogenbad
 (Netherlands/1:45.23)
Bronze – Phelps (1:45.32)

Aug. 17 – 200-meter butterfly
Gold – Phelps (1:54.04)
Silver – Takashi Yamamoto
 (Japan/1:54.56)
Bronze – Stephen Parry (Great
 Britain/1:55.52)

Aug. 17 – 4x200-meter freestyle relay
Gold – USA (7:07.33)
Silver – Australia (7:07.46)
Bronze – Italy (7:11.83)

Aug. 19 – 200-meter individual medley

Gold – Phelps (1:57.14)
Silver – Ryan Lochte (USA/1:58.78)
Bronze – George Bovell (Trinidad and
 Tobago/1:58.80)

Aug. 20 – 100-meter butterfly
Gold – Phelps (51.25)
Silver – Ian Crocker (USA/51.29)
Bronze – Andriy Serdinov
 (Ukraine/51.36)

Aug. 21 – 4x100-meter medley relay
Gold – USA (3:30.68)
Silver – Germany (3:33.62)
Bronze – Japan (3:35.22)

2008 BEIJING OLYMPICS – eight gold medals

Aug. 10 – 400-meter individual medley
Gold – Phelps (4:03.84)
Silver – László Cseh
 (Hungary/4:06.16)
Bronze – Ryan Lochte (USA/ 4:08.09)

Aug. 11 – 4x100-meter freestyle relay
Gold – USA (3:08.24)
Silver – France (3:08.32)
Bronze – Australia (3:09.31)

Aug. 12 – 200-meter freestyle
Gold – Phelps (1:42.96)
Silver – Park Tae–Hwan (South

Korea/1:44.85)

Bronze – Peter Vanderkaay
(USA/1:45.14)

Aug. 13 – 200-meter butterfly
Gold – Phelps (1:52.03)
Silver – László Cseh (Hungary/1:52.70)
Bronze – Takeshi Matsuda
(Japan/1:52.97)

Aug. 13 – 4x200-meter freestyle relay
Gold – Phelps (6:58.56)
Silver – Russia (7:03.70)
Bronze – Australia (7:04.98)

Aug. 15 – 200-meter individual medley
Gold – Phelps (1:54.23)
Silver – László Cseh (Hungary/1:56.52)
Bronze – Ryan Lochte (USA/1:56.53)

Aug. 16 – 100-meter butterfly
Gold – Phelps (50.58)
Silver – Milorad Čavić (Serbia/50.59)
Bronze – Andrew Lauterstein
(Australia/51.12)

Aug. 17 – 4x100-meter medley relay
Gold – USA (3:29.34)
Silver – Australia (3:30.04)
Bronze – Japan (3:31.18)

2012 LONDON OLYMPICS – four gold
medals, two silver medals

July 28 – 400-meter individual medley
Gold – Ryan Lochte (USA/4:05.28)
Silver – Thiago Pereira (Brazil/4:08.86)
Bronze – Kosuke Hagino (Japan/4:08.94)

Phelps places fourth (4:09.28)

July 29 – 4x100-meter freestyle
Gold – France (3:09.93)
Silver – USA (3:10.38)
Bronze – Russia (3:11.41)

July 31 – 200-meter butterfly
Gold – Chad le Clos (South
Africa/1:52.96)
Silver – Phelps (1:53.01)
Bronze – Takeshi Matsuda
(Japan/1:53.21)

July 31 – 4x200-meter freestyle relay
Gold – USA (6:59.70)
Silver – France (7:02.77)
Bronze – China (7:06.30)

Aug. 2 – 200-meter individual medley
Gold – Phelps (1:54.27)
Silver – Ryan Lochte (USA/1:54.90)
Bronze – László Cseh
(Hungary/1:56.22)

Aug. 3 – 100-meter butterfly
Gold – Phelps (51.21)
Silver – Chad le Clos (South
Africa/51.44)
Bronze – Evgeny Korotyshkin (Russian
Federation/51.44)

Aug. 4 – 4x100-meter medley relay
Gold – USA (3:29.35)
Silver – Japan (3:31.26)
Bronze – Australia (3:31.56)

2016 Rio Olympics – five gold medals, one silver medal

Aug. 7 – **4x100-meter freestyle relay**
Gold – USA (3:09.92)
Silver – France (3:10.53)
Bronze – Australia (3:11.37)

Aug. 9 – **200-meter butterfly**
Gold – Phelps (1:53.36)
Silver – Masato Sakai (Japan/1:53.40)
Bronze – Tamás Kenderesi
   (Hungary/1:53.62)

Aug. 9 – **4x200-meter freestyle relay**
Gold – USA (7:00.66)
Silver – Great Britain (7:03.13)
Bronze – Japan (7:03.50)

Aug. 11 – **200-meter individual medley**
Gold – Phelps (1:54.66)
Silver – Kosuke Hagino (Japan/1:56.61)
Bronze – Wang Shun (China/1:57.05)

Aug. 12 – **100-meter butterfly**
Gold – Joseph Schooling
   (Singapore/50.39)
Silver – Phelps (51.14); Laszlo Cseh
   (Hungary/51.14); Chad le Clos (South
   Africa/51.14)

Aug. 13 – **4x100-meter medley relay**
Gold – USA (3:27.95)
Silver – Great Britain (3:29.24)
Bronze – Australia (3:29.93)

FOREWORD

Not too long ago, at an NBC Olympics event in New York, I walked into a back room where a few people were milling around, and Michael Phelps was seated on a small couch. In front of him, on a coffee table, was a large, empty pizza box. Phelps was downing the last morsels, so I waited a moment before confirming my suspicion.

"Michael, did you eat that whole pizza by yourself?" I asked.

His smile, framed by some lingering crumbs on the sides of his mouth, was a mixture of sheepishness and pride.

"Yeah," he said. "I housed it."

Okay, I know Olympic athletes in training burn ridiculous amounts of carbs and calories. But still. . . .

As he turns 23, Michael Phelps is a peculiar combination of a typical American young man and thoroughly extraordinary American athlete. Sure, he's already well on his way to becoming the most decorated Olympian ever, and he might only be halfway through his career. But in the handful of times we've met over the past several years, what's struck me as much as the superhuman aspects of him is the normal stuff. The kid from Baltimore raised by his single mom and older sisters. The football fan who goes to a bar in a purple jersey every Sunday in the fall when he's training in Ann Arbor to watch his hometown Ravens (cleaning out the kitchen of chicken wings, mozzarella sticks, and potato skins by halftime, I'm guessing). The video game fanatic who has to schedule his day around his housemate: an English bulldog named Herman.

Maybe what accentuates Phelps' normalcy on dry land are the freakish gifts he has when water is involved. We've heard and read a lot about how Phelps was born to swim—how his elongated torso, large feet, and massive hands are a racer's dream combination. But to understand what makes him so phenomenally successful, you have to know the level of his dedication. In the year leading up to the Athens Games, Phelps took just one day off from training—that includes weekends—and it was the day his wisdom teeth were removed. In the four years since his dominance in Greece, his coach says he's somehow found a way to step up the intensity another notch. Like Michael Jordan and Tiger Woods, two athletes he's sometimes compared to, Phelps has the most talent. But like that esteemed pair, he wins so often because he understands that while talent is huge, hard work takes it to other levels. And also because, like Jordan and Woods, he loves nothing more than competing, and hates nothing more than losing.

Since he last was on the Olympic stage, Phelps' life has been, sure enough, a combination of the normal and the remarkable. He's made a wrong turn or two, but afterwards, he's taken full responsibility. He talks about what he's learned from those missteps in this update to his book. Meanwhile, in the pool, while you may have been turned away, he's set eight more world records and counting, won 12 more gold medals at the World Championships, and done everything he can to put himself in position for his monumental goal in Beijing: eight events, eight gold medals. It would be the greatest achievement in the history of the Games.

As Phelps himself might put it, he's looking to "house" the Olympics.

I'm not going to bet against him. That pizza box was empty, but it sure looked like he had room for more.

—Bob Costas, June 2008

ACKNOWLEDGMENTS

To Mom, Coach Bob,
and in memory of Gran and Stevie

This is the fourth edition of my book. I want to thank everyone I mention throughout the book and those who were mentioned in the previous editions. I would also like to acknowledge a few people who have been and continue to be an instrumental part of my life.

Mom, there really isn't anything I can put into words. You are the best. I cannot thank you enough for everything you have done for me and continue to do—none of this would be possible without you. To my sisters Hilary and Whitney, for letting me follow you around as a little brother, giving me space and support as I grow, and for accepting me for who I am now (even if that includes forgetting to call you back). To my new brother-in-law, Bob, welcome to our family; to my niece, Taylor, and nephew, Connor, I look forward to watching you grow; to Gran, who taught me so many lessons and who I miss every day; to my dad, Fred, for the take-no-prisoners attitude I bring with me to the starting blocks; to Uncle BJ, Aunt Krista, Uncle David, Aunt Dee Dee, Uncle David, and Aunt Amy, Sara, Andrew, and everyone in our extended but close family.

Thanks to my coach, Bob Bowman, the world's greatest swim coach, who has guided me in and out of the water and who I couldn't have accomplished any of this without. Thanks for seeing my dreams before I did. To Eddie Reese and Mark Schubert, my head Olympic coaches; to Tom Himes for showing me how much fun swimming can be; to Murray Stephens, for creating an environment where any dream is possible; to Cathy Lears, John Cadigan, and the supporting families at the NBAC, one of the best swim clubs in the nation; to Jon Urbanchek for helping me laugh while at Michigan; to Club Wolverine including Fernando Canales, for letting me be a part of your team; to MoJo Isaac and Stefanie Kerska, for helping with the transition to Michigan; to Keenan Robinson, for doing his best to keep me healthy for four years; to Greg Harden, for listening and helping me grow up; and to Bill Martin, Go Blue! I'll miss the Big House.

To the Hansen family: Steve, Betsy, Gracie, and, of course, Stevie, who continues to be my inspiration and will always be part of my life.

Thank you to Octagon for helping me grow the sport of swimming: to Peter Carlisle for taking on challenges (including racing me in Beijing in 2007), being a great agent, and a caring and understanding friend (and to the Carlisle family—Justine, Aidan, who at seven has an amazing underwater dolphin kick, and Kenny, who loves the water—for sharing so much of Peter's time); to Marissa Gagnon, aka Bubbles, for somehow managing to keep everything together for me and making me feel like I'm working with family; to Drew Johnson for his "unbelievable" commitment and for supporting me as I grow in the public eye; to Frank Zecca for keeping my financial life balanced, which is often not an easy task.

To Mike Unger, for always being there when I needed you; to the staff of USA Swimming, USOC, NBC, and IOC for everything you do for the spirit of the Games; to all my USA teammates for giving your best for our country.

To Dick Ebersol, thank you for your support, guidance, and belief in the sport of swimming, passion for the Olympics, and the personal relationship we have developed along the way.

To my partners at the Pathfinders for Autism, Johns Hopkins Children's Center, Boys and Girls Clubs of America, and Sport Legends Museum at Camden Yards; to Baltimore County Public Schools, especially my teachers that understood my dream.

To my sponsors: AT&T, Hilton, Kellogg's, Omega, PowerBar, PureSport, Rosetta Stone, Speedo, and VISA.

Thanks to Brian Cazeneuve of *Sports Illustrated* for his continued dedication to help me share my story as it is an ongoing journey.

To Peter Sawyer, the agent for *Beneath the Surface*; Dean Miller and Doug Hoepker, the editors on the book; Courtney Leeper and Noah Amstadter for all of their hard work.

To the city of Baltimore, home of the Ravens, I am looking forward to my return. Lastly, thanks to everyone who supports the great sport of swimming!

1

MY OWN MIRACLE

The night before my first Olympic race in Athens, I could see myself in a movie. Hold on, it isn't as fun as it sounds. I was in my room at the Olympic village, watching *Miracle*, the story about the 1980 U.S. hockey team. I had watched the movie twice before, and there was one scene that really hit home. About four months before the team won the gold medal in Lake Placid and inspired the whole country, it played an exhibition game in Norway that the players never forgot. The Americans tied that night, but the listless way they played enraged their head coach, Herb Brooks. After the game was over and the players figured they'd have time to rest, Brooks made them skate from one end of the ice to the other, no matter how tired they were. After they finished one round, he'd blow his whistle and shout out, "Again." And away they'd go. "Again." The players were gasping for air. "Again." The players were falling over from exhaustion. "Again." Soon one of the workmen came by and turned off the lights in the arena, but Brooks wasn't satisfied. "Again." After a few dozen "agains," Coach Brooks finally let the players go back to their locker rooms, and they knew after that, no matter what the score, it was his job to drive them until they gave their best effort. They knew that no matter what obstacle they faced at the Olympics, even a game against the seemingly unbeatable Soviets, they had already overcome something more difficult—that night of endless "agains." They may have hated Brooks for it at the time, but how could they have been that good without him?

Fast forward 24 years to a pool at the North Baltimore Aquatic Club. It was a Friday in February 2004, a day that was supposed to mean a light workout of about 5,000 easy yards. That's almost three miles, which for us is almost a day off. Instead it was the day Herb Brooks reappeared as my coach, Bob Bowman. We started doing these kicking drills: 75 yards of kicking only, at full speed, followed by 50 yards easy. After a couple of those, you start to feel a burn in your legs, so they get a little wobbly as you get out of the pool. But do enough of them, and your legs get stronger and you're able to kick harder and more efficiently during competitions. We were supposed to do eight sets of these drills, but apparently we didn't do them very well. "C'mon, get it right," I remember Bob saying that day. So eight sets became ten. "No loafing," Bob shouted. And we were up to 12. "If you're not serious, why show up?" Fifteen and counting. "I said full speed." Eighteen. You know, when Bob gets really angry, there's a vein in the right side of his neck that just gets bigger and more pronounced. By the time we were on our 24th set, his vein looked like a second neck.

When I got out of the pool that day, you could have twirled up my legs and put tomato sauce on them because they felt like spaghetti. That was a serious burn. Could even the Olympics be this hard? The movie resonated with me because without all the hard work they put in, without a few days of spaghetti legs, the U.S. hockey players would never have been capable of their miracle. They worked at it. They needed someone to push them. They needed to push themselves. They became a family. They grew up. They understood that commitment—real commitment you never knew you could make—comes before winning. And they could never have done it alone. At the Olympic Village the night before the biggest meet of my life, I fell asleep to *Miracle*.

❋❋❋

I woke up the next morning at 7 a.m. and I had never been so pumped for anything in my life. Usually I get fidgety when I'm in the middle of the most intense part of my training. As I get closer to a big meet, I relax and get laid back, because the hard work is done and the fun part, the thrill of competition, is in front of me. On the first Saturday of competition, I couldn't wait to get back in the water. I had the 400-meter individual medley that day, with the top eight swimmers from the morning heats advancing to the evening finals. Before the morning swim, I followed the routine Bob had meticulously planned for me: I ate a light oatmeal breakfast, stretched for half an hour exactly two hours before the race, did 35 minutes of drills and light swimming, relaxed up to half an hour before the event, put on the racing suit, took a light swim ten minutes before and then got on the blocks to race. Bob has the internal stopwatch of a mad scientist. If daily plans are off by minutes or if split times are off by hundredths of seconds, the vein starts popping and the lungs start shouting. He doesn't want anything to be random.

Bob and I didn't say much about the morning prelim, which was a good sign. I had the fastest time in the heats and I was considered the favorite to win that night. A year earlier I won the 400 IM at the World Championships in Barcelona in world-record time. With a possible eight events staring at me, Bob and I both thought it was a good thing that the final of the 400 IM, a "safe" race, was ahead of me on the first night.

Between sessions, I talked briefly to Erik Vendt, the other U.S.

swimmer in the race. Erik and I had talked about finishing one-two as we had at the Olympic Trials the previous month in Long Beach. Unfortunately, he didn't swim that well in the morning and barely qualified for the final, in eighth position. "Forget about it," I told him. "This wasn't you and you know that. We'll get 'em tonight."

An hour later I was back at the village, hoping to rest and try-ing to figure out why I couldn't mash my pillow into the right shape. Usually, I'm so spent after being in the water, I fall asleep like a rock and you can give me a gold medal for power napping. No luck that day. I stared at the ceiling in my room for two solid hours. Try telling a kid to fall asleep on Christmas Eve. Can't do it. The anticipation is way too intense, except that this wasn't some-thing I'd been waiting for since last December 26; I had been wait-ing for this for as long as I can remember having goals. One gold medal. That's what I thought about since 1992, the year I realized I could swim. Every time reporters asked me about tying or break-ing Mark Spitz's record of seven gold medals at one Olympics, I'd keep reminding them that it was my dream to win one gold medal. Maybe that's why I couldn't shut my eyes that afternoon—my dream was in front of me, hours away. There are times in my sleep when I literally dream my race from start to finish. Other nights, when I'm about to fall asleep, I visualize to the point that I know exactly what I want to do: dive, glide, stroke, flip, reach the wall, hit the split time to the hundredth, then swim back again for as many times as I need to finish the race. It's pretty vivid the first time I do it, but eventually it puts me to sleep as if I'm counting sheep. But two hours of visualization! Know what happens when you stare at a ceiling for two hours? It's still the same ceiling. Get me out of here. I want to swim again.

At 4:30 an overflow of athletes and coaches started pushing their way to get on the bus to take us to the swim stadium. "Michael, be aggressive. Move up towards the door," Bob prod-ded. "Need to make this one or we're behind schedule." At that point I turned around and snapped. "What can I do? There's nothing I can do about it! Everyone's leaving at the same time, okay?" Bob and I made the bus, but we didn't talk when we were inside. He knew I was nervous, wound tighter than he'd ever seen me before a race.

I went through the same warmup at the pool and the minutes before the race went by pretty slowly. Finally I walked onto the deck with Eminem's "Til I Collapse" blaring on my headphones. I'm a huge hip-hop fan, and for the last year I've listened to that song before each race. I won't repeat all the words, but it begins like this:

> Sometimes you feel tired, feel weak
> When you feel weak, you feel like you wanna just give up
> But you gotta search within you, find that inner strength.

I toweled off the block in my lane, Lane 4, took the headphones off, and stretched my legs against the block, right leg first and left leg second. On the blocks I have a ritual of bending down, reaching my arms above my head and swinging them back down three times across my chest very fast. Then I get into a track start (one leg behind the other), wait for the loud beep, and go.

As I jumped into the pool, Rowdy Gaines, an Olympic champion from 1984 and an NBC analyst in Athens, was telling his audience, "This event is going to introduce America to Michael Phelps." The 400 IM consists of 100 meters, or two poollengths, of each stroke; butterfly, backstroke, breaststroke and freestyle. My plan for the race was pretty straightforward: take as big a lead as I could—two bodylengths, if possible—before the breaststroke, which is my weakest stroke. Bob wanted me to stay just ahead of my record pace without blasting it too fast.

My butterfly split, 55.57 seconds, put me ahead of the 55.66 I swam at the Olympic Trials in Long Beach a month earlier when I broke the world record. I didn't actually know the time, but I felt very strong.

I have a habit of looking up at the clock during the backstroke, because I can face the scoreboard. I knew I was on target, and I could feel that I was starting to pull away from the swimmers next to me by the two bodylengths I'd wanted.

The breaststroke leg always seems to take forever. Since your hands aren't supposed to break the surface of the water, it takes about ten seconds longer to swim 100 meters in the breaststroke than it does, for example, in the freestyle. I got through it without losing much of my lead. I was 100 meters away.

When I came off the last wall with 50 meters to go, I looked to my left and saw Italy's Alessio Boggiatto approaching the wall in Lane 3. Then I looked to my right and saw Hungary's Laszlo Cseh just getting to the wall in Lane 5. Since the people who swim the fastest in the heats get the middle lanes in the finals, those swimmers can usually keep a close eye on their competition. At that point I knew I was about to win the gold medal I'd been thinking about, talking about, even dreaming about, for most of my life. I smiled through the water for the last 25 meters. I rarely do that during practice unless someone cracks me up in the middle of easy laps, and I *never* do that during a race. That night I remember smiling as I glided into the wall.

Immediately after every race I look up and try to find my mom, Debbie, in the stands. It isn't just because she's been there for all my meets, but because she's been there for everything else. She raised me as a single parent since I was seven and supported me unconditionally through everything, not just at moments when I was smiling at the ends of my races. So before I looked at the scoreboard, I looked up and saw my mom standing next to my sisters, Whitney and Hilary, who were all cheering. After that, I glanced at the clock and saw the WR, signifying world record, next to my name. I put my arm in the air, but I was in a trance. Even though I had been ahead in the race, it still didn't sink in that I had won until I looked up and saw the #1 next to my name. I was waiting for that switch to go off, so I could let my emotions go. The switch came from Lane 1. "Mike! Mike!" It was Erik, swimming over across the lane lines to get me. I hadn't even noticed that he had finished second. We went one-two. "Yeah, Vendt, yeah," I shouted. "Yeah, we did it."

At that moment I was as happy for Erik as I was for myself. He had won a silver, behind our teammate, Tom Dolan, four years earlier at the Sydney Olympics. Nobody worked harder or deserved his medal more than Erik. Our team book lists him at about 5-10, but that's pretty generous. He doesn't have the physical gifts that other swimmers have, but he just works harder than other people. I never thought I'd celebrate like that with a Red Sox fan, but something like this is twice as sweet when you can share it with your teammates.

"Yah, Vendt, we did it!" Erik and I hugged and got out of the pool. I was still in a fog when we passed the mixed zone, an area underneath the stands where reporters stand behind some barriers and ask quick questions. I was too giddy to remember what I said. Bob caught up to me then and handed me an instant breakfast drink. As much energy as I expend, I need to try to keep weight on and keep nutrients in my body after races and long training days. "So proud of you," he said. "It felt great," I told him.

At that point, Bob was trying to get me back into the practice pool as fast as possible, so I could swim down and get some of the lactic acid out of my legs. Especially with three more races the next day, a warm down at the end of a race was as important as a warm-up before one.

After our events, we have to go into doping control. While we don't have to go right away, we always have to check in with a drug control steward and sign a form right after that race to confirm that we've been notified to be tested. That night, the steward came up to me and started talking in slow motion. "Mee-ster Phelps, you have, you've been, I tell you have been see-lec-ted for the doh-ping control. You may take, you have the op-shun, Mee-ster Phelps, to have, if I may ex-plain." At that point, Bob jumped in. "Just give him the paper and have him sign it." Now, Bob was the one who was wound up. It's his job to keep me grounded through the highs and lows, but this was a tough one. It was as big a high as I've ever felt. I got into the practice pool behind the stands and started swimming, still smiling through the water. Another official came over to tell Bob to get me ready for the medal ceremony. "We need your swimmer in five minutes," they told him.

"The schedule says it's not for 20 minutes," Bob said.

"Yes, but they must wait . . . "

"Sorry, you'll get him in 15."

The medal ceremony was awesome. I had stood on podiums before, but I had never won an Olympic medal, and this one was over too quickly. We were introduced and given our medals. Then, to honor the ancient Games in Greece, they gave us wreaths to wear on top of our heads during the ceremony. We didn't know they were planning to do that, and we were a little unsure what to do once our music started playing. I took the wreath off my head and put it over my heart.

My mom had always taught me to try to keep calm in the face of tension and excitement. I was singing the anthem through my teeth and trying not to lose my composure at the same time. As I stared at the flags, I could see snapshots of a kid from Baltimore who was afraid of the water and a schoolteacher who said the kid wouldn't amount to anything because he couldn't concentrate. I saw a coach driving the kid through 24 laps and a family who supported him through everything. Was I really that kid standing on up here? At "Home of the Brave," I closed my eyes, almost as if I were snapping one more picture I could look at again and again in my mind.

I started walking with Erik past a photographers' well, where we stood and posed for pictures. I was looking up into the stands at Hilary, who was shooting me with a camcorder. I looked up and saw Dolan, who usually says things twice when he gets a little excited. "Yah, yah, yah, yah, great, great, great," he screamed, apparently hyper-excited. At that point, my mom passed by and I threw my flowers up to her in the stands before I went back to the practice pool.

I swam down for 45 minutes, had a massage and got on the cell phone with Hilary. "Where are you guys?" I asked her. "We're over by a fence, behind you, and they're going to kick us out." "Hold on," I told her. "I want to see you guys." A minute later, I saw my mom and my sisters waving at me through the fence. I hoisted myself up to kiss Whitney and Hilary. Then they each held a small cement box in place for my mom to step up and do the same. Thankfully, the guards gave us our space. We were away from the hoard of reporters, and I didn't have to keep my emotions in check because Hilary was the only one taking pictures. The spotlight was gone and it was our moment. I put my wrists through the holes in the fence so my mom could hold my hands. Next I pointed to the medal and said, "Mom, look. Here it is." Then I put the medal in her hand so she could hold it. My eyes welled up again and so did hers. It was one of those moments when you want to say a million things because so much is running through your head. Yet for some reason, you say almost nothing. I'm sure I said more than, "I did it, Mom. I did it," but I was too semiconscious to remember much else.

"Hello, how's it going, everyone?" a voice said. Okay, I was conscious again. It was Bob. He had been standing on the side, letting us savor the occasion, but now there was work to do.

"Michael, you have a press conference, a drug test, and a lot of work to do tomorrow."

Even at a time like this, Bob always thought about tomorrow and the next challenge. He never let me look back during the entire Olympics.

So I'll do it now.

2

CLOSE CALLS

My mom knew she'd have her hands full from the moment I was born on June 30, 1985. At nine pounds and six ounces, I was probably destined to run her into the ground. I can't say I was accident prone as a child, because a lot of things happened without my control. Other things happened because I was restless and had to get into everything. Whatever it was, if it was breakable, I usually found it, so let's just say I was incident prone.

I was two years old on Christmas Eve in 1987. I started developing a fever that kept getting worse. My parents called my pediatrician who told them to get me to an emergency room right away. My dad, Fred, was a Maryland State trooper, so he put me into his police car and started flying toward Franklin Square Hospital, 45 minutes away from our house in Whiteford, Maryland. He flashed his lights and blared his siren and got me there just in time for them to diagnose a pretty serious viral infection that was lowering my white blood cell count, sapping my strength and driving up my temperature to 104. The doctor told my parents afterward that if the infection hadn't been treated within a few hours, I probably wouldn't have pulled through. The stopwatch was important in my life even then.

I used to love to jump around in the garden in our backyard. We grew tomatoes, potatoes, corn, beans, onions, radishes, melons, you name it. We had a dog named Thadeus, a white German Shepherd who usually had a pretty friendly personality when the girls would walk into his pen to feed him. Thadeus' previous owner used to give him these baby dolls to play with. He would shake them around, chew them up, toss them as far as he could across the pen and then race after them and start chewing again. Of course, Hilary and Whitney were ten and eight at the time and Thadeus was used to the company of kids who were bigger and older than me. I was only three, so one morning when I went into the pen to feed Thadeus, he thought I was one of the dolls. He bit me in the back of the neck and started chewing. Then he tossed me from one end of the pen to the other. He was much bigger than I was, and I couldn't do anything to get free. Hilary started screaming and trying to pull him off, but he was having too much fun. To Thadeus, I was a play toy, and he was as full of restless energy as I often was. It took a few minutes, but finally my dad came and pulled the dog off me. Thadeus broke my skin in several places, but thankfully, he didn't decide to take a piece out of my neck.

A few months earlier, two raccoons had died near our house, one from rabies and the other from distemper. My dad had Thadeus put down and he told me we would have to get another dog because, with all the diseases going around, we couldn't take a chance that he'd bite one of us again. If I try to remember my early, early childhood, the day Thadeus mistook me for a rag doll was my first memory of anything.

Of course my parents had warned me to be careful of Thadeus, but parental warnings didn't usually stop me from experimenting with danger or discomfort. The first story about Michael Phelps and water had nothing to do with a swimming pool. Mom and Dad took us to dinner one night when I was seven at a Mexican place called Chi Chi's and they tried to explain that I should be careful of the hot sauce in the bowl on the side. What happens when you tell a kid to be careful? You awaken his inner daredevil. The red sauce looked a lot like ketchup, and that wasn't too hot, was it? So I took a nacho, slathered on a huge spoonful of five-alarm chili sauce and took a bite. Whoa! Whoa! Whoa! Within seconds I was waving my arms like a windmill and my eyes were like faucets. Water, water, I need water. "Michael, we told you to be careful." More water, Mom's water. Dad's too. "If we tell you it's too hot . . ." Where's Hilary's water? ". . . then you have to be careful." Waiter, more water, please. I was drinking it so fast that about half of it ran down my cheeks. I was like a beached fish trying to find his way to moisture. I guess my parents figured if I didn't listen to their warnings, I might as well learn for myself.

I was a handful at the dinner table, because I always had to do something with my hands. In my middle fingers I liked to twirl pens and pencils, but if they weren't available at dinner, I might try to substitute a salt shaker or a steak knife. I should have known I couldn't twirl glasses of milk. Until food arrived, it was up to my mom to keep me away from anything that could break, spill, cause bodily harm or overseason the lasagna. Once I was finished eating my food, I used to play with it. Take some ketchup, some mayonnaise, some sugar, a few potatoes, some spinach and just mix them all together as if you're making a casserole. It drove my mom crazy. Sometimes I'd realize I was still hungry, so I'd try a bite of the casserole and it was usually okay—especially if you poured milk on it. And ice cream was always better in some melted, mashed, or otherwise altered state.

I simply could never sit still. I made faces at cameras, answered questions with questions and climbed on things that weren't meant

for climbing. Most people had patience with me, but one particular primary teacher took her case to my mom. "Michael just can't
focus on anything," she told my mom. "Well," she answered,
"maybe he's bored with what he's being taught." That didn't go
over well. "Mrs. Phelps, you're not insinuating that Michael is
especially gifted, are you? I just don't ever see him being able to
focus on anything in his life."

I was a hyperactive kid who loved being with his friends and
his family, but still caused trouble for everyone. The year I turned
seven, two things happened that would change my life.

I walked into my parents' room at our old house on
Chesapeake Avenue one day. My mom had a very sad look on her
face and my sisters were crying. You know how you walk into a
room and realize you've interrupted a heavy conversation and you
don't know how to make a graceful exit? I felt like that. I didn't
know what I'd walked into, but I knew it wasn't good. Sometimes
I've walked in on situations where my sisters or my mom were
upset or people were having an argument, just as they do in any
family, but I remember that this was something I'd never seen
before, because everyone was sad. I figured it was just something I,
as the little kid, wasn't supposed to understand, so I began to leave.

"Michael," my mom said, "I need to tell you something." I don't
know if I had ever heard the words "separation" or "divorce"
before. Parents are always together. There is a mom and there is a
dad and they will always be there to look after kids like me, to
teach us, guide us, pat us on the back, have all the answers because
parents just know these things, and they basically tell us what's
what. I heard my mom explain to me that my dad really wasn't
going to be living with us anymore, but it didn't make sense. Dad
must have gone out to get something.

I began to grasp the whole thing one day when I went to play
a video game. I used to bounce into our den and wait anxiously for
my dad to get off the computer so I could play a game. Suddenly I

didn't have to wait anymore. Maybe my dad really wasn't coming back. Maybe he wasn't going to be in my life the way he had been. Maybe this was more of a change than I realized.

I'd ask my mom why and my sisters why, but they didn't offer an answer. Perhaps nobody really had one, because Mom and Dad had been together so long. Both of my parents had grown up in small industrial Maryland towns, where people played sports and relied on families for support and incomes from the local paper mill. Dad came from Luke, which only had a population of around 100. Mom grew up a mile away in Westernport (pop. 2,000). They were school sweethearts at Bruce High and later at Fairmont State. She was a cheerleader and he was an outstanding football player who set the school record for interceptions as a defensive back, and was eventually the last man cut from the Washington Redskins training camp. They both earned education degrees. Mom became a home economics teacher; Dad was a state police officer. Neither of my parents were swimmers.

Mom was always the one with irrefutable logic and unconditional love. She taught school kids about health and nutrition, and twice she was voted Maryland State Teacher of the Year. It's a pretty strong negative statement about the higher education system that Mom got a "C" in a parenting class at Fairmont State. Upon further review, professors, I'd like to upgrade that to an A-plus.

Dad had his share of scraps in his early life, went hunting and fishing in his spare time and once had a job as a bouncer in Atlantic City. He would sometimes describe arguments he might have with someone by saying, "Let's just say he and I had a discussion." He became a sergeant and would spend almost three decades on the force before working as an independent security officer.

As I began to grasp that my dad would be away for a long time, I needed something that could grab my attention. My mom had started Hilary and Whitney in swimming because a family physician, Dr. Charles Wax, had convinced her that she should introduce her kids to water safety. The girls swam in the pool at Loyola High School, the original home of the North Baltimore Aquatic Club (NBAC) before it moved to its present home at the Meadowbrook complex. I knew they worked hard, because I remember alarm clocks going off at 4 a.m. so that my dad could drive Hilary to practice. I also remember seeing my sister have a blast during the club's annual July 4th celebration. They used to sit in these blow-up boats and paddle forward in the water with their arms. I was starting to play other sports, but I wanted to get in the water, too. It was time for my first swim lesson.

You would think that on the first day I hit the water I just sort of turned into a dolphin and never wanted to leave the pool. No way. I hated it. We're talking screaming, kicking, fit-throwing, goggle-tossing hate. It wasn't anything like I expected. The NBAC was offering stroke clinics and I had my first lesson from Cathy Lears, a neighbor and close friend of my mom. I drove her crazy. I may have been the younger brother of two great swimmers, but as soon as I got in the pool, with Miss Cathy guiding me along, I realized I was scared to get my face wet. We tried it a few times without Miss Cathy holding on to me, but I just didn't feel comfortable. In the shallow end, I was okay, because I realized that if I had to, I could simply stand up on the bottom and not worry about sinking. But when I knew I couldn't stand, I started getting tense, becoming more rigid, less buoyant, unable to swim. Miss Cathy sensed my nervousness, but she also wanted to make sure I kept going and she didn't let me make excuses: "I'm cold. I have to go to the bathroom. Maybe if I just sit on the side and watch the other kids do it. . . ."

No luck. "That's your problem, Michael Phelps. Your mom wants you to learn how to swim, so you're going to swim."

"But I don't want to get my face wet." I raised a screaming stink about it.

Miss Cathy was one of many people who were determined to get the best out of me no matter how difficult I made it for her. She finally offered me a compromise. "Well, you can start on your back and learn to swim that way," she said, "but you're going to learn one way or another." At least on my back I couldn't see how deep the water was, and so I couldn't see myself sink. I started to figure out how to float. Then after a few sessions I realized how to flail my arms and legs without sinking. I don't remember how long it took for this flailing to turn into swimming or how many lessons it took me to turn over on my stomach and work on the Australian crawl, but once I figured out how to swim, I felt so free. It was like I had this new toy that my sisters enjoyed all this time. I went to the pool every day and it usually took a while to get me to leave. I had grown up around the pool so much. The more I swam, the more it became a part of me and the more I wanted to get back.

Not so fast. Later that year, I was at a friend's house, wrestling around on the lawn with Russell Fitzell, a buddy from the swim team. I don't remember getting hit especially hard or taking an especially bad fall during the day, but when I went back into the Fitzells' living room and sat down, I started to complain without saying what was bothering me. It was a time when I was still upset and confused about my parents' separation, so I complained pretty often about nearly anything. Russell's mother, Loretta, put me in a recliner and gave me some juice, hoping that would quiet me down. I started watching cartoons and almost fell asleep. Then one time when I started wiggling around in the chair, I let out an odd sound, sort of like a puppy's yelp. Miss Loretta called my mom and they decided she should take me to the doctor. Good thing, too. I had broken my collarbone.

I wore a thick brace on my back for the summer. It was so hot and I wanted to get in the water and play around the pool with my friends, but instead I just sat there, because I had no choice. By the time I got the brace off in the fall, I was fired up to swim again.

3

INTO THE WATER

I don't remember my first race. People find that hard to believe, but before we had age-group races, club races, zone meets, national meets, international events and, of course, the Olympics, there was probably some small, informal race that kick started my career, but I don't remember it as much as I remember loving the water.

I remember swimming in an open-water mile contest in the Chesapeake Bay and it was a blast. We started out of the water, ran into it and tried not to collide with all the other swimmers as we elbowed for position. Everyone tried to cut each other off as we got closer to the finish, but it finally came down to me and Brad Schertle, the son of one of the NBAC coaches. I won a very close race at the end, mainly because Brad, um, tripped and fell on his own, sort of. I told my mom afterward that when I grew up, my future job would probably involve swimming.

I guess I started on my professional aspirations when I was still in elementary school. Greg Eggert is a swim official who used to own a swimwear business called Metro Sports. When I went to Eastern Zone meets to watch Whitney or Hilary in places like

Princeton, New Jersey, and Gloucester, Pennsylvania, Greg usually brought along samples from his business and set up a travelling store at the meets. Greg sold suits, caps, goggles, towels, and, most of all, posters. If I disappeared into his store long enough, I figured I could at least try to get my mom to buy me a poster. At some point I sort of appointed myself as Greg's sales assistant. I would show people to the right aisles, take the swimsuits on and off hangers for them and help them find the right size or color. "This is my associate, Mr. Phelps," Greg would tell his customers. My mom liked the fact that he looked after me and kept me occupied. I think I also helped him sell a few suits to people who would have flipped through and walked out, if not for the pushy sales assistant.

People in swimming like Greg made me feel I could fit in. That was important, because even though I had a lot of friends at school, some things could make me pretty sensitive. Because I didn't like listening to people and looking them in the eye when they spoke to me, I often had to ask people to repeat themselves. When I talked fast, I'd drop my Ls and add Ss to words, and if I tried to tell people I didn't have a lisp, I'd usually lisp the word lisp. And I would have given anything not to have such big ears. I used to wear a hat all the time because I thought it made them look smaller. Other kids knew they could get under my skin by flicking my ears, exposing my ears, or even talking about my ears. When our school bus stopped in front of my house, the older kids would take off my hat, fling it onto the driveway and make some reference to Spock, the Vulcan character in *Star Trek*.

I'm not sure if it was because of my big ears or short attention span, but I always appreciated people who were patient and supportive and I always identified with underdogs. My third-grade teacher, Barbara Kines, was one of the people who really encouraged me, telling me I had an "active personality" that was healthy for young boys. Instead of always telling me what to do, she often

asked me what I liked to do. Eventually, I invited her and her husband, Rodge, to some of my meets. Rodge was legally blind and I
knew that whenever I walked up to speak to him, I needed to say,
"Hi, Mr. Rodge, it's Michael." I even told the other kids to make
sure they did the same thing, so he wouldn't be embarrassed to ask
who was in front of him. Rodge would talk with the kids about
how he had to rely on his other senses because he wasn't able to
see. I guess because Rodge was so honest with us and so open
about what he had and didn't have, we really admired him.

One day, I won a freestyle race at Towson State and walked up
to share my excitement with him. I tapped his arm, but before I
could say anything, he told me, "Michael, that was great." I was
surprised. I asked how he knew it was me and how he knew the
result of the race. "Didn't you hear them cheering after they said
your name? Michael, the cheering was for you. You were great."

I was just starting to build a collection of small ribbons from
good results at swim events, when I began working at NBAC with
Tom Himes, the first coach who really enhanced my feelings about
swimming. Hilary and I were both working with him at the time,
when she was 16 and I was nine. He was the perfect age-group
coach who taught the basics well and encouraged kids to have fun.
Tom would show up at the pool in a Santa Claus outfit around
Christmastime. When Hilary's group won a zone meet it wasn't
expected to win, Tom made good on a promise that she could shave
off his moustache. Every Friday after practice, Tom would take
Whitney and me to TCBY for yogurt. He always looked after me
and would tell a joke or do something funny when I would go from
being hyper to being moody.

On the days I worked with Tom, I'd start looking at the clock
and calculating split times in my head. *Let's see: If that guy wants to
swim X, that means he has to hit the 50-yard mark in Y.* My mom realized
I was getting serious when I started talking to her about tenths of

seconds and negative splitting. If my math teachers had used text-books that related questions to swim calculations, I might have been ready for calculus.

And have you ever heard of sleepswimming? Mom also remembers me sitting up in my bed and waking the family in the middle of the night by yelling: "One, two, three . . . go."

Swimmers did serious work at NBAC, but there was also time for fun. We played a game called Categories in which guys would line up 20 feet from the wall. We would have a topic for the game—ice cream, for instance. We'd go along the wall, with a swimmer in each lane, and if another swimmer named your flavor of ice cream, you'd have to race against him.

Before practice, we also played Wall Ball, which could some-times be kind of painful. In that game, you threw a tennis ball against the wall as hard as you could. A designated "fielder" then had to catch the ball as it bounced back off the wall. If he couldn't catch it, he had to run to the wall. If I, the thrower, got to the ball before the fielder reached the wall, then he would be charged with an out. Once a person had three outs, he had to line up against the wall and let everyone else take a shot at him with the tennis ball. I was the youngest one in my group, and I soon discovered that the other kids knew how to throw.

Swimming with older kids made me feel important and accomplished, but that also came with a price. Two of the older guys, Matt McDonough and Justin Freidman, sort of adopted me as the group mascot. They used to pick me up and toss me back and forth over the lane lines. Michael Phelps, Human Volleyball. The pool also had these rubber trash cans that were full of medicine balls. Matt and Justin would take the medicine balls out of the cans, put me in the cans and then put the balls on top of me. Once you passed the point of no return, you were really in trouble. The far-ther I'd sink into the cans with my arms and legs flailing on the out-side, the harder it would be for me to get out. My only hope was to keep my head above the line of the balls, push myself to one side, and then knock over the cans until the balls spilled out and I could extract myself from the bottom. I actually didn't mind being picked on by Matt, Justin, and the older kids. They pretty much left my ears alone and at least they didn't ignore me. After a while I just accepted the fact that since I was the youngest kid in the group, I was also the entertainment.

My mom loved the fact that I swam, because she wanted me to drain as much energy out of my body as I possibly could. I was a pool rat, running around, sneaking up behind people, stealing their snacks and goggles, tapping them on the shoulder and running away and just causing general havoc. It seemed I was always getting "benched" at the pool. A benching was a kind of detention. You had to sit by the lifeguard stand and stay silent before you went back to play. It was terrible being benched and having to watch other people have fun. It was only supposed to last 10 or 15 minutes, but I always thought it lasted longer, and it happened to me a lot.

I was also an active spectator. When we went to zone meets, each state would have about 75 to 80 swimmers on a team, but only half of them would swim in the evening finals. The other 40 or so would support the teams with whatever traditions they had. The extras on the Maryland team, known as the Indians, used to paint their faces in the Indian team colors, red, yellow, and black. Some painted their noses; others painted faces. A few of the guys came out of the warm-down pools without shirts and painted their chests. So that's what I did. Sometimes it took the ink days to rub off. Other times it blended with my shirts in the wash and made life difficult for my mom. But if other swimmers painted their faces, I wanted to do it, too.

I had to be in the middle of everything, especially when I was around my best friends, Matt Townsend and Ayo Osho. When we were in fifth grade, Matt and I were watching a school talent show and I sort of convinced him to join in. "We both know how to juggle pretty well," I told him. "We're better than a lot of these kids." It was pretty embarrassing. Whenever he was juggling okay, I was dropping balls on the stage. When I had them in the air, his collided and bounced away. At some point we started laughing, then we tried to make up for it, so we tried to be funny by throwing the balls at each other. The kids and teachers in the audience weren't cheering or booing; instead they were just hoping we'd get off the stage.

I used to hang out in the back of the room with Ayo during sixth grade science class. We would turn on the natural gas burners for about five seconds and then watch for our classmates to start crinkling their noses at the strange smell in the distance. Fortunately nothing bad happened, but our hours of mischief also had practical applications. Ayo and I used to practice signing our names in the back of that class, in case we ever had to give someone an autograph. Some days our autographs would be from Ayo and Michael; other days they'd be to Ayo and Michael from Michael Jordan.

I simply couldn't sit still, because it was difficult for me to focus on one thing at a time. When I was in sixth grade, Dr. Wax diagnosed me with Attention Deficit Hyperactivity Disorder (ADHD), a condition that afflicts roughly two million elementary-school children who seem hyperactive, inattentive, and impulsive. ADHD can be pretty serious. Some kids who have it will have related learning problems such as dyslexia. Others become antisocial and don't try to make any friends. Others suffer from severe depression. I was lucky that those things didn't happen to me, but Dr. Wax wasn't taking any chances. He prescribed a medication called Ritalin to help me control the condition.

I started taking Ritalin three times a day: in the morning, at lunchtime, and before dinner. The second dose used to bug me. If I didn't go downstairs to get it either before or after lunch, the nurse would call me out of my next class to remind me to go downstairs. Other kids used to ask me why I would just disappear like that and what my problem was that I had to go to the nurse's office all the time. At first, my mom didn't tell me what it was or what it was supposed to do, but I did notice that it calmed me down and made me less jumpy in class. Once I became used to the drill, it wasn't really a big deal, but the medication didn't solve everything. I didn't take it one weekend, when my schedule could be monitored and when we would often have swim meets. It showed.

Sometimes there were so many kids swimming in so many heats at the smaller competitions, the parents needed to figure out a way to make sure that everyone made it to the starting blocks in time for their races. They managed this by placing kickboards in rows of eight along the deck. We were told to stand or sit on top of our boards and move them up one place until the start of the next race. The fastest heat was usually the last, so I was supposed to wait in the back. I could never sit still. I was either running off to the side to play with the other kids, banging my kickboard against the pooldeck or sneaking to the front of the line to jump into someone else's race. Parents and officials would have to pull me away from the front row of boards, while my board often sat there unoccupied six or seven rows in the back. "No, Michael, you have to wait your turn," they'd tell me.

Some kids threw fits when things didn't go well; I'd throw my goggles. With an outfielder's throwing arm, I could get some pretty good distance from a very energetic windup. To be fair, I had a lot of practice.

One afternoon, a kid from Delaware beat me in the 200-yard freestyle at a meet in Princeton, New Jersey, and I remember feeling the goggle-tossing urge inside me. This could be a really good heave, I thought. I'm really mad about this. Instead, I kept it inside, let it simmer and waited for it to boil over during the remaining races. I had five more events at that meet, won each of them and equaled a national age-group record. It was uncharacteristic of me not to vent publicly, because that's what I did back then when things didn't go well, but it was a good lesson that I could find more constructive outlets for my frustrations by keeping my mouth shut, getting back in the pool, and kicking everyone's butt. If I could only remember that all the time.

I had a well-earned reputation as a source of mischief at NBAC, but sometimes when trouble struck, people just naturally assumed I was responsible even if I wasn't. Our team was swimming at Towson State one day and two of our kids started throwing soap and clothes around the men's bathroom. I walked in and some of the older kids started picking on me and shouting out my name, as if I had been the instigator. I hadn't been formally introduced to one of NBAC's new coaches, but he already knew my history. "Michael Phelps, what did you do?" he asked.

"I didn't do anything," I shouted back. "It was them."

"Well then why were they shouting *your* name?"

"Ask them."

"No, Michael, I'm asking *you*. What did *you* do?"

I didn't get into real trouble, but I remember leaving that day saying under my breath, "I'm glad he doesn't coach my group. It'll really stink if I ever have to work with him." At the same time, the coach walked away, mumbling to himself, "Thank goodness, I will never have to coach that kid."

We were both wrong.

4

COACH BOB

Later that spring the new coach who cornered me at the meet in Towson took over an advanced set of swimmers at the NBAC, made up of 13-year-olds, 14-year-olds and me, an 11-year-old. I didn't know what to make of Bob Bowman at first, but I remember I couldn't put anything past him. If he told 20 of us to swim ten laps at different intervals and I only swam nine, he called me on it. If he asked us to show up at the top of the hour and I arrived at 5:01, he'd be at the front door to ask why. If I splashed a teammate when he wasn't looking, those eyes in the back of Bob's head would let him know, and he would be sure to let me know that he knew. Bob scared me.

I remember the first set he gave us: a 400 freestyle, a 4x100 stroke, one 400 IM and a 4x100 freestyle. I did each set three times. I remember it because it hurt. Is every set going to be like this? What did I do wrong? In fact, Bob wanted to see how we would react. When Bob watched the final set of four 100 frees, I didn't realize that I was actually coming back faster at the end of the set—

one minute, five seconds for each hundred—than at the beginning. Bob realized it, but he didn't know yet what to do about it.

For several months, whenever I wanted to talk to Bob, I usually confided first in Erin Lears, Miss Cathy's daughter, who also swam at Meadowbrook. "Erin, will this be okay? Do you think we can do that in this lane? Erin, let's ask him together." I wasn't the only one he intimidated. Swimmers swiped and hid each other's backpacks, food, and attire all the time, but when Bob put that rickety plastic chair down by the side of the pool, nobody dared touch it or go near it. Eventually, somebody decided to stick a "Beware of Bob" sign on his door.

I tried to hide my anxiety about Bob by driving him crazy. I was getting in and out of the water, hiding caps and goggles and chasing a girl I liked with a cap full of water. "Aren't you supposed to be tired?" Bob asked.

"I don't get tired," I told him.

Soon enough, Bob would help me find myself through swimming, and I would help him find his niche in swimming.

Bob had gone to Florida State on a swim scholarship and was elected team captain of the Seminoles as a junior. He majored in child psychology at FSU, but tended to overanalyze what he did in the pool. The expression "cut your head off and let your body go to work" would have suited him, but he just couldn't do it.

Bob made it to Senior Nationals in the 100 fly, but he got frustrated with his times and decided to stop swimming after his junior year at FSU. Bob quit the pool, feeling he hadn't achieved his goals, yet he knew so much about the sport, it made sense that he would work his way into coaching. He took a job as an assistant with the Area Tallahassee Aquatic Club in early 1986. There, the head coach, Terry Maul, handed him a stack of books, magazines, and pamphlets about motivation, strategy, and coaching technique. It was about two months worth of material, but Bob pulled an all-nighter and had it finished by the next morning. Then he went up to Terry and asked if he had any more material.

Bob later took another position in Cincinnati with a club called the Marlins. He taught a breaststroker there named Michele Shroder who was a very positive person and very influential in Bob's approach to coaching. There were times when Michele told Bob that she was going to accomplish something, even when Bob doubted her abilities. He learned to feed off her confidence and I think we've had days when he's fed off mine. Michele went on to swim at Texas. Meanwhile, Bob kept moving around. He had a job in Birmingham, Alabama, and two others at the Napa Valley Swim Club, where he coached Eric Wunderlich, one of the country's top breaststrokers. In all, he had coached in seven places in five states over a nine-year span.

In 1995, Bob's coaching career was going very well. Eric seemed primed to become his first pupil to make the '96 Olympic team, but in the meantime, Bob had interviewed for his dream job as head coach of the prestigious Dynamo Swim Club in Atlanta. It was Bob's second attempt at landing a job there. In 1990, they interviewed him for an assistant coaching position but hired someone else, sensing that he was going to get along better with swimmers than he would with parents and administrators.

But in '95, word had gotten to Bob that he was the front runner for the Dynamo job. Instead, the club offered the position to someone else, and later that week, Eric told Bob he was switching clubs. That was it, Bob thought. It was time to try another profession. He decided to pursue a degree in farm management at Auburn University so he could eventually run a horse farm for a living. In the meantime, he would take a part-time job as an assistant with the team at Auburn, but only until he earned his degree. That was going to be the end of his coaching career.

Then, with the Atlanta Olympics around the corner, Bob had a phone conversation with Murray Stephens, the head coach at NBAC. Murray had trained Anita Nall, an Olympic breaststroker at age 16 in 1992, and he was training Beth Botsford, who would go on to win the 100-meter backstroke in Atlanta. He respected Bob and wanted a chance to bring him on board.

"Bob, we're looking for somebody here."

"Murray, I don't think this is my future. I just want to go back to school."

"Okay, but you can go to school somewhere in Baltimore. Just help us out on a part-time basis."

"Well . . ."

"How much is Auburn paying you?"

"Ten thousand a year. That's not bad for a part-time . . ."

"I'll pay you thirty-five. When can you start?"

"Um, how is next week?"

By then I was training full time at the Meadowbrook pool, which is really an inclusive environment for all ages, the kind of place where potential Olympians cross paths with beginners all the time and where swim parents always pitch in to help one another. Before you get to the pool after entering the front door, you have to pass a sign on the wall that reads: "Meadowbrook requires the use of swim diapers and/or plastic pants on children who are not toilet trained or marginally trained and prone to accidents."

Bob and I didn't seem like a good match at all. I was the goofball; he was the taskmaster. Before I discovered football and hiphop, I liked baseball and Top-40 hits; Bob liked racehorses and classical music. I did without thinking; he thought before doing. If a ball rolled under a couch in front of me, I would ask: "Why don't I have a big brother or a small dog to either move the couch or crawl under it?" If a ball rolled under a couch in front of Bob, he would ask: "Does the ball really exist?" We came at everything from different places, which was why we often went at each other.

Early that fall, Bob wanted my technique to mature, so he tried to get me to switch from a two-beat kick to a six-beat kick. I fought him. Sometimes I'd start swimming a lap the way he wanted and then I'd lapse into my old style. Sometimes I did it out of rebellion, other times out of laziness. Bob's antidote was simple: if I couldn't swim with a six-beat kick, he'd kick me out of practice and send me home. The next day he did the same thing. For a week, Bob kicked me out each day until I got fed up and started doing what I was supposed to. I was furious with him, but when he told me I wasn't old enough or mature enough to go through a whole day of using a six-beat kick, that was the first day I proved to him that I could.

Bob never really told me how talented he thought I was or that, based on my skills, I would probably soon join the club's Senior Performance Group, the elite set of potential Olympians at the NBAC. In some respects he didn't want to deal with me any more than I wanted to deal with him, but he also figured he had nothing to lose, because he knew once I jumped to the next level, he'd never coach me again.

Bob also saw me making improvements, lowering my times in meets and practices. He also knew that I rarely got tired and if someone could just push the right buttons with me, they could also push me pretty far in the right direction, even one day, to the Olympics. In October, Bob called a meeting with my mom and dad to confide some of his projections with them.

"But Bob, he's only 12."

"I know, Debbie, but in 2008, for instance, he'll be 23 and . . ."

Bob was very frank about my talents, my attitude, my inconsistent focus, and my dueling moments of indifference and determination. He also said that I had a realistic opportunity other kids didn't have. Bob talked to them about where they were planning to send me to high school, what my hours might look like in a typical day and what sort of sacrifices we would all have to make in order for me to be the best swimmer I could be.

It was a huge commitment for a number of reasons. First of all, that kind of dedication meant that I would have to start gradually sacrificing my time playing other sports in order to focus on swimming. That would be rough. I loved other sports, and I had the bruises and trophies to prove it.

In fifth grade, I won a school contest called the vortex throw. The vortex was actually a small football with bells and a tail. It was shaped so you could really heave the thing a long way. I threw the ball farther than anyone in the grade, and I felt like I was on top of the world. It felt like the ball sailed about a mile. Maybe a block. Okay, maybe from home plate to the pitcher's mound. But it felt like a mile.

I had a huge trophy in my room for being named best player in home run derby. The derby's "fence" was a series of cones about 20 feet beyond the infield. I played catcher and always wore number 13. I used to love watching major league catchers throw their mask off and take off after pop-ups. It just looked cool. I remember one day when a player on the other team hit a pop-up just behind me. I grabbed the mask, ripped it off my head, flung it over near the on-deck circle and took off after the ball. I missed it. What's worse, when I threw the mask away, I also tossed the helmet that was underneath it and broke the helmet. It wasn't a play for the highlight reels, but it made me feel like I was in the majors. I strategically put my trophy near the entrance to my bedroom and didn't mind if my friends happened to pass through and see it.

At the time of that meeting I had also just started playing midfield in the Towson Rec. lacrosse league and I loved running up and down the field. I scored once in a while, but other players on the team were better than I was. The part I loved, even at age 11, was the hitting. It was unreal. I was a tall, skinny kid, so I often got the worst of it. But I remember one day when a kid was chasing after the ball with his head down. I stepped into his path and he just ran into me and fell over. I loved being in the center of the action. I remember my mom driving me to a lacrosse game and asking: "Do you have a cup in case you have to play goalie?" All goalies were required to wear cups, and my mom had reminded me twice before we left that morning to bring mine because the kids sometimes took turns playing goal. I didn't like having to stand there and wait for the action to come to me, so I sort of forgot the cup, accidentally, on purpose. "Michael, what if you have to play goalie?"

"Mom, I'm not going to play goalie. That's why I forgot my cup."

I didn't take Ritalin on Saturdays because I had so many outlets for energy release. I'd go from a lacrosse game to a baseball game to swim practice. That was a blast. I played three sports with three different sets of rules and goals. If that didn't make me tired, I'd usually come home, eat and shoot baskets with Matt. We played one-on-one, of course, but we also played a game called Fifty in which you'd try to make a foul shot for ten points and then subsequent shots for five points each. You could keep shooting until you missed, and the first one to 50 would win the game. It was our version of H-O-R-S-E.

The balance of sports was a saving grace for a mother's son and it would be hard to disrupt that balance. As easily as I tended to lose my temper, what if I got so fed up with swimming that I decided to quit? At least the way things were now, I had multiple outlets for my restless energy, and if I was angry about something that happened on the baseball diamond, I always had the lacrosse field to look forward to. But if my parents needed a reason to think twice about having one of their children focus so intensely on swimming, they only needed to think about what happened to Whitney.

5

A SISTER'S
BRAVE FIGHT

If you look at our family photos, you'll notice something interesting about the first baby pictures taken of my sisters and me: Hilary has both of her eyes open, Whitney has both of her eyes closed and I have one eye open and one eye closed. I'm not sure what that means, but many people think I split the difference between my sisters, that my personality is a cross between Hilary and Whitney. Both of my sisters had great careers in the pool, where their favorite stroke, like mine, was the butterfly, but I gained a lot from each of them well beyond their enjoyment of swimming that helped me as I got older.

Hilary is very nurturing and modest, and she has a strong sense of right and wrong. My parents always told us to be honest, no matter what the consequences. One time when we were having a catch, Hilary was helping me get a ball that had rolled right under the center of my mom's car. She had just started to drive, so when it rolled underneath, she started to move the car. The door wasn't completely closed, so it banged against the garage as she opened it.

The nick on the side of the car was barely noticeable, but Hilary apologized as if she had rolled over the house. She called my mom from the kitchen and then called my dad at work to tell them what she had done and how sorry she was. She didn't get in trouble for it and she didn't need a scolding from our parents that she wasn't already giving herself. That's Hilary.

Eventually, she swam mostly to have fun, but still set three school records at the University of Richmond, where she went to college. Over the last few years, Hilary and I have become really close. She is an easy person to joke around with and have fun with.

Whitney was one of my best pals growing up and we had a lot of fun together doing things like shooting baskets and slinging balls against a bounce-back lacrosse net. Every morning, she'd come back from swim practice with the unenviable task of waking me up. Don't let the hyperactivity fool you. At 7 a.m., I was a zombie, barely emerging from my coma. After my mom would leave to go to her teaching job in Harford County, Whitney would always fix me an egg sandwich and since she knew I ate everything, she would throw almost anything on that sandwich, from cinnamon to peppers, and I wouldn't notice, because I'd smother the bread in heaps of mayonnaise. Afterward, Whitney would pack my lunch and we'd sit in the kitchen and watch the cartoon *Bobby's World* together until it was time for the bus to pick me up for school. She always watched the clock and made sure to walk me outside in time to catch that bus, before her boyfriend, Victor, arrived to pick her up and take her to high school.

Whitney often refused to compromise, just as my dad did. We were visiting my dad's mother in western Maryland one day, when my sisters got into an argument. Hilary pushed Whitney because of something nobody can quite remember and Whitney headed back downstairs to tell my dad about it. "So, get her back," he told her. That was Whitney's green light. The next thing we heard was a loud squeal. Then Hilary came downstairs sporting one less tooth. It wasn't as though Whitney and Hilary were enemies. Even though Hilary was the older one, Whitney once scared away a bratty girl in Hilary's middle school class by telling her to "leave my sister alone."

Whitney didn't take no for an answer and she applied that zeal to her swimming. She was named outstanding swimmer in the state of Maryland from 1990 to 1993. In '94, she was 13 when she qualified for her first world team by placing second in the 200 fly at spring nationals. She went to Worlds in Rome four months later as the U.S. team's only 14-year-old and finished ninth there. I remember her coming back from Europe with free watches, tales of travel, and an optimism about the future.

It's amazing for me to think that Whitney first resisted swimming when she was six. She cried about it as much as I did, and her coaches had to bribe her with a Snickers bar to get her to stay in the water. But once she started improving, they couldn't get her out, and she never complained about anything. If a coach told her to do ten of something, she'd do 12; if he told her to be someplace by noon, she would be waiting for him at 11:30. She didn't really hang out much with kids from school, because it wasn't her scene and she was pretty mature for her age. She and Victor would usually rent movies or she would do things with us or with my dad. The rules were different for her, though. I went rollerblading around the house with Whitney, wearing whatever I wanted and going wherever my legs would take me. Whitney dressed up in kneepads, elbow pads, and a helmet and wasn't allowed to skate past the driveway to make sure she wouldn't get hurt. None of that seemed to bother her. She didn't see her lifestyle as a sacrifice, because she enjoyed swimming so much. She also heard the buzz around swim circles: Whitney Phelps will be the next star of USA Swimming. The gold medals are a matter of time.

Unfortunately, two things were standing in Whitney's way. First, when she was nine or ten, she began to have problems with a sore back. They were minor at first, but they would recur more and more frequently. In early 1995, Murray Stephens, who was also Whitney's coach at the club, placed a training device called a monofin on Whitney's feet and had her swim with it. The idea was to add resistance to the stroke in the water and, therefore, make you stroke harder in order to get from here to there. The device didn't cause the problem, but for the first time Whitney felt a serious strain in her back after practice was over; only she didn't tell Murray about it. In 1995, she went to the Pan-Pacific meet in Atlanta, where she won a bronze medal, representing the U.S. in the 200 fly. But Whitney also left the pool in pain that day. Every time she had to do a flip turn, the motion would cause the nerves to tug at her back. Whitney wasn't one to speak up about pain, but she really felt the effects. Her arms and legs would sometimes go numb when she bent over.

Whitney was doing training sets that I never had to do. If that extra lap was going to take an extra hundredth off her time, she'd plow through it, trying to gain an advantage. She wanted to be the fittest in order to be the best. There was another way to accomplish that, she figured: by eating less. *If I'm skinny and small*, she thought, *it will make me faster. If I drop fat, it will make me faster.* The spiral began innocently enough, when she started skipping between-meal snacks and treats like ice cream and donuts. Then she began eating less at meals. It happened so slowly, people around her didn't realize it. Even she didn't realize it. Susan Teeter, one of the U.S. team officials, was already getting worried before the Pan Pacific meet and mentioned to my mom that she noticed Whitney had really gotten thin. My mom confronted Whitney about it periodically, but each time, she downplayed it, made light of it or simply denied that there was a problem. Of course, I had no idea. If Whitney and I sat together on the couch in front of a movie and a box of Oreos,

I might offer her one of my cookies, but if she declined, I'd be glad to finish the carton by myself while she sat and watched me. I didn't think anything of it.

Over the next few months, Whitney did not train well at all. She was losing energy and turning blue after long sessions in the water because she had no body fat and low glycogen supplies an active body needs. She aggravated her back injury and sometimes couldn't finish practice, yet she became good at hiding the warning signs by staying under water until her color came back and trying to shake off the back pain as if it were a scratch.

At home, food was still an issue. On the advice of Whitney's nutritionist, my mom insisted that Whitney keep a calendar of what she ate during the day. She would also try to sneak calories into Whitney's dinner by putting extra butter on potatoes or whatever she could think of. My mom also made it a point to buy as many healthy snacks as possible, deliberately leaving some out on the kitchen tables in case Whitney should walk by.

Whitney got worse before she got better. She made increasingly frequent trips to the bathroom to purge herself of her most recent meals. My mom would go in minutes after she left the bathroom to see if Whitney had purged her food, but she was good at cleaning up the telltale signs. She denied what she was losing from her body to my mom and exaggerated what she was putting into her body to her nutritionist. If she had a problem, she would handle it herself, the way big girls were supposed to handle problems, but she didn't think it was an unmanageable situation.

Against this backdrop, Whitney somehow made it to the '96 Olympic Trials in Indianapolis. She came in with the fastest time of all the swimmers in the 200 fly, 2:11.04, and was favored to make the Olympic team that summer. I knew nothing about Whitney's health problems or about my mom's concern about what would happen to Whitney after the Trials were done. To me, the Trials were an opportunity to see swimmers I had watched on TV or read about in swim magazines and a chance to get autographs. When I wasn't watching races, I waited by the door that led from the stands downstairs to the pool. I took a cap off my head and collected signatures from Beth Botsford, Whitney Metzler and Jenny Thompson. "Michael," my mom said, "why don't you let Whitney be the first one to autograph your hat?"

"Mom, some people already signed it."

"Well, let her sign the center."

Whitney qualified for the finals of the 200 fly and finished sixth. It was a great result given her condition, but I remember Hilary and my mom being in tears after the race. Why is everyone so sad, I thought to myself? We've been to other events before where things have gone well and events where things have gone badly, but nobody cried. I remember wanting to say something to cheer up my mom, but I didn't know what to say. Somebody either tell me what I'm supposed to say or come over and say it themselves. As we walked into a waiting area outside the stands, Eric Wunderlich, the breaststroker who used to work with Bob, stopped by. "Whitney's going to be okay," he said. "You know how tough she is."

At a competition five months after the Trials, Whitney finished second in a time that would have allowed her to win the trials, even though she was having trouble stretching and bending over. Whitney realized she would have to stop swimming for a while to take care of her back. She confided in people that her pain was more than had let on and she was diagnosed with two bulging disks and a stress fracture that affected both her back and neck. Her support system circled around her and also helped her improve her eating habits, even if it wasn't something we discussed at the dinner table. It wasn't an easy thing for Whitney to welcome, because as she saw it, she didn't want to be a burden on people by sharing her problems. Those are common traits among people with eating disorders.

So after all that Whitney had to overcome, here was Bob telling the family that another Phelps might be good enough to make a run at the Olympics.

6

A BIG STEP

I especially enjoyed it when my dad worked as a swim official at my meets, because it allowed us to stay close. When I was behind the blocks, he'd ask what time I was shooting for. If I didn't reach my goal time, I could always count on him to say, "Oh, so close. You'll get it next time." Whenever he said that, I always figured he knew what he was talking about and it gave me a lot of confidence. Since he was at the starting end of the block, there wasn't much chance I'd get disqualified, even if I dove in a week early and threw fishnets in the other seven lanes.

For a while our relationship was pretty good. Dad taught me the importance of a firm handshake and had me practice it on him so I didn't greet somebody with a fist full of mush. I also learned about good and bad ways to handle autographs while I was with him at Baltimore Orioles baseball games. I remember one afternoon when I saw an Orioles pitcher standing over by the railing, near third base, talking to a friend of his. "I'm going to get his autograph," I told my dad. "Michael, he's talking to someone," Dad said. "If you interrupt him now, it would be rude. Just stand near them and wait until they're finished. Then you can ask him for his autograph, and I'm sure he'll give it to you." It didn't quite work that way. As soon as the pitcher was finished talking, I spoke up, but he waved me off, because he didn't feel like signing. My dad had been sitting in the background watching all this, but he shot up to the railing and just about undressed the pitcher in front of everyone.

"Now why are you so special that you can't sign one autograph for this boy? He was waiting for you for ten minutes. I know you saw him. He was the only one waiting and he was very polite. Do you really think you'd be playing baseball in Camden Yards if you didn't have kids looking up to you like that?"

The pitcher never did come back to sign anything, but he did sort of crawl away.

As a kid, I didn't understand why an athlete would behave that way. I understood that the players sometimes needed to prepare for games, so it never phased me if a player said, "Sorry, I can't. I have to go take batting practice." But this player was simply rude. He didn't acknowledge us. Before that, I thought all players were nice guys. I thought for some reason that you had to be an especially good person in order to be a great athlete, and that being an especially good person meant that you treated other people well. The pitcher's attitude was a shock to the system.

I try to accommodate everyone who asks for an autograph. Until 2004, that's been pretty easy to do. But at times when I can't because I have to catch a plane or I have Bob screaming at me to get in the pool, I try to be polite about it. I try to apologize and, if I know I'll be available later, I'll tell people when practice is over and where I'll be. I remember how I felt after the exchange with the pitcher and it kind of blows me away when I think of how I'm in a position to make or break a kid's day based on how I respond to him for a few seconds. Fortunately, I also had a good example to draw from.

My dad worked security detail at a number of functions and often met prominent people from the area during his assignments. At different times, he worked on the security team for President Reagan and the Pope. While working at one of the local hotels, he struck up a friendship with Ben McDonald and Chris Hoiles, two Oriole players who were very good guys. Through his connection with them, he was able to get me into the clubhouse one day to meet the players, and my dad had already prepped them about the trophy in my room from my home run derby days. "You don't know those guys," I told him. "Michael, yes, I do," he said, "and you're going to meet them." I saw McDonald, one of Baltimore's top pitchers, first. "This must be Michael," McDonald said. I must have had the goofiest grin on my face. "I understand you're a tremendous baseball player." Now my grin was as big as the ballpark. "I wish I could hit like you, but I'm just a pitcher." Okay, bigger than the ballpark. It wasn't just that this was Ben McDonald, an Orioles pitcher, taking time to scribble his name or pose for a picture because I knew something about him; he actually knew something about me. So maybe I really was a pretty good player. Way to go, Dad.

We went fishing a lot, too, but I only liked it when I was catching something. Otherwise, I'd get bored and start throwing rocks in the water, which, of course, would scare off the fish and defeat the whole purpose of going fishing in the first place.

If dad could introduce me to fishing, I could coax him into playing video games. One of our favorites was Zelda, an old-school Nintendo game with a little guy who wore a green outfit and carried a little sword. The guy would start the game with two hearts of life and along the way accumulate feats of magic and more hearts. It was a cool game back in the day and it was cool to bond with my dad. I even told him one day that I wanted to be a state trooper, inspecting vehicles and keeping the roads safe as he did. "No, Michael, you'll probably want to do something else," he said.

As time went on, we spent less time together. That happens as kids grow up and become more independent, I guess. Both of my parents were always behind decisions I made. If I wanted to hang out with my friends instead of going to Dad's house on the weekends, he was fine with that. If I wanted to sleep in on the weekends and get ready for a meet, it was okay. There was a fine line for my dad between staying active in our lives on the one hand and giving us space to grow up on the other. As time went on, I stopped trying to involve him in my activities and he stopped trying to involve himself.

It also got really awkward for Hilary, Whitney, or me to see him in the company of another woman. *Was this a girlfriend? Was this woman becoming a special part of his life and was she, therefore, supposed to become a special part of our lives?* I just didn't want to see him with anyone except my mom. She didn't seem interested in anyone else's company, because she was always taking care of us and putting us first.

I tested the limits of her unconditional support when I discovered rap music. Whitney's boyfriend Victor had a Jeep CJ7 and I used to love getting in that car. He played hip-hop CDs and cranked up the sound system and I thought it was awesome. I'd listen to the beat, nod my head and feel like I could fit in with older kids. After I listened to A Tribe Called Quest, I started saving up money to buy the CDs. I turned on MTV to watch the rappers in their houses and their tricked-out cars with spinners on the rims and TVs in the seats. I just liked the whole culture of it. Rap lyrics can be pretty raw, but I explained to Mom that I tuned in for the beat and not the message. She listened to the songs and to my explanation with an open mind and she never objected, because it was part of growing up.

So was my note-passing fling. I was in sixth grade at Dumbarton Middle School and had been passing notes in the hallway to an eighth-grade girl named Molly, who was one of Erin's friends. Molly would say something funny; I'd respond. I'd ask about her friends; she would give me a funny note in return. We didn't have any classes together, so we couldn't pass notes during classtime. Of course we could just talk in the hallway, but this became a sort of game we played, to write things that would make the other person laugh through the next class. Eventually, I got up the courage to ask Molly to the movies in one of those notes. She agreed, and suddenly, the pressure was on. I didn't tell too many people about this date, but Matt McDonough started telling me about the yawn, stretch your hand out and put your arm around her trick. It's easy to think about, but doing it in a subtle way is practically impossible. That night we met up with a bunch of her friends and saw *Jurassic Park II*. I didn't drive yet, so my mom was going to pick us up. I'm not exactly sure what inspired the moment—maybe T-Rex roaring or actors screaming, but at some point during the movie, we both went for it. My first kiss. It felt weird. It felt great. It felt, wow, what is it supposed to feel like? It was a new feeling, exciting, scary, everything. Honestly, I don't know about her, but that's all I thought about during the movie.

I couldn't help myself when we went back to school. People knew we were going out, so they asked and I told. It's a rite of passage and I felt different after it happened. In a few months, the summer came. I bought my first rose to give to Molly for her graduation and she got ready to go to ninth grade at a different school, while I was heading for seventh. Nothing ruins a lifelong relationship more than seventh grade, so we split. High school seemed so far away at that point. I still had a lot of growing up to do and some important decisions to make.

Remember the primary teacher who said I'd never amount to anything because I couldn't focus? Well, my mom didn't tell me about those comments then, but she did tell me about a discussion

she had with Ms. Myers, my seventh-grade English teacher. She
said that I was having an extreme amount of difficulty with writing,
that I couldn't, or didn't, take the effort to express my thoughts on
paper as readily as I would when I spoke. I had to hand in journal
entries for her class, and on many days I didn't feel I had much to
say, so I didn't hand anything in. When I did write something, I
didn't take time to think things through or to proofread what I
wrote. My mom tried to explain to me that writing was not a one-
shot deal, that it took as much patience and detail to tell a story or
write a journal entry just as it would to write someone a letter,
something else I didn't like to do unless I was slipping notes to
girls in hallways. "Michael, not only does Ms. Myers think you
aren't doing a good job on your journals, but she thinks you simply
can't do a better job on them. Now, what are we going to do about
that?"

What we did was work and work some more. For hours after
swim practice, we'd sit in front of the computer together and Mom
would help me complete my journal.

"Michael, what's the topic today?"

"Summer vacation."

"And what was the first thing you thought of when they told
you the topic?"

"The beach."

"So write about what happened at the beach."

"Nothing happened at the beach."

"Really, so you slept at the beach the whole time?"

"No, we did things."

"So, write about three things you did."

"I can think of two, maybe."

"Good, two. . . and then one more."

"But Mohhhm . . ."

My mom would rarely say no to anything I did, even if she

thought it wasn't a good idea. Instead she'd say, "Oh, I see" and start nodding. That meant that she wanted me to rethink the idea on my own so she didn't have to give me a lecture. I can read the nods (that mean no) pretty well by now. They're usually followed by a list of every consequence under the sun to make me reach the conclusion that the plan just won't fly.

"All right, Michael, but if you do that, you realize that this will happen and that will happen and you have to do this and give up that and I won't be there to help with this and . . ."

"Okay Mom, I'll do something else."

"Michael, I'm glad you feel that way. I think you made a smart decision. Michael, I really support the decision you just made."

"Thanks, Mom."

Each time, my mind processed the consequences, there would be this chain collision of objections to something that told me no.

I can only think of one time when I really tried to override her. It was seventh grade and I was fed up with having to take Ritalin. I looked at it as a crutch, and I didn't need to be slinking off to the nurse anymore. This wasn't coming from anyone else. This was me. I wanted to be rid of it.

"Michael, you know how you lose concentration."

"I'll concentrate harder."

"You know how you don't like to read a whole chapter in one sitting. . ."

"Mom, I'll concentrate harder."

"You know how you start talking to other kids in the middle of lectures. . ."

"Mom, I know I have to work harder."

"If I start hearing from your teachers . . ."

"Mom, I really want to do this. I need to do this. It's time."

On my mom's face, I saw a combination of concern and pride. Inside, I knew how much she wanted me to take this step, too. We spoke to Dr. Wax about it and he gradually started weaning me off the medication, first eliminating the afternoon dose so I wouldn't have to take it during school, then the frequency of the other doses, and by the next year, all of it. The crutch was gone, and I had learned what it was like to set a goal that was difficult to achieve—and to win.

7

BREAKING **OUT**

Just because I was growing up, it didn't mean I was growing out of old habits. It was January, 1998 and Bob wanted me to warm down at the end of a long practice by swimming an easy 400 yards. After giving his instructions, he ran upstairs to make some copies from a glass-enclosed room that overlooked the pool. From there, he could see that I only swam 150 yards before getting out of the water, so he came downstairs to confront me. At some point as he was walking down the staircase, he mumbled something a little off-color under his breath, but without realizing it, he said it as he passed Whitney, who was walking in the other direction. She told my mom about it later that night and Mom sent Bob a one-page let-ter that asked, among other things, why he was being so tough on me, given my age. The upshot of the letter was that Bob apologized for one word, but he stood by his disappointment over the fact that I left early. I realized that Bob looked after the little things and he was going to make sure I did, too.

I never liked practices the day before a meet. Get me to the blocks and tell me when to go. I thought I could cruise through one of those training sessions one afternoon as we were preparing for the annual meet that NBAC hosted in June. We had an easy practice scheduled: 16 sets of 50s starting once a minute, with each set going a little faster. We lined up to do our sets in a row, so if the swimmer in front of you slowed down, it meant that you had to slow down, too. I was really swimming in quicksand. "Michael, speed up," the girl behind me was saying. "You'll have to go faster." I didn't and finally Bob had had enough. "That's it, Michael, get out of the pool. You're not going to swim another stroke for NBAC until you do the set properly. Not another stroke." Of course I had to explain to my mom why I was done early that afternoon. I was convinced that Bob wasn't serious, that he'd let it blow over because it was just a throwaway training set and we had races to swim. Wrong again. Bob got on the phone with Mom and called for a 5:30 a.m. meeting with my parents and me the next day. It was as much fun as going to the dentist.

Bob held court in his usual plastic seat. Mom brought her usual arsenal of logic and called for calm compromise. Dad sat in full uniform and listened. I pouted and kept my face under my cap. "Michael is not on the team until he does the set I told him to do yesterday," Bob said. "Michael, I don't care if you like it, and I really don't care if you like me, but if you want to be on this team, you have to get in the pool and finish what you were supposed to do yesterday."

Honestly, Bob never expected he'd coach me for very long. He figured one of us would give up on the other sooner or later. He knew I was talented, but he figured either I would convince my mom to take me to some other coach or he would go somewhere else. He had nothing to lose. He didn't lose, either. I went downstairs, stretched and completed the drill properly from start to finish.

It was a rare joy when we got away with doing anything behind

Bob's back (Bong), but you take your victories where you can get them (Bong). Since it seemed we could never say anything without Bob catching on (Bong), the kids at the pool came up with our own language. We called it Bong. It was our version of Pig Latin, and Erin and I could speak it fluently a mile a minute. If a tense moment called for a conversation we couldn't have in present company, one of us would cover our mouth as if to cough. Out would come the word "bong" and everything else that followed was a flurry of syllables that flew straight over Bob's head. Essentially, we added the letters ONG to consonants, spoke all vowels and got away with verbal murder. Bob never wanted us to complain about the heat, but whenever it was really steaming during one of our workouts, in or out of the pool, the phrase I-tong-song Hong-oh-tong would get tossed around like a beachball. Verbal warfare is fun when you bring camouflage.

Other times, well, it can lead to trouble. I was playing volleyball at school in seventh grade when some kids began talking smack on the other side of the net. Then one of the kids came over and started flicking my ears. I told him to knock it off, but he wouldn't. Finally I slugged him, got suspended from school and had to sit through long talks with my parents. My mom talked to me about conflict resolution, since she never wanted to me to hit anybody and always figured there were better ways to handle arguments. My dad talked to me about punching technique, since he wanted to make sure I got in a good shot. "Michael, if you're going to hit the kid," he said, "make it a good one."

Some days, my temper would get the better of me. I was sitting in eighth-grade math class when my teacher, Mr. De Stefano, told me to stop leaning back in my chair. It was a way for him to prove a point. I had a habit of rocking back in my seat, so I was only resting on two chair legs and I was making an outline into the floor. "But I'm not doing anything," I yelled at him. Then I left the room.

I was furious and I was convinced that he singled me out and over-reacted. But after that I never leaned back in my chair again.

On the other hand, I loved eighth-grade home economics class. I've never taken such detailed notes or given such undivided attention to a teacher. Of course a lot of that had to do with the teacher. Ms. Schwan was right out of college and gorgeous. The girls in the room sometimes gave her trouble, but I don't think one guy ever misbehaved in that class for a minute. If she had asked us to collect a million milk coupons, jump into a barrel of onions and calculate tax in Swahili, we would have done it. We all had killer crushes on her. I got an A.

I had another breakthrough of sorts that year: I shaved. Boys love it when they are able to shave. It means they have to shave, which is a sign of manliness to compensate for that crackling voice. It's different, though, for swimmers. When we train for big meets, we go through a cycle we call "shave and taper." As the competition approaches, we gradually reduce our training load so that our bodies will be able to draw from the training base while still being rested enough so we aren't too tired and sore. That's the taper. Swimmers also shave their bodies before big competitions on the theory that body hair creates resistance as the body moves through the water. That's why, if you watch the Olympics or other major swim meets, most of the swimmers will be wearing swim caps. Some will even be bald. When swimmers compete without being shaved and tapered, chances are they are competing while still in the middle of a training cycle and won't be able to swim at their peak.

A swimmer's shave extends well beyond sideburns. You need to shave everywhere that isn't covered by your suit. And nobody is more capable of self-inflicted injury than a rookie shaver. *How hard do you press down? Where do you press down? How do you reach this spot? And that spot? How much do you (ouch!).* ... By the end of that first shaving session, I had nice road maps running up and down my legs with crowded intersections forming at my knees.

Meanwhile, I was starting to take part in bigger competitions. My breakout meet was the '99 juniors in Orlando, where I made my first national cut at age 13. I didn't win any events, but I finished in the top four three times. I swam the 200 fly in 2:04, which was an astounding ten-second improvement from what I had done in training just six weeks earlier. I was a little disappointed to swim so well and not win any titles, but Bob congratulated me after the race and said that he thought first place might have been bad luck. He said he had never coached a swimmer who won juniors and then went on to win Nationals as a senior.

I was in for some heavy reading after that meet. Every six months, *Swimming World* magazine would list the top 16 times in each race throughout the country. I would read through the entire list the first day I got it and then read through it again the next day. The magazine also listed the top age-group swimmers in the country. I got a real charge out of looking in the magazine and seeing my name in its pages. So what if you had to skim through what seemed like ten thousand pages to get to it on one of the last pages. And maybe it was listed in microscopic print, visible only by a high-powered lens. There it was: M. Phelps.

I felt I was really hitting the big time. I gave my first interview to our local paper, the *Baltimore Sun*. What did a 13-year-old have to say for himself? I really don't remember. I was shocked, rather than nervous. Cal Ripken Jr. belonged on the sports pages, not me.

I went to Senior Nationals later that summer in Minneapolis and finished 41st in the 400 IM in my first race. In my next race, I swam a 2:07 in the 200 fly and was dead last in my heat. The time was more than two seconds slower than I had just swum at juniors. It was a good lesson for Bob that perhaps I just wasn't ready yet. Logically, I should have been able swim as fast there as I had in

Orlando, but this was a different atmosphere altogether. I remember being on the deck, getting ready for my heat and thinking: *Wow, there's Tom Dolan.* Later I was sitting in the stands, watching Tom Malchow walk across the pooldeck. I wasn't really trying to see what his practice habits were, but I was just watching him because I was in awe of him and, more important, in awe of the fact that I was swimming at the same meet as the defending Olympic silver medalist. I got to see the elite swimmers up close, but I was focusing on what they were doing rather than what I was doing.

I wasn't due to compete on the last day of the event, but that didn't mean Bob didn't want me to swim. "Get ready, Michael, you're doing a practice today." I thought, *wait a second, he isn't going to make me practice today. We're already at the pool and I didn't even bring my suit. Hey, it worked in lacrosse: no cup, no goalie; why wouldn't it work at the pool?* Because Bob was my coach now.

"I thought I was resting today."

"You're training."

"But I don't have a suit. What can I do?"

"You can get in the car with me."

"You're kidding."

He wasn't kidding. It took us 40 minutes to go back and get the suit. I had a pouty face and a serious attitude all day, but it didn't change the fact the we got the suit and I went back in the water.

Bob tried to nudge me in the right direction by instituting double sessions in training, but it didn't last a week. "I'm spending 80 percent of my time at the pool," I told him. Bob rebuffed that with a notebook and pen and some simple math. So it was only 20 percent; it sure felt like 80 percent. I mean nothing ruins a good argument like a bunch of facts.

That year, Dynamo called to offer Bob another interview for a job at their club. After 18 months of coaching my group, a position he assumed would be temporary, Bob finally saw his dream job staring at him in the face, so he went up to talk to Murray about it. "Bob, I don't want to do anything to keep you from moving on," Murray said. "I know how much you want this job. Maybe you should take it." Bob was reassured he was doing the right thing and he figured he would leave . . . for about three seconds. "Of course if you stay, I see you being Michael's coach for the duration. It wouldn't be right to give him to anyone else. Let me know what you think." Bob called the Dynamo club back the next day to tell them no. We were in this together for the long haul.

8

NOW FOR THE LONG HAUL

Not only was Bob my coach for life, but he was on to me. When I arrived at a morning practice, he told me one day that after practice was over, he was going to give me a note with some of what he thought were realistic goal times for the next few meets. The times weren't listed in numerals; they were written in Bong—are no secrets safe? I still have the paper. It was his way of letting us know he was aware of the language and that he was relating to us. It was also Big Brother springing into action. Apparently, Bob had known about Bong for a while, but he hadn't told people. Fortunately, even though Bob realized what we were doing, he didn't necessarily understand what we were saying. We made sure we spoke too quickly for him to keep up, but there was still an inherent danger in gabbing in Bong, because the cong-aye-tong was out of the bong-aye-gong.

I headed off to Towson High School in the fall of 1999 and rediscovered my urge to play other sports. I hit it off with a government teacher there named Gerry Brewster, a former state delegate (Anyone remember 'I'm a Brewster Booster?'). On our first day of class, we listed our interests on a piece of paper and I wrote down swimming.

"Are you any good, Michael?"

"Pretty good."

"Have you won any races?"

"A few."

It turned out Mr. Brewster was also the high school golf coach. He told me about the team and it sounded like fun, even though I told him at first that I couldn't try out because of swimming.

A few weeks later, some friends of mine won spots on the Towson High football team. Away from Towson, Matt, who went to a different school, Calvert Hall, for freshman and sophomore years, also made his team as a lineman. I really wanted to join them and I started calculating the hours for homework, swim training, and football practice in my head. The numbers almost made sense if you turned them sideways and removed those futile eight hours for sleep. I couldn't do without meal and snacktime.

"Hey, Mom, I was thinking of trying to join the football team."

(Silence from Mom. Oh, that's not good.)

"Mom?"

"Michael, let's talk about this."

(Silence from me. This could be painful.)

"Michael, I know you're proud of your friend and you should be, but how many hours of practice do you think the football team has? And how many games?"

"Well, they practice in the afternoons . . . and then they play games . . ."

" . . . about the same time you have your swim meets?"

"Not all the time."

"Where can his football career take him? First string? County championships? All-Metro? A Division I school? Will he be pro?"

"He's kinda small for the pros."

"Now what can you do with swimming?"

"Mom, how about golf?"

(Long self-explanatory silence.)

"Maybe I can go to one or two of Matt's games."

"Good idea."

I always respected my mom's opinion, so it was ironic that a couple of adults thought I was being disrespectful toward her because I called her Debs at meets. In fact, that was a Mom-approved means of address. See, pooldecks are chaotic places with swimmers, officials, coaches, and family. Kids shout out "Mom" or "Dad" into a mass of people and 40 heads turn around to see if that scream is for them. So whenever I couldn't find my mom or just wanted to get her attention, I'd yell for Debs instead.

Training went well that fall and winter. Bob had reached into his bag of tricks to improve every one of my strokes. I did butter-fly and backstroke laps, using only the right or left arm, in order to isolate the arm and work on the way it moved through the water. We improved my freestyle technique by doing a drill that kept my elbows high and had me pull through with my fingertips, so my legs would do more of the work and get stronger. He often had me swim with arms only, legs only, or with one arm or one leg.

One day, Bob had me train in sneakers. Other days, I'd either swim while tethered to a pulley, while wearing a scuba vest or with an innertube around my ankles. Those impediments allowed me to increase resistance the way a hitter in the on-deck circle would take some practice swings with a donut on his bat. The extra weight would make the bat feel lighter and easier to swing once he actually faced live pitching. The weights on the swimmers would make swimming feel easier once the weights were gone.

The variety kept it interesting and challenging. Bob gradually worked me back into double sessions until I was ready to handle them on a regular basis. He didn't want to tell me just how much my times were improving in practice, but in February of 2000, a week before we left for the Spring Nationals in Federal Way,

Washington, Bob pulled my mom aside outside of Meadowbrook to speak to her.

"Debbie, when we get back from Seattle, we should sit down and talk."

"Why, Bob? What's wrong?"

"Nothing is wrong at all. In fact, it's good, but it's a matter of time before things start to change for Michael and nothing is going to be the same."

"What do you mean?"

"He's way ahead of schedule right now and at some point—I don't know when—we're going to need to get ready for media attention, hype, expectation. He'll need to prepare for that, and it will be on us sooner than we think."

Somewhere in the back of Bob's mind was the remote possibility that I could finish in the top two at trials in Indianapolis five months later and qualify for the Olympics at 15. It seemed less remote to him after my prelim swim in the 200 fly in Federal Way. I usually feed off a noisy crowd, but it was 1 p.m. on the first day of the meet. Almost nobody was in the stands and so there was no atmosphere. I broke two minutes for the first time, finishing in 1:59.4, an age-group record for 13- and 14-year-olds that was also faster than the 15s and 16s. I didn't have perspective on that swim, but Bob and Murray were hiding their excitement. "Okay, that was good, Michael. Swim down and we'll go get lunch," Bob told me.

During that trip, I ate every single meal at a place called Mitzell's, which was located next to our hotel. And at every meal—we're talking 21 meals over seven days—I ate clam chowder as my appetizer and a slice of cheesecake for dessert. Only the entrée changed. That's how people on the team began to know me as Mr. Clam Chowder. Why change it if it works? As he was getting ready to take me to Mitzell's, Bob was walking out to the parking lot to pick up the car, which was a long way from the front door. During the walk, he told himself under his breath, "Okay, he's going to make the Olympic team. This Olympic team. The 2000 Olympic team. I better get him ready." Even though Bob had the Olympic inkling, he didn't act very different at lunch. But after he dropped me off at the hotel, he went out for a long jog to run off some of his energy. I came back at night and lowered my time to 1:59.0, finishing third behind Stephen Parry of Great Britain and Malchow.

The day after, I set another age group record in the 400 IM and dropped my time in that race by seven seconds to 4:24. Bob told me how well I was swimming, which gave me a false sense of relaxation. I wasn't swimming in any finals the next day and Bob had talked about doing some sightseeing in the afternoon, so I figured I had earned a rare day off from training. What was I thinking? Of course, we trained anyway.

In the afternoon, Bob and I went to the Seattle fish market where customers have to catch their own fish. Confused? It's a tradition that after people place their orders while standing on street level, a man wraps their fish while on a raised platform and throws it down to them. You don't want a turnover there. Imagine going back to school or to work after missing the fish and having it hit you in the chest? I don't get some traditions. Later we went up in the Space Needle that overlooks the city. It was an amazing view, but I couldn't help bringing up swimming once or twice. Each time, Bob sort of deflected the conversation, telling me that I was doing well and then talking about other things. He didn't want me getting carried away about the future.

On the final day I swam my one 1,500 free of the year and recorded the second-fastest time ever for my age group. On the outside, Bob was being very positive; on the inside, his mind was in overdrive, planning an accelerated schedule. I wondered why he couldn't sleep on the flight home.

We came back from Seattle on a Monday and Bob brought me back to my house, when my mom was off at work. On the front lawn, she had placed a large banner with the word "congratula-tions" on it and trimmings around the lawn in red, white and blue. I thought it looked great. Bob grabbed all of it and took it down. My mom was pretty upset with Bob when she came home a little while later.

"Bob, do you realize what he just accomplished?"

"Debbie, this is like step number 180 in a 10,000-step process. We're just getting started here."

They compromised and left the sign up for 48 hours. I never saw the other decorations again. Bob asked my mom for her help in not letting people get too excited and in keeping people's expecta-tions in check. He decreed that nobody around Meadowbrook could say the word "Olympic" in my presence.

That week, USA Swimming sent an invitation for an orienta-tion camp in Colorado to over a hundred swimmers the organiza-tion felt had a chance to make the Olympic team. The agenda included discussions about jet lag, what the pool was like at the Olympic venue in Sydney, suggestions for things to pack on the trip and so on. My mom told me about it and I wanted to go, but Bob said no. "You're not on the team yet," he told me. "Don't get ahead of yourself." I made it pretty clear that I was disappointed. "Michael, the way you'll give yourself the best chance to go to Sydney is by staying here and training."

Still there was one thing he couldn't avoid. I had never been out of the country before, so he made sure I went to get a passport application. "What's this about?" I asked. "Nothing yet," he said. "Just fill it out. You may need it some day."

Right after Nationals, it seemed I was spending a lot of time with people in medical robes. First, I was added to the U.S. Olympic Committee's pool of athletes who needed to be drug test-ed. As a 14-year-old, growing up into the sport, I found it weird having someone stand next to you and watch you go, especially the first couple of times. But now that I've been tested on hundreds of occasions in my career, it's really not that big a deal.

There are two types of tests: those we take immediately after competitions, when we win an international medal or qualify for a national team; and unannounced tests that officials can conduct at any time. Yup, people can either show up at your front door or at your training facility and insist that you provide a urine sample for drug testing. I can usually sense when I'm due for a random test. Sure enough, I'll show up at Meadowbrook and the two local testers will be the first people I see when I walk through the door. Really the complicated part is making sure people know your schedule, since the anti-doping officials can call on you at any time. My mom and Bob always know my itinerary, because if I'm unavailable for a random test, that can count as a doping violation and I would be subject to the same penalties as I would be if they found an illegal substance in my system.

The person who conducts the tests probably has the worst job on the planet. But it's a necessary process. Without it, people would be tempted to cheat. That's why there are proctors to monitor school tests. Even with it, athletes have been caught taking substances to enhance their performance illegally. We need testing in order to have a clean sport, and I believe we do, especially if you compare swimming to some other sports. The fact is that an anti-drug policy is there to protect the clean athletes, to make sure the competition is fair, to make sure athletes aren't doing things to their bodies that can hurt them badly in the long run.

I also learned, at that meet, that swimmers are careful never to drink from a cooler that isn't taped up. The tape indicates that an official was in charge of pouring the water or sports drink into the cooler and he watched to make sure nobody tampered with what's inside.

Soon after my first doping test, I also went to get checked out for something else. I could feel something wrong one day when I dove into the water at practice. My heart rate was accelerating and Bob suggested I see the doctor. Because I was very flexible and had long hands and feet, I had some early symptoms of Marfan Syndrome, a disease that affects connective tissues and can be fatal if there is leakage to the vessels that lead to the heart. If you reach out your arms and form a T and your wingspan is longer than your height, you can be at risk. In my case, those measurements have always been very close. I didn't know at the time why the doctor decided to look into this. My mom and Bob didn't want me to freak out, so they told me that it was simply a good idea for young athletes to have an EKG test in order to look at the heart.

Fortunately everything was, and still is, okay. I have been tested once a year ever since at John's Hopkins under the direction of Dr. Peter Roe, and the tissues are strong, the aortic route is clear and my heart is in good shape—as long as my Baltimore Ravens are winning.

Next issue: After one of my growth spurts, I had a protruding bone in my shoulder that would grind and shift when I took a stroke. The bone grew faster than the rest of my body could handle, and when I moved my shoulders around, both of them popped out toward the back side. I went to see Scott Heinlein, a local physical therapist, who had me do a few exercises to correct the problem. By having me push against him at a certain angle, he was able to loosen the motions of the joints and reduce the grinding. Since then I've gone to see Scott for problems with my shoulders, knees, back and ankles. I'm convinced he does magic. "Here, Mike, move your hips like this, and your knees will get better." It doesn't matter how disconnected the pieces seem, he finds the connections. One of these days, he'll tell me to cure a headache by moving my toes. All I knew after those initial sessions was that he had me ready for Trials in Indianapolis.

Despite Bob's optimism, I was still swimming under the Olympic radar screen. No male swimmer my age had qualified for a U.S. Olympic team since 1932. In its Olympic Trials forecast that summer, *Swimming World* magazine wrote the following: "Fourteen-year-old Michael Phelps swam a phenomenal 1:59.02 at spring nationals, but is probably a year or two away from being a factor on the world scene."

9

ME, SECOND?

The Olympic Trials are not for the faint of heart. In years past, it used to be that countries could send three swimmers per individual event to the Games. But in part because the U.S. teams were so strong, the International Olympic Committee voted to reduce that number to two per individual event. You can measure the margin of error on your fingernail. Gary Hall Jr., a three-time Olympian, once compared the stress levels at the two events by saying: "If I'm third at the Olympics, it means I'm on the medal stand in a few minutes; if I'm third at the Trials, it means I'm on the couch for a month." All the best swimmers in the country were there: Tom Dolan, Lenny Krayzelburg, Jenny Thompson, Dara Torres. I wasn't as awed by them as I had been at other meets, but I was still unproven.

In Indy, we stayed at the Adam's Mark. I was in a room by myself and it marked the first trip when I really took advantage of room service. Every night I'd order a chicken sandwich and cheesecake, and I became attached to that meal as I did with clam chowder in Federal Way. I'm glad to report that nobody started calling me Mr. Chicken Sandwich.

The competition was a sort of mixed blessing for us. Over the previous year, Whitney had worked tirelessly to rehab her back and straighten out her diet. After a year out of the pool, she came back and had a great year at the University of Nevada-Las Vegas. She was the team's outstanding newcomer and she made her cut for the Olympic Trials. We were so psyched for her that she won her conference title and was doing so well. After talking it over with her coach at UNLV, Whitney decided to come home in May and train at North Baltimore to work with Murray and Bob and to re-chase her Olympic dream. It was great having her around the pool, but it didn't take long for the spasms to return to her upper back and for doctors to warn her about a bulging disk. It was a tough decision for her to withdraw, but she didn't want to represent herself or her club at a sub-par level and she didn't want to jeopardize her long-term health. It wasn't fair. We should have been going after our dream together. Instead, it was just me.

I entered in three events: the 200 fly, 200 IM and 400 IM. I had also qualified for the 1,500 free, but I agreed I wouldn't enter it. Every year since I was 13, I have had a deal with Bob that I would swim exactly one competitive mile race each year. It's been one a year ever since.

On the second day, I swam the 400 IM and finished 11th with a time (4:25.97) that was well off my personal best. Bob told me to put it behind me and concentrate on the 200 fly, which was the event in which I had my one realistic chance to make the team. I came into the final as the third seed. Malchow, the defending Olympic silver medalist and world-record holder at 1:55.18, was the clear favorite. Behind him was a group of four swimmers who were capable of breaking 1:58: Jeff Somensatto of Auburn, Steve Brown of Stanford, Andrew Mahaney from the Atlantis Swim Club, and me.

Up in the stands, my family's seats weren't very good, so my mom moved down to a standing position in a no-standing area. She wasn't obstructing anyone's view, but an usher came by and told her to find her seat. Politely, but firmly, she told him, "My son is about to swim in the finals of the Olympic trials. Please give me two minutes. After this race, you can do what you need to do."

Bob had told me before the race that I'd have a chance to make up ground over the last 50 meters, but I'd need to be within striking range at the third turn. Instead, I was fifth at the 150 wall. Ironically my mom and Bob each told me the same thing, that they were preparing their "We still love you" speeches in their minds. My mom actually turned her head away from the pool and started watching the scoreboard. She missed the last 50 entirely. At the far end of the pool deck, Bob and Murray were standing on blocks, trying to look over the people in front of them and get a clear view of the race. As Bob began squinting to see how far back I was, Murray started broadcasting the details of the race into his ear. At 150 meters, Murray said, "Uh oh, he's pretty far back. It doesn't look good."

I could feel myself getting faster over that last 50, even though I didn't see where I was compared to the rest of the field. After I touched the wall, I couldn't look up at the board right away. I heard the announcer say my name and I wasn't sure I heard him correctly. *Second? But second is on the Olympic team. Really, second?* I had to remove my goggles to make sure I was seeing it correctly. Sure enough, there it was on the board: Malchow first in 1:56.87; Phelps second in 1:57.48. I had this ear-to-ear smile come across my face. I looked up into the stands and couldn't find my mom right away, because she had moved.

On the opposite end of the arena, Murray and Bob jumped up and down, tried to high-five each other, missed badly and fell off the blocks they were standing on. Anyone possessing a tape of that momentous celebration should please send one copy to *America's Funniest Home Videos*, a second to ESPN's *Top-Ten Bloopers* and another one to me. I'll handle the rest.

Malchow and I first congratulated one another in the water. Then as I started walking along the pooldeck, Whitney came up and put her arms around me. That hug meant more than I could say. I knew how hard the last four years had been for her. I knew how much she wanted to swim at the trials. I knew her bad luck was eating away at her, but at that moment, there was nobody else I wanted to see more than Whitney. I was too excited—and too young and new to everything—to find the words to tell her, but if I hadn't seen her put in all that work, if I hadn't seen the sacrifices she made and if I hadn't seen firsthand that you can't take success for granted, there is no way I would have been on that Olympic team. Every time I blew up at Bob or decided some level of extra effort wasn't necessary, I knew, because of Whitney, that I needed to blow off my steam and get back to work, because if I wasn't willing to do that, somebody else certainly was and he would kick my butt when we got into the pool. In a very real way, her hard work had put a Phelps on the Olympic team after all.

***

In some ways, the post-race press conference was almost harder than the event. I sat at a table and stared out at many more reporters than I had ever seen in one place. I had been used to one or two, but a whole colony of them? I talked about the race, what it meant to be going to the Olympics and what I did at school. Then came the curveball. "So, do you have a girlfriend?" I had no idea what to do or say or how to answer that. My face got pretty red as I told them I did. Then they asked her name, which I gave them. I also told them the fact that she was attending Dulaney High, a rival school. They practically asked me for her social security number. Then someone asked, "Did you kiss her?" Bob was sitting next to me and watching me squirm with every question. He covered the microphone with his hands and quietly said, "No comment," to let me know I didn't have to answer everything. I told them "No comment," but I had mentioned her name without her permission because I was just so caught off guard by the line of questioning. I apologized to her the next time we spoke and even though she was okay with it, I felt like an idiot. I was pretty on edge about doing interviews after that if I didn't know who I was talking to.

I went into drug testing afterward and happened to sit next to Jeff Somensatto in the waiting room. I felt weird about it, because I had just touched him out of a spot on the Olympic team, and I remember thinking how lousy it would have felt to finish third. Jeff was a complete gentleman about it, congratulating me and telling me to bring back a medal in Sydney. *A medal? Me? Wow.*

Bob and I were getting testy on the flight back to Baltimore. We flew back late and Bob had told me to come in at 9 a.m. the next day. I was tired and called him that morning to ask if we could train in the afternoon instead, and he said 9 a.m. would be just fine, thank you. After practice, Bob drove me to a local studio for my first live TV interview on CNN. They sat me behind a huge desk in a chair that swiveled. The words that came out of my mouth were fine, but I was pretty nervous about the first big interview—the open space, the microphone, the earpiece, the lights. So what did I do? I spent the whole interview swiveling. Hello, America, this is Michael. Here's Michael's left side and now here is his right side. Which side do you like best?

Bob came over to the house afterward with a two-page list of to-dos and things he wanted to discuss with my mom. At the top of the list were the reasons I should come back home immediately after the end of the swimming competition during the first week of the Games rather than stay for the second week, which traditionally has no swimming events.

First of all, athletes who went to Olympic Games were housed in a dedicated Olympic village, a series of dorm rooms surrounded by shops such as restaurants, a post office, a movie house, a souvenir shop, a laundromat and a large cafeteria. It's a pretty cool set up, with access limited to people with official accreditation. Athletes living in the village had a history of living double lives. Until they completed their events, they would turn in at 10, drink carrot juice and barely make a sound. Once they were done, they would have a lot of pent-up energy to release, and the village could become a very different place. Bob figured it wasn't a great place for a 15-year-old to be during the second week of the Olympics, since I wasn't used to fending for myself yet. Because Bob wasn't one of the official coaching staff, he would be in Sydney, but wouldn't have access to the village. My family couldn't be in the village either, so Susan Teeter, our team manager, kept a close eye on me. "If you get to the next Olympics," Bob said, "I promise you can do whatever you want during the second week."

Bob didn't really talk about my chances of winning a medal, but he suggested a goal of trying to drop my personal best by one second during the Games. It sounded like a reasonable plan. On August 20, I left my home for Pasadena. We were planning to head for Australia from the West Coast, so my first overseas adventure was just beginning. My mom had been through a long (think textbook-sized) checklist of things to pack or take care of before I left. But she couldn't make me remember everything. I was always losing my room key at the Doubletree Pasadena. One morning when Bob had planned to meet me for breakfast, he walked by the front desk and there I was standing in a bathroom towel at the front desk of the Doubletree, asking for a new room key. I roomed with Aaron Peirsol, a 17-year-old backstroker, during the trip. We spent a lot of time talking about how we could be the youngest American guys to medal. Each time Aaron talked about winning a medal, he used the word "sweet." The word was starting to grow on me. It sounded like a sweet idea.

10

THE OLYMPIAN

On our way to Sydney, one of the flight attendants came up to the three teenagers on the U.S. swim team: Aaron, Megan Quann and me. It was still a year before the tragedy of September 11, so rules were more relaxed then. "We have a surprise for you guys," the woman said. "The captain wants to know if you would like to join him in the cockpit." Wow, what a thrill. We were overlooking Sydney Harbor and we stared down into the Sydney Opera House, an open-air theater right on the water.

Soon after we arrived and went through team processing at the Olympic village, we took a short flight to Brisbane for another training camp. Practices went well and one day I went with my teammates to one of the local casinos. I had no money to wager and couldn't do it anyway because I was too young, but it was like a mini-Las Vegas. I had a 10 p.m. curfew during the trip to make sure I couldn't get into trouble. I sort of did anyway.

A day before the swimming competition started, we moved back into the village. Aaron and I roomed together and he and I would hang out with Jamie Rauch and Tommy Hannan, two of our teammates, to play Tony Hawk and James Bond video games all the time. I didn't know about the electricity conversion between the U.S. and Australia, so when I tried to hook up the system when Aaron and Tommy weren't around, I fried the video game. When the guys walked back into the room, I sort of played dumb for a while, but I had to fess up. To make matters worse, the system actually belonged to Brian Jones, a swimmer who narrowly missed making the Olympic team at the trials.

At big competitions, especially the Olympics, you can't go anywhere without your ID badge hanging from your neck. It's usually a laminated piece of thick paper with your picture, a bar code, your name and nationality and a list of where you can and can't go while attending the competition. You take it off to train, compete, and sleep, but it stays around your neck for almost everything else. Lose it at the Olympics and you can't go to the village, you can't go to the pool; it's like you're stuck in glue.

In my first morning swim, I had qualified for the semifinal of the 200 fly, winning my heat in 1:57.30 and finishing with the third fastest time overall behind Malchow and Denis Sylant'yev of Ukraine. Somehow, I heard Hilary call my name after the race, even though I had no idea where she was sitting.

In the semifinal, I lowered my time to 1:57.00, but placed third in my heat, which Tom won. As usual, Bob and I had a little side drama. In the States, the public address announcer will usually introduce the swimmers in numerical lane order, starting with Lane 1 and ending with Lane 8. In Sydney, they did it differently. Because the swimmers with the fastest times were in the middle lanes and the ones in the end lanes were the ones with slowest qualifying times, they began the introductions with lanes 1 and 8, then 2 and 7, 3 and 6 and 4 and 5. I was seeded into Lane 4 for my preliminary swim, but I wasn't prepared for the fact that I would be the last person announced. When they said my name, everyone jumped onto the blocks and I jumped on before tying my suit and tucking the strings inside. After the race, Bob jokingly told me I should be prepared the next time and look after the suit. It stayed on, thankfully, but the strings flapped around, which was like showing up for a business meeting with your tie untied. That evening, I forgot about the order of swimmers and forgot to tie my suit again. The time was okay with Bob, but not the suit. "Michael, these are the Olympic Games," he told me. "You are going to treat them right. What did we say about preparation?"

Yes, preparation. The next night, I planned to leave the village early to get to the pool for the final with plenty of time to spare. Bob wanted me there two and a half hours before the race and, as always, he had the prerace time meticulously planned, from warmup to stretching to swim down to racing. We traveled separately because as mentioned, Bob wasn't an official member of the coaching staff and couldn't stay in the village. But I had very precise instructions. What could go wrong? Ring. Ring. Ring.

"Hello."

"Hello, Bob . . ."

"Michael, are you here at the pool?"

"No, I'm going back to the village."

"What! Now! Why?"

"I took the wrong credential. I was heading out the door and I grabbed Aaron's instead."

This was bad. Of all days to have a brain cramp, this was the worst. I could tell Bob was upset, but yelling would have done no good at that point. "Well, okay, let's get here and figure out what to do," he said. I got to the pool with a little over an hour to spare. Bob was outwardly calm and we shortened our warmup to get me ready. I was jittery as I walked to the blocks, so instead of stretching behind my lane, I walked over to wish Tom luck behind his lane. Swimmers don't usually do that, and I'm not sure what I was thinking. I guess I was living the atmosphere and blowing off nervous energy. I was kind of scared to tell you the truth. I told Tom,

"Let's go, baby. We can do this." It was more a sign of nerves than sportsmanship.

I swam a good race. Just as I had hoped, I lowered my personal best again, this time to 1:56.50, but I never quite caught up to the leaders. Tom won the race in 1:55.35. I was fifth, .33 seconds behind the bronze medalist. After the race, the Malchow family was encouraging the Phelps family all over the building. Tom patted me on the back. "The best is ahead of you," he said. In the stands, Tom's parents graciously came up to my mom and told her, "Michael's time will come." I had to sort through my emotions after the race. I had lowered my PR by nearly a second, but I had also watched Tom's victory ceremony and really wanted to be on the stand with him.

Bob sent me back to the pool for a workout the next day and got some criticism from some of my teammates for not letting me blow off some steam in Sydney all day. Bob wanted to get me psyched up about next season, starting with the Spring Nationals in Austin next March, so he showed me my workout for the day on a piece of graph paper. In the margin, he wrote, *Austin WR*. It didn't take much to get me fired up. I was tired from the travel, the expectation, the whole experience, but I was already getting edgy about starting the next season. After the workout, we went to a waterpark that was adjacent to the warm-down pool. I slid down a few runs with some of the guys and basically screwed around and did nothing for most of the day. It was great to have time off to not think about the race for a few hours.

Soon I was back in the village, trying to take advantage of the 15-hour time difference and call some people back home. I wasn't getting much support from Tom, Jamie, and Aaron, who overheard one of my conversations and started making background noises. "Guys, I'm trying to talk to my girlfriend," I'd tell them, as my face turned into a tomato. Then the word started bouncing back at me like a tennis ball.

"Girlfriend, huh?"

"Girlfriend? Mike's got a girlfriend."

"Michael Phelps, paging Michael Phelps, would you please report to your girlfriend." "Hey," I told her, "can we talk later? There's bad static everywhere except on the phone. I need to call you back."

I also called Whitney, who had stayed home to start classes at UNLV and reconcile herself with a swimming career that was coming to an end. I told her I understood her decision not to come to Sydney. I knew it was hard for her to be around swimming and especially to watch swimmers she used to beat win medals at the Olympics. Reporters have noticed over the years that she hasn't come to as many meets as my mom and Hilary. They ask about jealousy, but they misread that completely. Whitney has always been incredibly supportive of me, but it was hard for her to go to meets and not be able to participate herself. I know she wishes she'd had a chance to see how good she could have been, but she has always been happy for my success. Whatever she's felt inside, I love her for the way she puts a smile on for me. I told her how much I missed her and was looking forward to catching up on her next visit home.

The next day I went to the AT&T family center, a dedicated place created by one of the Olympic sponsors where athletes can spend time with their families and their families can relax, eat, and watch other events on television. I was there with my aunts Amy and Krista, my uncle BJ and Pat Calhoun, one of the breaststrokers on the team. My dad was there, too. He had flown over on his own. It was good to see him, but we hadn't spent nearly as much time together in the months leading up to the Games. I knew for a long time that he had been seeing a woman named Lois. They moved in together for a while and we got along with her reasonably well. It was hard for me to like a different woman besides my mom, but I appreciated the fact that Lois tried to make an effort with us. A couple of times, I remember her suggesting to my dad that he should take us somewhere, either with or without her, but I always had the sense that she respected the fact that we were a part of his life and, therefore, a part of her life. For that reason, awkward as it was, we got along with her okay.

After my dad split up with Lois, he started dating a woman named Jackie. I hadn't spoken with her much, so I didn't know much about her. She was with my dad that day. At one point, I got up to go to the bathroom and he followed me over there. I guess none of us really noticed his hand in the few minutes we were there with him, but as we walked into the bathroom, Dad reached his hand out and said, "Hey, look what I got." I was stunned. It was a ring. What do you say after seeing something like that? "Oh, um, cool," I told him, and I tried to change the topic. Did it mean he was engaged or already married? *Can we talk about something else?* I was there to enjoy the Olympic experience and have some fun. Now I wanted to crawl under something. When we rejoined the group, my dad made a formal introduction. "This is my new wife, Jackie," he said. Wife it was. He and Jackie had married after the Trials. *Why didn't he tell anyone? Why weren't we invited? Sure he had grown apart from people, but did he not want us to be a part of something in his life as important as that?*

In the blur that followed, I forget who called whom. I was on the phone with Mom who told me that I should talk to Dad about it if I felt I had something to say. Say? What could I say? I felt as though I was the odd man out, that we were all left out. Whatever Mom may have felt, she was careful not to badmouth Dad behind his back. She told me she'd support me any way I wanted to handle it. For a while I just decided not to speak to him about it. Eventually he said he didn't want to give me one more thing to think about so close to the Olympics, so it was better to tell me after the Olympics. Whatever. It was done. It was time to move on.

The next day I walked around the Olympic Park with Bob and was amazed at all the people. It was my first chance to sightsee. Bob knew about what had happened with Dad and he spent the day trying to cheer me up. That would have been the day to forget a credential and oversleep practice. I bought a silver charm for my Mom around Sydney Harbour and tried to find an escape. I could deal with swimming my best and not winning a medal, but I was having trouble blocking out what happened the day before.

The final day of swimming was fun, because it was relay day for our medley teams. I love relays, probably because I didn't get to swim in many of them with NBAC and I loved feeling like a part of a team. I painted my face half red and half blue for the occasion and I had *Team USA* written across my chest. We won both relays in world-record times and boosted the team medal total to 33 swimming medals, more than a third of what all the U.S. teams combined won in Sydney. Out of the 48 swimmers on our team, 41 came home with at least one medal. I was one of the seven who hadn't and I was already starting to think about the 2004 Olympics in Athens.

11

ON TOP OF
THE WORLD

As planned, I came home early from Sydney, a day after the swimming ended and a week before the closing ceremonies. In Baltimore I was treated to one celebration after another. Mom arranged for a limousine to bring me in from the airport. A group of friends came out to meet me there, and so we went where any other 15-year-old would go in his limo—to 7-Eleven for Slurpees. I was blown away by the novelty of being in that kind of car for the first time. We had some odd looks from people who must have thought we were lost, and one of the guys in the car joked that a real limo would have had ready-made Slurpees in the backs of the seats. I came back to a front yard that was dotted with American flags. It was good to be home, even if I missed out on the razor scooter the athletes received at the end of the Games.

I was ready to go back to school to catch up on organic chemistry, French, English, and geometry at Towson High School. I wanted to get there early on my first day back, but Hilary was awfully slow getting me from the pool to school. She fumbled around with the car keys, went back inside to get something she'd forgotten and suddenly had a coffee craving that could only be cured by a trip to Starbucks that was a little out of our way.

"Hilary, hurry up."

"Michael, I'm going as fast as I can."

She wasn't. It was 8:25 and she still needed to waste 20 minutes to make sure I didn't arrive before the 8:45 surprise party the school had planned. It worked. I was surprised. As we drove down Cedar Avenue, I could see the banners, television cameras and 1,200 students lining the street. I shot Hilary a look. *You sneak.*

Our principal, Gwen Grant, greeted me by saying: "The Olympic champion has arrived." Mr. Brewster passed out some "Fly Michael Fly" T-shirts and buttons he'd distributed before the Games. My girlfriend was there to needle me with the news that her school, Dulaney High, had beaten my Towson team 26-0 in the opening game of the football season. Students asked for my autograph. I signed somebody's arm. It was overwhelming.

Later, my English teacher Jeff Brotman welcomed me back and asked in jest, "Michael, do you have any excuse for your absences?" The kids in Mr. Brotman's class had created a satirical contest entitled *I Know Him*. It was a trivia game in which the girls would have to guess some fact about me from swimming results to favorite foods and music. The girls who knew the answers would then have to tread water for as long as they could and the one left treading would win a date with me. There was no date, and I'm not sure who won.

I was enjoying the spoils of being an Olympian, but there was still one more thing I wanted to do. There was a tradition among swimmers to get tattoos on our hips once we made the Olympic team. Almost everybody got one and I didn't want to be left out. I told my mom I wanted to do it before we left for our first pre-Olympic training camps in Pasadena, but I didn't say anything about when. She didn't raise much of an objection, especially since I told her the rings would be pretty small.

So one day I went to get the tattoo. About halfway through the process, I was talking to the guy painting the rings on me and he told me he had just gotten out of jail. "Oh, really." I didn't ask what he had done, but I was pretty aware that I wasn't going to joke around with him. "Yes, Sir. No, Sir. Thank you, Sir." I got home that day and I must have had the goofiest smile on my face. My mom gave me the old slow motion, "My-kull, where have you been to-day?" She rolled her eyes and tilted her head toward me as if to say, "Now I know something is up, so you might as well just tell me what it is." She was fine with the tattoo. I think on a scale of off-spring independence, a small, discreet tattoo that stood for something positive and upheld a team tradition was something she could tolerate. Whew.

I actually became the answer to a trivia question on ESPN's *Two-Minute Drill*: Who is the youngest male to make an U.S. Olympic swim team in 68 years? Answer: Michael Phelps of Towson.

I threw out the first pitch before an Orioles game at Camden Yards and was introduced to the crowd at a scrimmage of my favorite football team, the Baltimore Ravens, at their training facility in Westminster. The players surprised me with a team jersey and the kids collecting autographs came by with footballs to ask for my signature. "You the new kicker?" one of them asked. I walked around with Ray Lewis, one of the NFL's best linebackers, and he introduced me to Elvis Grbac, Jonathan Ogden, Jamal Lewis, Peter Boulware, and some of the other players. Some of them joked around with me. "I'll swim you, boy," a voice shouted. Ray gave me a Phelps jersey with the number 00 on the back. I was loving it.

Later that month, the Olympic team was invited to the White House. Lenny presented President Clinton with a team jacket. The President gave a speech in which he cited numbers about an increase in overweight teenagers. We also had jackets for Mrs. Clinton and their daughter, Chelsea, who was then dating a swimmer in her class at Stanford. We stood for a group picture with the president on the South Lawn and we lined up to shake his hand and pose for individual photos. There were several hundred Olympians present, so the photos were, um, taken in a flash. I remember we had police escorts of 30 vehicles on our way to and from the ceremony. I hung out with Dominique Dawes and Elise Ray, two of the Olympic gymnasts from the area, and invited them to come to one of my meets. The Olympics felt like an extended honeymoon.

The honeymoon ended in the fall, when Bob and I had one of our worst meltdowns. I was still feeling the mixed emotions of everything that happened in Sydney, and I was also going through my most accelerated growth spurt. In a blink, Mom would line me up against the doorway, take out the tape measure and I'd be two inches taller. We were bickering a lot in practice over seemingly little things. One Sunday, Bob came over to the house and we laced into one another. Mom listened for a while, then left, then came back and we were still arguing—about commitment and direction in the pool and attitude out of it. Both of us kicked furniture and threw books on the floor. It was bad.

Bob decided we needed to go for a ride and we headed for his sanctuary. Bob had always wanted to be involved with horses, and if it hadn't been for me, he might have trained Kentucky Derby and Preakness winners by now. These days he owns several horses by himself and shares ownership with my lawyer, Frank Morgan, in several others. At the time, he was just getting involved in the business at Bonita Farms and he would occasionally use terminology like "he travels well" to describe his swimmers as well as his animals. "There are two kinds of people," Bob insists, "those who own horses and those who want to." I was pouting all the way up to the farm, a place I had never seen before. There were no buildings and no cell phones and you could hear the autumn leaves fall off the trees. If any place was going to calm somebody's soul, this was it.

Bob asked if I wanted to get on a horse and I told him it was one of the things that really freaked me out. Another, for some reason, is picking up somebody else's baby, because I'm always afraid I'll drop it. Bob and I talked for hours and finally walked back into my house after dark, carrying McDonald's bags full of food. We didn't solve everything that day, but we understood how much we needed one another in order to succeed.

WR Austin. Bob had been writing that on almost every note he had left for me since the Olympic swim in Sydney. I hadn't won a medal there and that drove me for the next six months. I was grabbing for a goal. I needed a goal the way a car needs fuel. I desperately wanted to break a world record to make a statement that I had arrived, to validate the work we'd put in. The Nationals that year also served as trials for the World Championships later that summer in Fukuoka, Japan. I was the only 15-year-old guy entered at Nationals that year. In the days leading up to the meet, Bob would email me a different motivational quote each day. It might have been something as simple as "No pain, no gain," but I looked forward to getting them. Case in point: "The greatest thing in the world is not so much where we stand; it's where we're going."— Oliver Wendell Holmes.

At each competition it seems there are certain habits I like to fall into for the duration of the meet. When we first arrived in Texas, I started playing the song "Perfect Gentleman" by Wyclef Jean on my CD player. I thought *oh, I can get into this.* So I played it on my headphones while I was waiting in the ready room before the races. After the song was over, I hit repeat, then repeat again. If something works, why change?

On the first day, I finished third in the 400 IM behind Erik Vendt and Tom Wilkens and missed making the team by three-

tenths of a second. Still, our focus had been on that 200-meter butterfly race.

Murray Stephens is a good role model for Bob, because he is as
calm before big races as Bob is nervous. I was late getting a rub-
down before the start of the 200 fly final. Murray could see that Bob
was flustered about something before the start of the race, so he
asked Bob what was wrong. "Michael's behind schedule," he said.
"He's screwing up the 200 fly. He's taking too much time getting
ready." Murray nodded, looked at Bob and said to him, "I'm going
to go get a Coke. You want one?" That calmed Bob down. If Murray
wasn't worried, he didn't need to worry either. Ever since that
exchange, whenever Bob starts to panic before the start of one my
races, he walks away and gets a Coke.

Before I went to the ready room, Bob told me to "stay with Tom
Malchow for the first 100 or 150, then kill it coming home and you'll
have a great shot." I made my surge later than Bob had wanted,
trailing Tom by almost a bodylength at the third wall, catching him
with 25 meters left, then hitting the overdrive button and hoping
for a time that would be faster than the 1:55.18 Tom had swum in
Charlotte in 2000 to set the world record.

I looked up and saw 1:54.92 and didn't quite believe it at first.
For a split second I just floated, squinting through my goggles to
make sure I saw the numbers right. Then I went spazo. I starting
flapping my arms like a bird trying to shake bubble gum off its
wings. I was on top of the world, thinking, "nobody has ever done
that race faster than you. That's awesome." At 15, I became the
youngest person ever to hold a world record, breaking the standard set by Ian Thorpe when he lowered the 200 freestyle world
record in 1999 at 16 years, 10 months. It was the first swim that had
really meant something.

Again Bob had a long walk to the garage. Honestly as much as
the world record meant to me, I think it meant even more to him.

I had been thinking about this record since the end of the Olympics, seven months earlier. Bob had been thinking about it for 15 years, since I was born. He told me later that after the race, he had another long walk to get the car from the garage and he couldn't get the smile off his face. He actually had to hide it in his hands as he walked past random people on his way to the car. He had moved around so much trying to find the right fit and this moment was sweet vindication for a lot of uncertainty.

Meanwhile, I called home to tell Mom about the result:

"Michael, did you swim?"

"Yeah."

"And . . ."

Before I could say anything, I just started giggling, like a kid in a candy store who is embarrassed by how good he feels. "Mom, I broke a world record." I could tell my mom was trying to stay calm on the other end, but we were both ready to start dancing on the walls. Make that two kids in a candy store.

Bob and I flew back to Baltimore where there were other sports stories making much bigger headlines. It was the weekend of the Orioles' season opener and Maryland's first appearance ever in the Final Four basketball tournament, so I kind of flew under the radar screen. Hilary visited from Florida with her boyfriend and they wanted to take me out to dinner with Mom in the Inner Harbor to celebrate. When we arrived at a Cheesecake Factory, we got hit with a two-and-a-half-hour wait. "If you tell them about the world record . . ." Hilary suggested. We didn't. Instead, we left and went to a California Pizza Kitchen where the wait was a lot shorter. Setting a world record doesn't make you a celebrity, even in your hometown. But there would be time for that later.

The next day, a Japanese television crew visited Meadowbrook to film us there. It was the first time a member of the international press came to visit me and they wanted to talk about the World

Championships later that summer. Mom thought this was a huge
honor to have people in from overseas, so she invited them over for
dinner and served an Asian chicken salad, Baltimore style.

Before the trip to Fukuoka, the swim staff briefed us on some
of the things we should be aware of over in Japan, given their cul-
tural traditions. They told us we might be asked to take our shoes
off and put on slippers before entering rooms. They also told us we
didn't need to leave tips in restaurants because tipping wasn't usually done there.

I adjusted pretty well to the new time zone, as I had in
Australia, but I was careful not to touch the street food, because I
didn't know what it was. There were soda machines in front of
stores, as you would find in the States, but the flavors included
things like watermelon and pear. I was rooming with Jamie Rauch,
a breaststroker on the U.S. team. We stayed at a great hotel. We
had two huge beds and a computer station in the main room. There
was even a television in the bathroom and a seat warmer on the toilet. Bob ate sushi for the first time there, but I was a little too timid
to try it. On the first day, I walked around an adjacent mall with
two teammates, Anthony Robinson and Randall Bal. Anthony
would make this noise that was like a little siren, so people gave us
a lot of room as we were walking by.

Jamie was a fun guy to hang out with. We had a deal that every
morning the person who got up first could wake the other one by
whacking him over the head with a pillow. I think I got in more
whacks than Jamie, but if you ask him, he was ahead. I could be
pretty sleepy in the morning, so whenever I went downstairs to
leave for the pool with the other swimmers, Jamie would egg me
on.

"C'mon, say the word 'lisp.' Say it. C'mon, Mike, I know you
have it in you."

"Nope, not gonna do it."

"C'mon."

"No, I'm not doing it. I'm not saying the word 'lisp.'"

Of course I had just lisped the word lisp exactly as Jamie wanted me to. Now I was sure to walk around mad for the rest of the day practicing my L-words under my breath. "L-l-l-i-s-s-p."

Again, I had three rounds in the 200 fly. I swam the first heat reasonably well, but in the semis, Bob wanted me to go out a little faster and cut my time more than I did. I qualified third in 1:56.41 behind Malchow and Franck Esposito of France and Bob was livid.

Some swimmers have problems with going out too fast, and their coaches need to convince them to conserve energy. I still had a problem with starting too slowly, with being too tentative. That had nearly cost me a spot on the Olympic team in Indianapolis and it may have cost me a medal in Sydney. Bob wanted to make sure it didn't happen again. "Michael, get back in the water," he said after the semi. "You need to swim 1,500."

I didn't try to pout my way through this practice. I knew Bob would test me from time to time, but I also knew that I had to pay attention to him at a meet like this. I don't necessarily want Bob to get on me at meets, because there is only so much training and preparation you can do at the last minute, but I did want him to be around, and I really didn't want to disappoint him. After I got out of the pool, he really got on my case. I didn't realize Bob was being strategic. He knew that Jamie wasn't far away, so after he was done yapping at me, he went over to Jamie and started playing good cop-bad cop.

"Hey, Jamie, can you go over and talk to Michael," he said. "I gave him some strong words and he's pretty down right now. "

"What do you want me to tell him?" Jamie asked.

"Tell him to keep his head up, that this was only one day, that he's going to swim a great race tomorrow, because he's done it before and he knows he can do it again. Just pick him up a little."

That's pretty much what Jamie told me. It worked. Afterward, I knew I had work to do, but I couldn't wait to get back in the water to do it. I was ready to attack the water and prove to Bob and everyone that I could race on the world stage against the best swimmers and just conquer everyone.

I didn't speak to Bob the next day until we arrived at the pool. It was an unusual exchange, because he was walking past me as if he was too busy to hear what I had to say.

"Bob I want to speak to you. Bob, where are you going?"

"Michael, I'm on the staff. I have to go to the meeting. What's up?"

"Well, I have to swim the final and should I . . . can I take it out?"

I remember he just stared at me for a few seconds before saying, "Hell, yes." Then he walked off. After all that, I was completely psyched up to swim fast.

I charged through the first 50 meters and turned first, .83 seconds ahead of my world-record pace. I had never done that in a big meet. I turned first at the next two walls and touched the last one in 1:54.58. For the first time in my life I was a world champion. I was on top of the world and Bob was a genius.

Before I knew it, I was back in the water getting ready for the next day. Because of the expense and distance, my family had stayed home for this particular trip. It was the middle of the night in Baltimore, so I figured I would wait until I got back to the hotel to call my mom.

But I did call Erin Lears. A long time before I was capable of breaking records, she and I had made a pact one day at Meadowbrook that if either of us should ever break a world record, we would have to call the other person, day or night. "Really, Michael, no matter what time it is, you have to call and tell me, okay?" So I called. Miss Cathy answered and knew right away who it was and why I was calling. "Congratulations, Michael," she said. "Hold on, I'll get Erin."

I don't know if Erin was too groggy to figure it out right away, but I had to make some small talk first to be sure she was awake. "Michael, it's great to hear you, but um, Michael, why are you calling? Do you realize it's 3 a.m. here?"

"It is, but remember we had this agreement?"

Before I could finish, Erin started screaming into the phone. We talked for a long time and it was great to hear a friendly voice from home.

I mis-timed the call to my mom, who was already on her way to work by the time I got back to the hotel. I left her a long message, talking about different things in Japan and wishing her a good day. I almost forgot to let her know that I had won and broken the record.

The next day, I picked up a copy of the in-house daily newspaper put out in both Japanese and English by the Championships' organizing committee. My world record had actually been only the second one set the previous night. The first was broken in the men's 400-meter freestyle by Ian Thorpe, the 17-year-old from Australia who was his country's national hero and who was clearly recognized as the best swimmer in the world. Ian had won five medals, including three gold, before his home fans at the Sydney Olympics and he was even better in Fukuoka. The headline at the top of the paper that day read simply "Teenage Stars Thorpe, Phelps Break Records." Wow, what the heck was I doing in the same headline as Ian Thorpe? He was the man. I was just the kid. As soon as I saw the headline, I remember saying, "Wow, he's, like, all-world."

More like all-worldly. On the one hand, Ian and I were very similar. We both had mothers who were schoolteachers. We both had sisters in swimming; in fact, Christina Thorpe competed at the same 1995 Pan Pac meet as Whitney. But Ian had seen and done so much more than I had. He was already a millionaire because of his sport and had used his money to buy a house for parents and set up funding for a kids' cancer center. He had his nickname, "Thorpedo" copyrighted. He wrote a newspaper column. He attended fashion shows with Giorgio Armani and a movie premiere with Tom Cruise. Six companies had signed him to sponsorship contracts. In a contest held by the country's largest paper, the *Sydney Morning Herald*, Australians chose Ian as the person they would most like to have as a dinner guest, ahead of Russell Crowe, Nicole Kidman, Elle McPherson, Greg Norman and prime minister John Howard. I couldn't imagine I would ever be so good or so famous that people would make that sort of fuss over me. Ian finished the meet in Fukuoka with six gold medals.

Most of all, he impressed people with his composure and the way he carried himself. At a press conference after one of his races, a reporter asked Ian if he could recite some of the words and phrases he had learned in Japanese. Ian responded with a list of about 30 different words and phrases that weren't necessarily related to one another. Then the reporter followed up by asking him, if he wouldn't mind, to repeat the words in English. Again Ian obliged. Sitting among the reporters was a former swimmer, Daichi Suzuki, the 1988 Olympic champion in the 100-meter backstroke and now a newspaper columnist and reporter for Japanese television. Because Suzuki had lived in Boston for two years after he retired, he was perfectly fluent in English. He was the one who realized how amazing Ian's memory had actually been. After playing back the tape of the press conference, Suzuki realized that even though the words and phrases were random, Ian had repeated them back in English in exactly the same order as he had just said them in Japanese, without going out of order once.

Many people saw Ian as the person who was carrying the torch for international swimming both in and out of the pool. I didn't talk to him much in Fukuoka, but on the flight back to the States I thought a lot about how I wanted to be able to do something to make people pay more attention to the sport in the U.S. the way Ian had done in Australia.

We used Ian as a model. During that meet, Bob went up to Ian's coach, Doug Frost, and asked if he could pick his brain. Doug was very helpful. He talked to Bob about how Ian learned to handle the press, how he recovered from races, and when, during his training cycle, he would travel to altitude. Bob saw Ian as the prototype of the swimmer I could be. He was a great example to follow.

Back to Baltimore. Mom came to get me at the BWI airport at around 1 a.m. and I had a serious food craving.

"Michael, there's food at home."

"Mom, there's food at Taco Bell, too."

"Are they even open now?"

"Until two or three, something like that."

I ate dinner in the car in about three minutes. That night, with Bob's blessing to sleep in, I hit the pillow right away and didn't wake up for 12 hours.

The next day, Jamie Barone, one of the NBAC swimmers, drove me over to the pool and we blasted Dr. Dre on the stereo and told jokes until we cracked up. When I arrived, they had a little victory celebration for me at the pool. The kids were wearing "Fly, Michael Fly" T-shirts. Some people yelled, "Speech, speech," and all I could say was, "It's great to be home."

12

COMING TOGETHER

Jamie was going to school at Loyola when he joined NBAC and we hit it off right away. He had two other brothers and one of them was my age. That first summer, Jamie was in Baltimore by himself. I didn't have a driver's license, so Jamie drove me around a lot. We kept a running score in everything, and we were almost always dead even in Madden football. He also made a huge contribution to my life by introducing me to Pete's Grille. Pete's was a diner on Greenmount Avenue, not fancy, but really good. Think about the normal amount of fuel that most teenagers need. Then consider that the teenager is in the middle of a growth spurt. And he's an athlete. You have a recipe for . . . a lot of recipes.

Mom raised three kids on a schoolteacher's salary, but based on her food bills, it was like raising 12. Before I discovered Pete's I used to ask for four dippy eggs in the morning. That fall, I started asking for seconds. We're talking eight eggs for breakfast. That's why Pete's was huge. I started going two or three times a week, then almost every day. Within a few weeks I had probably tried everything on the menu, but I eventually settled on my "usual."

Ready? Here goes: Start with three sandwiches of fried eggs, cheese, lettuce, tomato, fried onions and mayonnaise; add one omelet, a bowl of grits and three slices of French toast with powdered sugar; then wash down with three chocolate chip pancakes that the owner, Lou Sharkey, serves only to me, unless it's a Sunday. And, no, there is no truth to the rumor that I have an army of elves living in my stomach.

When I walk into Pete's, I feel like the TV character Norm walking into Cheers. Everybody knows my name, as it says in the song. Lou says it's his regulars who count. Even Vinny Testaverde, the NFL quarterback, had to wait ten minutes for a seat when he went in.

My friends and I used to make bets about eating food. At an all-you-can-eat buffet one day, we decided to eat all we could. Our table tried to eat the place out of everything, and we nearly did. Of all my friends, Matt is the one who is usually up for a good eating challenge. And when teenage guys get together, some of the challenges can be kind of . . . teenage. Matt made $30 from me once by mixing wasabi paste with soy sauce and inhaling it through his nose. He won a DVD from me one night after we ate dinner and then went for burgers. There was no way we were ready for more food, but at the drop of a challenge, Matt added a quarter-pound burger for dessert. Three years ago, we were at my old girlfriend's house, watching a guy on TV trying to swallow some small fish, whole. He couldn't, so Matt and I figured we could. Swimming really came in handy, because I was able to hold my breath during the full swallow. Goldfish aren't that big, but they start flopping around in there and they can gross you out. The money is never an issue during these challenges. If you win a penny, you feel you've accomplished something, though I'm not really sure what it is. I only won a dollar for downing my 50th chicken wing at Bill Bateman's in Towson, but just think, with that dollar, I could buy

. . . another chicken wing. Believe it or not, there really is something I don't like to eat: angel hair pasta. I don't like the texture of it.

I have a teammate on the national squad named Ed Moses, who used to be a huge fan of junk food before he started to eat super healthy. His dad joked once that he knew Ed was serious about swimming the day he first requested lima beans for dinner. Let me state for the record that I will never request lima beans for dinner. I don't care how hungry I am, I will never resort to lima beans. Goldfish, yes. Lima beans, no.

Two days before we left for our summer nationals in Clovis, California, Jamie and I loaded up on food and headed off to the bowling alley. Jamie started talking about it really casually at practice the next day and Bob just flipped.

"You did what!"

"Bob, we just went bowling. It's not like we played football."

"Jamie, have you ever heard of Matt Gribble?"

"Ah, no."

"He had the 100 fly world record back in the '80s. He messed up his back bowling one night and it took him right out of Nationals the next day because of it."

That was our last frame.

We arrived in Clovis, and it was the hottest meet I've ever been to. We tried to think of it as mind over matter, but the temperatures were near a hundred each day and the swimmers regularly broke out into giant fits of Bong. Guys, I-tong-song Hong-oh-tong. I tong-song Rong-eee-aye-long-long-yong Hong-oh-tong. Despite the heat, I just missed American records in the 100 fly and 200 IM and finished second in one other race. It was a good ending to a great season.

Even in Baltimore, I hardly thought of myself as a celebrity then, but I first had a sense of being able to use my story and my accomplishments to help other people. I visited some schools in the area and started getting more comfortable with speaking in front of a large group. It was great to have kids ask about my swimming, my goals, my family. I've always been really at ease speaking to kids, because they always seem so interested in what I have to say and they want to be able to look up to older kids they'd like to emulate. Still, younger people are one thing; older people are another.

A gentleman who used to work out in the pool had moved into a retirement home in Parkville and asked if I could come by to visit. I arrived one day, forgetting that I was still wearing a baseball cap. One of the people who ran the hospital started to introduce me to people, explaining that I was an Olympian and a world champion. One of the first men I met skipped right over the handshake and was clearly not impressed. "Remove your cap, son," he told me. I know how older people are about manners, and I know we sometimes take them for granted. I had completely forgotten about taking my hat off. Since then, it's become force of habit that if I'm wearing a hat I always take it off when I enter a building, unless I'm just walking into a swimming pool. That's especially important with kids, because they model what they do after what you do.

I was just getting back into the groove of swimming and school, starting 10th grade and looking forward to another good year. I walked into U.S. history class one morning and I remember the somber looks on everyone's faces. Word was going around that our nation was under attack and planes had just hit the World Trade Center in New York. Soon after, we heard about the plane that crashed into the Pentagon, even closer to home. Nobody knew exactly what to do, so the teachers and students sat and watched television for updates throughout the day. For the most part, people were quiet and scared and there were tears in class, as there were throughout the country. To this day it's hard for me to watch video relating to what happened on September 11. I saw a special recently about the daughter of one of the pilots who had flown the planes. Her wish afterward was to meet Derek Jeter, the Yankee shortstop, and she was able to do it. Something like that is still pretty emotional for me. I think everyone from our generation will always remember where they were when they first learned about it, but I also remember the way people pitched in afterward to help each other out. The newspapers and TV shows were filled with stories about people donating clothes, food, money, and counseling to those who needed it. I know I was only 16 when it happened, but I think it brought this country together more than any other event in my life.

*** *** ***

Planes were back flying again on September 14. That day, Bob and I were heading out to Dulles Airport in Washington for a 6 a.m. flight to Portland, Oregon, where we were due to give a clinic. On our way, we stopped at Dunkin Donuts to get breakfast. I reached down for my wallet to pay for it and he said, "No, no, I have it." I figured it was no big deal at the time. After we got back into the car and rode for another half an hour, I thought I felt a little lighter than usual. I reached down and realized I had forgotten my wallet, with, among other things, my ID. "Mom, can you meet us at the airport with something?" Crisis averted.

Even before World Championships that summer, Mom and I talked about whether I should turn professional and accept prize money and sponsorship money. We also talked about getting an agent to help with things such as finding sponsors and negotiating contracts.

I consulted Anita Nall, who had spent many years swimming at NBAC and she offered some very helpful suggestions. Murray had originally discouraged Anita from getting an agent. "They just take your money," he told her. So she handled things on her own. Anita told me that if she could do it over again, she definitely would have hired someone to represent her. That conversation helped confirm my decision to turn pro and forego my eligibility to swim in NCAA meets. Of course, the decision didn't change my plans to go to college, attend classes and get a degree, since my education was still a priority. But once you accept any money that relates to your sport (prize money, endorsements), you lose your chance to compete in sports for your university.

I turned professional a month into my junior year at Towson High. With the help of Frank Morgan, the attorney who is a family friend and Bob's partner in the horse business, I signed a sponsorship deal with the Speedo swimwear company through 2005. A month later, I went with my mom to Phoenix for a photo shoot for Speedo. We had a driver pick us up at 5:45 and I had my own make-up person and hair stylist. Usually I just get a guy with scissors who says, "You want it short?" I did some question-and-answer sessions with a swim group and did another afternoon photo session with an underwater cameraman. At one point I told my mom, "There's a lot of work in this."

A week before that session, I had competed at the U.S. Open swim meet in New York. The thing I remember most about that meet is what I forgot. I walked onto the deck to swim the 200 back and as I reached up to start scratching my head, I realized that for the first time in my career, I'd forgotten my cap and goggles before the start of a race. This was a pretty embarrassing thing to do. I looked at my mom, sitting in the stands, and we both shrugged our shoulders. I looked over at Bob, who was standing at the side of the pool, and we shrugged our shoulders, too. At that point, there wasn't much else anyone could do. I finished second in the race and at least I didn't forget my suit. It was one of those learning experiences. Some days you learn from a book; other days you learn from hours of practice; and then there are the times you're so embarrassed by something, you know you'll never do it again.

That fall, Bob and I put together a training video about how to do the butterfly. It was a fun experience. We demonstrated some drills Bob used to get me to stroke and kick properly, how to work on bodyline, posture, rhythm, and timing. The filmmakers shot me from different angles going through the water, and we spliced in questions from an interview Bob conducted with me about my swimming and my preparation. I know he enjoyed that part, especially when I told him how much I loved to train and how I needed to work on my breaststroke. "And Michael, do you have any special diet?" he asked. "Well, I get all the nutrients I need," I said. "My mom makes sure I eat enough fruits and vegetables. I just want to cram in what I can." Watch that smirk, Coach.

13

LIFE AS A PRO

I still had to find an agent to handle my contracts and appearances. I talked about it with my mom and Bob. We spoke to different people at several agencies, but weren't really impressed with anyone. One day, we visited McLean, Virginia, home to the offices of Octagon, a large agency that represents Olympic athletes. We had made an inquiry about meeting with Peter Carlisle, who was handling a number of athletes competing at the Winter Olympics in Salt Lake City. Because of his commitments to those athletes, Peter couldn't meet with us until after the Games were over. I spoke to several of Octagon's people for a while in McLean, but just didn't connect with them, and we were set to cross them off our list. Then one morning during the Olympics, Bob was watching the *Today Show* and saw an interview with Peter. He was blown away. "Wow, this guy gets it," he thought. "That's who should represent Michael." Peter wasn't able to meet with us for another month, while he looked after his winter athletes who had just won Olympic medals. We finally arranged a meeting with him at Frank Morgan's office in April.

During that second meeting, I let the adults do the talking while I sat there for a good 20 minutes. It was weird to hear people sitting around, discussing my life, almost as if I wasn't there. At some point, Peter turned to me and asked: "So what do you want for your future, Michael? What are your goals?"

I looked around and saw everyone staring at me. I said the first thing that came to my mind: "I want to change the sport of swimming," I told them. That sounds like a boastful statement, but I didn't mean it to reflect me as much as the sport. How often do you see swimming highlights on *SportsCenter* next to the dunks and home runs and touchdowns? How often do guys hang out at the water cooler and talk about split times the way they talk about batting averages? In Australia, I saw swimming as the lead segment on the evening news, the lead topic on talk radio. Swimmers are on billboards, in commercials. Kids see them and want to be like them. When kids bug their parents about things they want to do, they want to jump in the pool. That's great for swimming and that's what swimming should be in the United States. "I want to change the sport of swimming. I want people to talk about it, think about it, and look forward to seeing it. I want them to want to jump in and do it. That's my goal."

After the meeting broke up, we walked around the offices for a while and then ate some sandwiches around the table. I wanted to leave a mature impression and so what did I do, but drop my plate full of food all over the carpet. Good one, Michael. It isn't as if adults don't think kids are goofy enough. *Ladies and gentlemen, we're marketing . . . a klutz.* Fortunately, Peter seemed to forget about it in about ten seconds. He sat down with me—and my second plate of food—to talk to me alone. He started to ask me about my favorite hobbies, what music I liked, what video games I played, what subjects I liked at school, what I watched on TV. I told him I was curious about the questions. "Michael, I need to know who you are, so I can tell people what you're about," he said.

I liked the fact that Peter asked me a lot of questions, that we talked less about money and more about goals than I thought we would. I liked the fact that he thought my opinion mattered and I wasn't just a prop in the room who wasn't supposed to be a part of the conversation just because I was only 16. We all liked Peter and we decided to hire him very enthusiastically.

I was a challenge for him. When we talked, I'd say, "Hey, did you hear Ian's launching a food line? He has underwear ads, too. And you should see what he has in Japan." It was a lot of pressure for Peter, because most companies think in terms of football and basketball players before they think of swimmers to market their products.

Soon after I began working with Octagon, Peter arranged for me to have media training. They brought in a crew with mics and lights for a mock interview session and had the interviewer come at me with aggressive questions, Jim Gray style. They tried to keep me from being nervous and defensive and, most of all, to feel as though I were in control.

They also taught me to relax. Interviews are like giving book reports in front of a classroom. You know everyone is looking at you and listening to you and you want to make sure you say something, so you say the first words that come into your head. Sometimes the words fly out of your mouth before your brain has time to edit them. Whenever I gave an interview, I had a problem with the word unbelievable. It was my crutchword. Lights, camera . . . "Michael, how did it go today?"

"It was an unbelievably unbelievable meet, if you can believe it."

I needed to stop that, so the Octagon people put an unofficial "unbelievable" meter on me, counting the number of unbelievables in an interview. Once I learned to think about not saying it, I started to relax, take my time with my answers and say what I was actually thinking. Believe it.

I was starting to get more requests for interviews when I went to swim meets. The autograph requests began picking up, too. One day a girl asked me to sign her shirt and there was a slight problem: she was still in it. I asked her to turn around and I signed the back. I've had a few other requests like that since then. It's awkward signing a body. I don't know what lines to cross; what's okay, what's inappropriate.

In 2002, I began taking some crank calls in my hotel rooms when I would travel to meets. There were some kids on one of the other teams who would call my room, ask to speak with me, tell their pals listening in that they had me on the phone and then hang up. So early that year for the first time I started registering under a different name in order to avoid those calls. It was an example of how you've arrived within your profession, kind of like an actor being featured in the *National Enquirer*.

That summer, we headed to Colorado Springs for altitude training three weeks before going to the Janet Evans Invitational in Los Angeles. I was giving Bob a hard time again and he was getting under my skin telling me to knock it off. I took that pretty hard and told Jamie Barone later that evening that I didn't deserve to be there and should probably go home. Instead, I went for a ride with Cathy Lears, who was acting as chaperone for the trip. We didn't say very much, but she let me look at some peaceful scenery, if only to soothe my mind. I slept off my anger and Bob and I gave each other the silent treatment at practice the next day. It's odd, but on race days we were already at the point where we really didn't need to talk in order to communicate. When I swim, especially at meets, there is no way for a coach to scream above the din of noise so he can be understood. Instead Bob will whistle in four or five different tones and I'll try to carry out the instructions encoded in his whistles. I can't describe exactly how each one is different from the others, but I can recognize each of them. There's the whistle that says: *C'mon, pick it up*. There's the one that says: *Good job. Keep up the same pace.* There's the whistle that says: *Good, but give it some more tempo.* And there's the half-whistle, half-slap of the hands that says: *What the heck is up with you today? Get that gorilla off your back and start swimming.*

I was frustrated by the meet in L.A., even though I swam well. Erik Vendt touched me out at the wall of an exciting race in the 400 IM. I remember standing on the podium with Erik and wanting to trade gifts with him. I got a mesh bag, he got a nice Speedo towel and hey, I needed a clean towel.

Three weeks later at the Nationals in Ft. Lauderdale, I set an American record in the 200 IM and was just off the world record in the 200 fly. I remember putting my head in my hands after the race. That was really my first taste of understanding what not training properly for butterfly could do. Bob made almost all the training decisions, but when it came to the butterfly, he'd occasionally throw me a little rope and give me a choice of doing extra butterfly sets at the ends of practices. I usually declined, because I was tired. Hey, it's my best stroke and I already did a full day's work. I thought I was the coach and I knew what I was talking about. I had no clue. He let me learn the hard way. It's always the best way to learn. I hadn't improved my time since the race in Fukuoka and it would take me a while to swim that fast again.

Still, if my butterfly was lagging, I was making strides in other areas. I used to watch videos of Ian Thorpe's races and marvel at how smoothly he swam the freestyle. Ian had the best underwater dolphin kick on the planet and I wanted to incorporate that into my training. I've always been a decent kicker, but Bob really stressed that I should maximize my strengths and so we made the dolphin kick a priority that summer. We gradually worked the kick into my IM sets in practice. If we did ten 400 IMs, he would say, "Michael, I really want you to use the dolphin on the last two, from breaststroke to freestyle." Then it would be the last four, then six and so on.

The dolphin kick was probably the deciding factor when I out-touched Vendt in the 400 IM in Fort Lauderdale. Erik and I turned even at 300 meters and I tried to get in as many dolphin kicks as I could after he came up. Erik turned before I did at 350, but I stayed under for another 12 meters. I watched the tape afterward and he had taken five strokes before I broke the surface. The race came down to the touch. After we hit the wall, we were both trying to look around a tent that obscured our view of the scoreboard at the opposite end of the pool. When I finally saw the results, I raised my arms up in the air and held up my fingers in a number-one pose. Some photographers caught the picture and I think photographers look out for it, because it always seems to be a pose they use in newspapers after I win a race.

I had two other close finishes in Fort Lauderdale. First, Klete Keller edged me in the 200 free and later I outtouched Ian Crocker for my first big victory in the 100 fly. After the race, Anthony Nesty, the gold medalist in that race at the 1988 Olympics, came up to me and said, "That's how I beat Matt Biondi in the hundred fly that day. It was the touch." Talk about close. Nesty hit the wall first in his race in 53.00 seconds, followed by Biondi in 53.01. That was really the first time I realized that if I nailed the touch at the perfect time, that could make the difference in the outcome of the race. It was weird because I had never swum short races against a field like that and it was the first time I stepped up and swam one that well at a world or national level. Bob was pretty excited when he came up to me afterward and asked: "Where the heck did that come from?"

We left three days after nationals for Pan-Pacs in Yokohama, Japan, and I didn't adapt well to the time change. The busride from the hotel to the pool took an hour, so it was hard to get my usual nap in between the morning prelims and the finals at night. Before the final of the 400 IM on the first day, I overslept and almost missed the bus. Bob had to get off the bus before it left, run upstairs and wake me. It was a good model for days when things don't go according to plan and you have to fight through anyway. I felt really grumpy before the race, but I touched Vendt out in a time that was two seconds slower than I had swum at Nationals.

I lost again to Tom in the 200 fly, which was my second indication that summer that I couldn't take butterfly training for granted just because I held a world record. I hated losing and I hated hearing Bob say, "You see what I mean?" From that day on, whenever Bob gave me a butterfly set, I did it and gave it my best effort. That's all he wants. Bob really has a feel for when I'm not swimming well because I have a technical problem and when I'm simply not trying my best. He's not the easiest guy to trick. If you do well, Bob will say "good job" and that's usually about it. He wants and expects as many consecutive days of hard training as possible. If you give him that, you're on his good list.

I finished the Pan Pac meet with three gold medals and two silvers. I won the 200 IM and swam in the 4x200 free relay, which the Australians won again. I had never been a part of a U.S. relay team that won a major event, but we had a good feeling about the team we'd put together for the 4x100 medley relay on the final day: Aaron Peirsol (backstroke), Brendan Hansen (breaststroke), me (butterfly) and Jason Lezak (freestyle). Brendan gave me a lead, ahead of the Australians, and I swam a 51.1, at the time the fastest split in history. Then Jason brought us home in 3:33.48, breaking the world mark we had set in Sydney by .25 seconds. After the race, we were jumping around in all different directions on the deck. It was an awesome feeling to be a part of a team with a common goal. Individual races are good, but relays are a blast.

Afterward, I got onto a bus that was nearly empty. The only other swimmer I recall being on the bus with me was Ian Thorpe. We had a really good conversation and I remember how much I liked talking to him. At one point he told me, "If you ever want to train together, I'd be more than happy to welcome you in

Australia." Really? I was thrilled. Training with Ian? Wow, what an
opportunity. I'd learn so much. "And you can train with us in
Baltimore, too," I told him. Ian was like a rock star at that meet. He
had left such a good impression with the Japanese people when we
were in Fukuoka the year before, and when we got off the bus,
everyone pushed past me and surrounded him. He was definitely
still the man.

Soon after I was back home, I saw Juan Dixon, the Maryland
hoop star, walking through the Towson Town Center. It was neat
just to walk by him, but I figured it must be weird to be recognized
a lot. There was only one woman in one of the stores who knew me.
Sort of. "You're that swimmer guy," she'd say.

As many hours as Swimmer Guy spent training for swimming,
he didn't always put in what was required in other areas. I had
worn braces for three or four years starting in 1996 and I couldn't
wait to get them off. During that time I almost never wore the clear
retainer the orthodontist had given me and I paid the consequences for it. I got the braces off in 2000 and I figured I was done,
but a year later, he told me I had to wear the retainer again at night.
I was mad about it, but I had nobody to blame but myself that I still
had to wear the retainer.

I was also lazy about driving, even though I was eager to get my
license. Bob often let me practice by driving his car in open parking lots and in places where there weren't any other vehicles
around. I was getting pretty comfortable behind the wheel, but
unfortunately, that was only half the battle. I didn't read the book,
so I failed my written test. I tried passing it off with the guys at
school as no big deal, but they ripped on me pretty hard when they
found out I failed the test. Mom made a good point later on when I
told her I chose to take the test on a computer rather than on paper.

"Michael, can you go back and check your answers on the computer?"

"No."

"Could you have checked them if you had taken the test on paper?"

"Yes."

Of course I still didn't read the book the second time and failed it again. The ribbing got really intense after that one.

"Mike, hire me. I'll drive you."

"Michael, want to borrow my bike?"

After that I read the book pretty intensely, passed the written test, got my learner's permit and eventually got my license in time for senior year. Ah, freedom.

With the extra money I was making through swimming, I was able to purchase my prized possession: a Cadillac Escalade, the kind you see a lot of pro athletes and rappers driving around. I spend a lot of time in the car, so I wanted to put my signature on it. I received a bonus from USA Swimming each time I broke a world record, but even with the money that would be coming in, I would have to okay any large purchase I made with my mom. Our deal was that any time I broke one of those records, I could buy something nice for myself. Usually, that meant adding something to the Escalade. After one record, I bought spinners for my rims, which I really loved. I got a kick out of watching people stare at the spinning rims after the car stops. I had TVs installed on the dash and in the backs of the seats and I've had the stereo system upgraded twice. I know Bob liked riding around in there and having me blast 50 Cent in his ear. It was good for him and it makes up for the fingernails on a chalkboard, known as country music, he subjects me to in his car.

That fall, USA Swimming voted me U.S. Swimmer of the Year and named Bob U.S. Coach of the Year. *Swimming World* magazine awarded Ian International Swimmer of the Year honors for the third year in a row. He had won 11 gold medals at his two major meets—the Pan Pacs and the Commonwealth Games in Manchester, England—and had lowered his world record in the 400 freestyle to 3:40.07, an event in which nobody could touch him. But unlike the previous two years, when he won the award going away, I finished a close second in the voting. I was in serious company.

14

HEROES AND INSPIRATIONS

A lot happened over the next few months to make me think about people who had either inspired me or looked after me, about people who were important in my life.

I think we overuse the word "hero" a lot. Being a good athlete, a good actor, or a good musician who happens to be in the public eye doesn't make you a hero; it makes you someone who has achieved something in a very public world. I've always admired other athletes both in and out of my sport. When I started in swimming, I was a huge fan of Pablo Morales. He was the Olympic champion in the butterfly and he was very friendly with fans and people in the swimming world. Outside of swimming, how can you not be in awe of Michael Jordan? I don't know that anyone has ever made people appreciate his sport more simply by playing it better than anyone else. Basketball just looks like a better game when he plays it. The last few years I've become a huge Ravens fan, and I love watching Ray Lewis put a big hit on somebody.

But a hero should be somebody who can lift up other people with his courage and dedication. I always think kids should have

role models within their families, as I've been lucky enough to have
with my mom. But actually, heroes don't have to be family and they
don't have to be in the newspapers. They don't even have to be
older than you.

Sometime in the fall, the Hansens, a family from Timonium,
Maryland, contacted Bob about their son Stevie. He swam for one
of the local clubs and was seven at the time. In October, he was
diagnosed with a brain tumor and was due to go to Johns Hopkins
for a brain surgery called a craniotomy. I went over to the Hansens'
house on Halloween to meet Stevie. I brought him a flag, some T-
shirts and a poster and shot some hoops with him in the Hansens'
driveway. Afterward, we talked about our favorite sports, favorite
TV shows, and favorite junk food and it felt good to see him laugh.
We also talked a lot about courage and not giving up. I could tell
Stevie was worried about what was in front of him, even though
I'm sure he didn't understand all of it, but I was amazed at how
strong he was. It was pretty neat being the older brother for a day
and I really hoped I made a difference. Stevie's surgery was on my
mind that night and the next day at practice. How would I face that
sort of thing if I had to? How bad is a bad day at the pool, if you
really think about it?

Stevie was too weak to see anyone after his craniotomy, except
for his family. I sent a basket of junk food and silver balloons over
to the hospital.

Stevie improved somewhat over the next year, and the following summer, I sent him an e-mail saying I wanted to come and see
him at one of his meets at Spring Lake, in Timonium. I went over
sort of unannounced. I found Stevie at the place called the kiddie
round out and gave him a hug. "Wow, you really showed up," he
said. And he proudly showed me the club's bulletin board that had
clippings about my progress. Stevie looked really good that day—
strong, smiling, almost carefree. The more I talked to him, the more
I forgot about his illness. I think he did, too. I heard one of his

ABOVE: Before I was known for diving into pools, I had fun diving into cake.

BELOW: Even as a young kid, I had a sense of adventure.

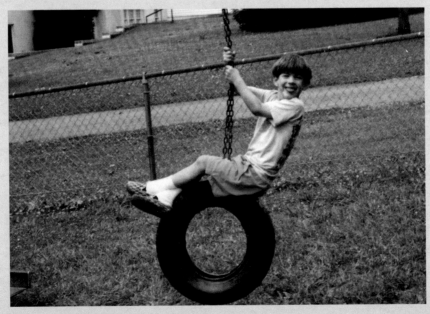

RIGHT: Growing up in Baltimore, I was expected to play lacrosse, which was okay for me since I loved the contact.

LEFT: Until I focused solely on swimming, I enjoyed many sports, including baseball.

RIGHT: Both Hilary (left) and Whitney (right) were swimmers, and they inspired me to try the sport.

LEFT: Dancing with my mom, who has provided me with so much support throughout my life.

RIGHT: My father and me.

LEFT: Whitney (left) and Hilary (right) have always been there for me.

RIGHT: Enjoying some time with Gran, who passed away following a brave fight against pancreatic cancer.
Photo courtesy of Edgar Sweren, D.D.S.

LEFT: Coach Bob Bowman molded me into the man I am today.

RIGHT: I loved spending time with one of my heroes, Stevie Hanson.
Patuxent Publishing Company, ©2003

RIGHT: Winning one gold medal at the 2004 Olympics was a dream come true; winning six gold and two bronze was unbelievable. AP Images

ABOVE: Waving to the crowd after receiving his gold medal for the 200-meter freestyle. He broke his own world record by nearly a second in that race. AP Images

ABOVE: Phelps and Milorad Čavić race in the 100-meter butterfly at the 2008 Beijing Olympics. AP Images

RIGHT: Celebrating his final win at the 2008 Beijing Olympics, the 4x100-meter medley relay. AP Images

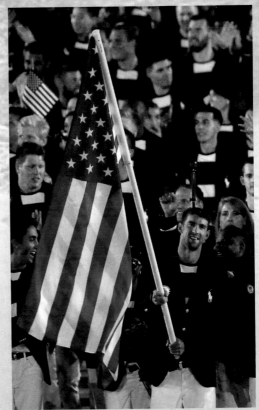

RIGHT: Phelps carries the US flag during the 2016 opening ceremony in Rio. AP Photo/Matt Slocum

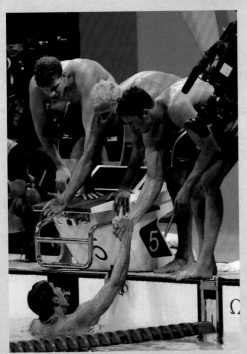

LEFT: Teammates Conor Dwyer, Townley Haas, and Ryan Lochte rejoice with Phelps after winning the gold medal in the 4x200-meter freestyle relay in 2016. AP Photo/Matt Slocum

ABOVE: Pictured during one of his gold-medal races at the 2016 Olympics—the 200-meter IM. AP Photo/Michael Sohn

ABOVE: Phelps shows off his gold medal from the 4x100-meter medley relay at the 2016 Rio Games. AP Photo/Michael Sohn

friends say, "Can you believe Michael Phelps came out to watch Stevie," and that really made him smile. I walked him up to the starting blocks for his races and watched him swim the free, fly, and relay. At one point when Stevie was on the blocks, the P.A. announcer told the crowd, "We have a special guest today, Michael Phelps." It was funny, because the kids who were already on the blocks turned around and started to clap. There is no place like home.

At some point I volunteered to swim a relay leg in a parents and coaches race. I didn't have a suit with me, so I borrowed one from one of the coaches. I took off from the shallow end of the pool and had to make sure I didn't dive in too deep. I posed for pictures after the race and Stevie's little sister, Gracie, wanted me to sign her forehead, so I put my name down in a red sharpie.

Three weeks later, Stevie came to Meadowbrook to watch me practice and we stayed in touch during the year. Later that summer, Stevie was re-diagnosed with tumors on his spinal cord. In the fall of 2003, Stevie developed severe back pain and had to undergo steroid and morphine treatment before they could get him to the operating room for another surgery.

The Hansens took a radical approach to radiation therapy, based on the St. Jude Medical Center in Tennessee. Stevie underwent six months of chemotherapy with two weeks on and two weeks off at a time. He tolerated all the pain with amazing courage, but his white blood cell count was down and he got tired very easily. He could train for about 45 minutes at a time before his body hit a wall.

I can't imagine how Stevie continued to swim through most of his treatments, but swimming was probably the best medicine he could have.

Before the 2004 Olympic Trials, I put a Roots hat and a basket of apparel in a duffel bag for Stevie. My mom gave Gracie and Mrs. Hansen a bag of 200 red, white and blue buttons with my name on them and Stevie handed them out to the other kids at an 8-and-under meet where he was the high-point scorer for his team. In 2004, the Timonium Recreation Council gave him its MVP award.

Say what you want about what makes a hero, but I can't think of a bigger one than Stevie.

✳ ✳ ✳

Jim Lears was the salt of the Earth. Miss Cathy's husband and Erin's father was like another member of the family. He was the treasurer of the NBAC and a very active parent. He began helping Whitney with her finances when she started earning a stipend from USA Swimming. Eventually he became Bob's accountant and mine. Most of all, he was one of the nicest men I've ever met. He always had a way of making you feel like you were talking to someone who wanted good things to happen for you. He was also a picture of health. Mr. Jimmy never smoked or drank; he jogged regularly and even finished the Boston Marathon. One day in November, he came in from his daily jog, went downstairs to do laundry and never made it upstairs. At 55 he had passed away from a heart attack. We were devastated.

I don't think Bob would have objected that day if I had asked for the afternoon off, but I tried to get through practice and was simply horrible. Bob felt it, too. He cut me all the slack I needed that afternoon and after shortening practice we sat and talked about Mr. Jimmy at the end of the day. Everybody at the pool knew him and loved him. Everybody was in shock.

We went to a viewing for Mr. Jimmy down the street from my home and I couldn't bring myself to stay very long. There were pictures of him throughout the funeral home. I walked up to his casket for five seconds and then went outside with Hilary and lost it in the parking lot. I walked home and cried myself to sleep.

I didn't know if there was anything I could do for Erin, except to try to be there for her. She's so much like Mr. Jimmy: peppy, giggly, full of energy and sweet. She can't go more than a few minutes without finding something to laugh about. A week after Mr. Jimmy's death, I passed by a Cadillac dealership and borrowed a Jaguar from someone I knew who worked there. I went to Erin's house and told her I had something special to show her. We got in the car, drove around and laughed about things that really didn't matter. It was a good release and a means of healing for both of us.

※ ※ ※

My mom had a black Jetta that was always giving her problems and she kept saying she needed to get a new car. The problem was that Mom always wanted to make sure we were okay before she would think to do something for herself. I figured I would practically have to lift her up and place her in the front seat before she'd buy something like that for herself.

We went to a Mercedes Benz dealership in December 2003 and took one of their silver ML320s home for the weekend. She really liked the way it felt, but at $35,000, she felt it was just too expensive. I knew that was about twice as much as she was willing to spend, so I put the down payment on the car and after I finished swim practice on Christmas morning (yes, you read that correctly), I left the keys in her stocking and had the car waiting for her in the driveway. What followed was definitely one of those Mom moments. She inhaled with surprise, put her hand over her mouth and gave me a hug that almost squeezed my head off my shoulders. Then I told her, "You know, this is for everything you've done for me—all the car rides to practice and meets, all the food and Gatorade you've bought, all the encouragement, all the patience. There's no way I could have done any of this without . . ." At that point she started smothering me with another hug and the words kind of got lost. The size of the gift was irrelevant; it was the fact that I had the chance to say thank you for so many things that seemed to slip by unnoticed. What would I have done without them? She's done so much and asked for so little in return over the years. When Dad left, she poured her heart and her resources into her kids. I don't acknowledge it all the time, but I had been looking forward to the day when I could do something like that for her. That was a great Christmas.

15

DOWN UNDER
AGAIN, MATE

Winter was here and there was nothing like a good snowfall. Near the Meadowbrook complex, there is a huge hill that is perfect for sledding. I was heading out after practice one day with Corey, Matt, and a group of their friends, and I casually told Mom where we were going. *Mom, why are you staring at me like that?*

"Michael, is it a good idea to go sledding?

"Why can't I go?"

"I didn't say you couldn't."

"Everybody else is going."

"Well, let's see, guys, are you going sledding, too?"

"Yes, Miss Debbie."

"And are you going to Barcelona next summer for World Championships?"

"No, Miss Debbie."

"Michael, are you going to Barcelona for World Championships?"

Oh, I know where this is going. I guess if Matt Gribble can tear a shoulder by bowling, I can always sled into a tree. Anyway, compromise is okay when you can still stand at the top of the hill and pelt everyone else with snowballs.

In April, we had a combination of two competitions in Indianapolis: our national championships, held over three days; and a competition called Duel in the Pool against the Australians, held on a single day—Bob's birthday, April 6. I won three races during Nationals—the 200 free, 200 back and 100 fly—becoming the first U.S. swimmer to win races in three different strokes at a national championship. I was pretty nervous about racing against Lenny for the first time. He was coming back from surgery on his shoulders after being the best backstroker in the world for a couple of years. At the airport in Indy, we compared training notes and he told me: "Dude, the times you're doing in practice are sick." Hear that, Coach?

When the Duel was first conceived, there was a real buzz to the Australians' visit. It was going to be the biggest meet held on U.S. soil since the Atlanta Olympics seven years earlier. Instead, most of the Aussies didn't show up. Not only Ian Thorpe, but also Ashley Callus, Geoff Huegill, Leisel Jones, and Jodie Henry all stayed home. The word was that many of them were injured, but we weren't completely convinced. I was especially sorry not to see Ian there. This was essentially a made-for-TV event and it would have been great to promote the sport by showcasing Australia's best swimmers against our best in one of our pools.

Bob doesn't always say things to me on the day of a race, but on the morning of the Duel, he came up to me and asked if I was ready. "I've been waiting for this day all year long," I told him. A few years earlier, Bob began using an analogy with me about training that came into play on that day. "When we practice long hours," he said, "we're depositing money into the bank. We need to deposit enough so that when we need to make a large withdrawal, we have enough funds to withdraw."

Until the Duel, I had never had a day this tiring or this rewarding in my career. The long training hours got me through four races
in the span of an afternoon. In the first event, I lowered the world
record in the 400 IM to 4:10.73. The atmosphere in the stands was
electric. Each time I'd come up for air in the breaststroke, the
crowd seemed to get louder. About 40 minutes later, I missed the
100-butterfly world record by .03 of a second, losing a chance to be
the first male swimmer to set two individual world records in one
day. I came back an hour and a half later and rallied from half a
bodylength down to touch out Tom and win the 200 fly. Up in the
stands, I could see a sign that my Mom had brought to the pool. It
wasn't your typical Go Michael sign. Instead, she wanted me to see
something I would recognize as hers because nobody else would
know what it meant. The sign contained one of those sayings I used
to think about before a big race, the type Bob used to email me once
a day before the 2001 Nationals. It said simply: *Actions Speak Louder
than Words.*

In my last race of the day, I swam a 51.61 on the butterfly leg as
we beat the Aussies in the medley relay. I had swum multiple
events on one day many times in my career, but never against a field
like this. It was a great litmus test of how I could come back from
one race, get a quick shake in the practice pool and get ready for
another race as quickly as possible.

It was especially important for us to monitor my lactate levels
in between races, something Bob and I had been doing since before
my first Olympics. Think of lactate as a sort of fatigue level that
your body builds up when it expends a lot of energy. If you swim a
fast race and ask a lot of your muscles in short period of time, the
lactate will accumulate in your legs and make it difficult to come
back right away and swim fast again. A lactate test measures the
amount of lactate in the blood, which indicates how quickly you go
into oxygen debt. Coaches use it to determine how efficiently

swimmers produce energy. Essentially, someone pricks your ear after each race and places a few drops of blood into a machine, which measures the number of millimoles of blood lactate per liter of blood. The level can rise to 10 or 12 after a hard race, but we try to get it to clear, or reduce, to a manageable level (below two), so that I can swim again without too much fatigue in my body. We try to get the rate down to 1.1 or less by having me swim down slowly after a race. The tests tell me how much I need to swim down afterwards, which is usually about 23 minutes. Hmm, Bob Bowman: Mad Scientist or Raging Genius . . . you decide.

Afterward, Grant Hackett, Australia's top distance swimmer, told a group of reporters that he thought I might be spreading myself too thin by swimming so many events. "I think Michael should focus on one or two events," he said, "because it nearly takes a world record to win an Olympic event." I was looking forward to having a chance to talk to Grant about that during my upcoming trip to Australia, and I was really looking forward to training with Ian.

Bob had worked on this for six months, trying to coordinate training schedules, pool time, flights, and an appearance at a training clinic. The plan was to train with Ian at his pool in Sutherland for three days and then to the Gold Coast to spend time training with Grant. A week before we were due to go, Ian's new coach, Tracy Menzies, emailed Bob to tell him they weren't going to be able to host us, because they had a sponsor commitment and they'd be out of town. I was really upset. I thought of Ian as the best freestyler in my lifetime and I was so eager to learn as much as I could from him. Bob tried to cheer me up, reminding me I'd still be able to train with Grant and see the Australian way of training up close, but I was really disappointed.

The trip was still great even without Ian. After the first day there, I remember saying: "Bob, what's this about? They swim freestyle every single workout. No wonder they're all such great freestylers." Bob arranged some independent time for me to work on the other strokes for the IM and for Jamie Barone, who was also on the trip, to work on the breaststroke.

Grant and I had a blast. We raced each other over 50 meters, both with and without fins, 30 times with a tenth of a second rest. Every time we raced with pulleys of some kind, he just destroyed me. Without them, we were pretty even. Just the adrenaline rush of racing Down Under, with somebody as fast as Grant got me through the workouts. I really think those workouts helped take me to where I am today.

Grant and I hung out away from the pool and kidded each other about a lot of things. Grant played that trick on me where you put a finger in someone's chest, say, "What's this?" and wait for the guy to put his head down, so you can pull your hand up and slap his chin. I tried to do the same, but he was too wise to it. It's hard to get a guy with his own jokes. Every time Grant kidded me about American football players, I just started ripping on Australian rugby players.

"Are you kidding? If Ray Lewis hit any one of those guys, they wouldn't have a chance."

"Yeah, well, your football players have to wear all that padding. Our players don't need it."

We laughed a lot in that week. It was the first time I ever tried to go surfing, but I wasn't very good. I went out on the water with Jamie and he managed to get up on his board a few times. I tried, too, but couldn't make it to a standing position, so I bodysurfed instead.

One night our group went to Benihana restaurant where the chef makes a show out of preparing steak, chicken, and the rest of the meal by juggling his utensils and flipping his food around. Grant was pretty good at catching flying shrimp in his mouth. I caught one eventually, but the first one nailed my chin and landed on the floor. See, every trip has a food story.

Bob and I conducted our clinic at a fitness center on the Gold Coast. We agreed to a request to speak to a "couple" of reporters there, and that couple turned out to be about 40 of them. At the end of the interview, we mentioned in passing to two reporters that our practice the next day would be open to the public. We arrived the next morning and didn't expect to see anyone, since it was 5:30 a.m. and it was pouring rain. Instead, the deck was lined with people, from end to end, waiting for us. I loved it. This was the way I wanted people to feel about swimming in the U.S. I looked at the people on the deck who were as wet as I was and I remember thinking that whatever I did in my career, whatever times I registered or medals I won, I wanted to do something to make people feel passionate about swimming. Our results are every bit as good as theirs. In fact in Sydney, they had been much better. Maybe the sport won't ever be as big for spectators at home as it is in Australia, because we have such a huge variety of other sports to do and to talk about, but I really wanted to do something to push it in that direction.

When I got back to Baltimore I had a new housemate. Kevin Clements was an outstanding IMer at Auburn University. He was a teammate of mine on a few national teams and he was looking for a change of training scenery. Bob was excited to have him come to North Baltimore, where he, Jamie and I pushed each other in training and hung out after training. When Kevin first arrived, he also needed a place to stay, so the plan was to have him stay with us for three weeks, while he made arrangements to move in with Jamie. Instead he stayed through the summer. It was good for him that Kevin liked hip-hop and video games, because he would have been dragged into them otherwise. I held my own at *Mario Kart*, but take away the console, and he beat me pretty badly at the billiard table. I think I helped Kevin rediscover his love for swimming, but he was also like a big brother to me. I had to be careful about Kevin because he and Hilary would synchronize made-up stories to make me think that I was late for something or that somebody had broken or stolen something that belonged to me. Of course, nobody's perfect. Kevin also listens to country music and I've been telling him to seek professional help.

Jamie's musical tastes were pretty close to mine, but he had more of a range. One day, we were listening to the radio as we were driving to practice and Kelly Osbourne started singing the words to her new single, "Papa Don't Preach." I hadn't heard it before, but Jamie knew the words right away.

"Dude, how do you know the words?" I asked him.

"It's a remake of a Madonna song. She did it like 15 years ago."

"She did? Oh."

Jamie and I teased each other about a lot of things—food, for instance.

"He'll have one Michael sandwich of deep fried cholesterol." (For the record, a Michael sandwich is buttered and jellied on both slices of bread and contains two eggs, four slices of bacon and one slice of American cheese.)

"And he'll have one Jamie sandwich with bread and lettuce, but go easy on the lettuce." (For the record, a Jamie sandwich sometimes contains extra lettuce. Oooo.)

I've always been grateful for my friends. When Matt and Ayo were both on the football team, they used to kid me about swimming being a non-contact sport. I'd offer to trade practices with them and see how long they lasted. We could rip one another at will and nobody would get mad . . . usually. Ayo is a big guy, about 6-5 and much stockier than I am. One day in junior high, Matt and I were sort of messing around with Ayo and it was getting to him more than we realized. We were walking back home from school and I tossed a stick in his direction. I didn't intend to conk him on the head, but my aim was off. He rushed at me and body-slammed me against the concrete. Five minutes later, we were all laughing again. It's a guy thing.

A few years later, I became good friends with a buddy of Matt's named Corey Fick. The four of us would hang out, shoot hoops and play cards and video games. Those guys always looked after me and didn't mind setting people straight if they overheard anyone saying negative things about me.

The guys have always been extremely supportive about my swimming, too, making sure we didn't do anything (apart from body slamming) that could affect my health. Because I'd have to get up for practice, I was an earlier riser than any of them. If I was hanging out at Corey's house and getting tired, I was always welcome to stay over and Corey always took the couch so I could have the bed.

If we played basketball, the guys would actually call out picks to make sure I didn't get knocked around:

"Mike, right here."

"Mike, behind you."

"Mike, watch out."

Corey always joked that he didn't want Tom Brokaw coming to his door asking, "How does it feel to ruin Michael's career?"

For the most part I'd limit my game to outside shots unless we fell behind and I got restless. Of course, if I airballed a jumper, I got no sympathy from anyone: "Getting tips from Stevie Wonder again, Mike?" It was funny to see the concerned reaction from Corey's mom after one of our games: "Michael, don't tell me you're sweating."

The three of us have a running joke about an imaginary character named Frank. We're not sure where he came from, how we met him or why we know him, but every time we have a question, a dispute or a problem, we invoke the name of Frank. I think it started one day when Corey and Matt were trying to fake me into saying I knew who they were talking about.

"Frank's a nice guy, isn't he, Mike?"

"Huh? Who's Frank?"

"C'mon, Mike, you know Frank."

"Never heard of him."

"We should call him right now."

"Yeah, but who is he?"

"Mike, he's the guy from Spain. Think he's awake right now?"

"I don't even know who he is."

The grins on the faces eventually revealed Frank as somebody's idea of a prank, but we've certainly asked enough people about him over the last year. I still have the hat Matt and Corey gave me that had Frank's name on the front and *Phelps '04* on the back. You can never replace friends, and I'm sure that wherever he is and whatever he's doing, even Frank would agree.

16

THE POWER
OF WORDS

NBC gave me a microphone to wear during my graduation ceremony from Towson High. First of all, I couldn't believe a) that the day
finally arrived and b) I agreed to let NBC throw a microphone on
me. It was pretty intimidating and I was very careful not to say anything I didn't want them to use on the air. Some guys around me
started talking trash and making funny noises, so I had my hand
over the microphone half the time. I was very aware of saying
something I'd regret. Actually, that's one of my biggest fears in
press conferences. I want to trust reporters who are there to do a
job, but sometimes I get very cautious. I don't like interviews to go
in directions I'm not expecting.

My media trainers worked with me on feeling more comfortable and on other details. They trained me to incorporate so-called
talking points into my press conferences, such as mentions of
sponsor names. If I can say Speedo or AT&T in my answers, they
want me to do that if it fits with the questions. If, for example,
somebody asks, Michael, tell us about the last 50 meters of the race,
I'm not going to talk about my favorite kind of watch, but if some-

body asks me about how I celebrate after a race, the fact is I text message my friends left and right with whatever free time I have. If they ask about swimsuits, I can talk all day about the FS2, the state-of-the-art Speedo suits. Sponsors are a big help, so I try to acknowledge them.

Sometimes I'll use what is called a bridging technique. If somebody asks me about the swimmer in the lane next to me, for instance, I'm glad to acknowledge his result, but I can't tell what he was thinking or feeling. So I try to guide my answer to a transition to a discussion about my race, since I do know what I was thinking about. If someone asks: "Michael, do you have a girlfriend?" My answer might be, "Right now, my focus is pretty much on getting ready for Trials, so I don't have much time for anything else. I'm sure I'll have time later this fall to relax and have some fun."

People have told me I've become more guarded in my answers than I used to be, but actually, one of my biggest fears is saying the wrong thing at a press conference. If you say something you don't quite mean, you can qualify, clarify, and re-state something a hundred times, but there are reporters who will jump on an opportunity to make a point that fits their story angle. If the angle is that you're a bad guy, they have a better chance to make you look like one the more you elaborate on your answers. I know that is only the case with a few people, but I have seen it happen enough. There is one reporter in Australia who seems intent on comparing me to Ian all the time and making the point that I am not as good a swimmer in the pool or as good a representative of swimming outside of the pool as he is.

So, to set the record straight about Ian Thorpe, nobody admires what Ian has accomplished more than I do. I am envious every time I see him swim freestyle, because his stroke is powerful and effortless and it is the blueprint for me when I swim freestyle events, as it should be for every other freestlyer in the world. Second, I have always admired the way Ian has conducted himself given all the attention he has received. I am only now starting to understand what it has been like for him for the past several years—ever since he was just 15!—because of the way Australians regard swimming. He is never flustered and always seems to know what to say and how to handle himself. Because of Ian, fans in Australia can admire swimming even more than they did ten or 15 years ago. He has taken a sport that was already number one in his country and moved it forward, which is a tremendous accomplishment. I have a strong desire to race against him and try to beat him because of how much I respect him. To compete in any race with Ian in the field is the ultimate, but it has always been competitive, not personal. I thrive on whatever will motivate me, whether it is another swimmer's presence or someone else's words, so I measure myself against him not to put him down, but to lift my performance up. That's as high a compliment as I can pay another swimmer.

Now, as for words . . . we were in Santa Clara training for the Janet Evans meet that was coming up in a few days when Bob came over to the pool and showed me a clip that had run in the Australian papers. The article quoted Don Talbot, a consultant to the Aussie team and its former head coach. In part, the article read: "We've got Ian Thorpe and they're trying to say they've got someone even better. In the major international meets, Phelps has done nothing yet. Obviously something's going to happen at the Worlds, but I think the Worlds will be a bit of a crossroads for him to see just what he can do when he gets up against the world's best. . . . We know Phelps is a good boy, but people trying to say he's a greater swimmer than Ian—that's absolute nonsense. . . . The promise for Phelps is there, but for people saying he's going to outdo Thorpie, I live to see that day."

I was furious. Done nothing yet? You mean winning a world championship and breaking a world record isn't proving yourself? There are ways to say certain things and stick up for your own swimmers without being disrespectful to someone else. I wanted to show him otherwise. I had a job to do and I wanted to prove I could do it. That lit a fire under my butt for the rest of the summer.

More fuel. Before the meet in Santa Clara, a Finnish journalist asked if I really thought I could break the world record in the 200 IM (1:58.16) held since 1994 by his countryman Jani Sievinen. I told him what I usually say, that anything is possible. I say that because I never want to assume I'll do something before I actually do it and because I never want to count anything out. "Yes, but then maybe you think it is too difficult," he said. "Nobody has done this for nine years, so maybe it will not happen. Why do you think you can do it?" I hadn't said that I could, but I wasn't ready to say that I couldn't. We went around in circles like that for a while and it was clear that he was a doubter. For a long time, I was too. To be honest, I thought Sievinen's record was the most impressive one on the books. He split the back half of his race in under a minute, which included his breaststroke leg, and he beat the previous record, 1:59.36 by Hungary's Tamas Darnyi, by over a second. I really wanted to wipe that one off the books, because it seemed so intimidating.

I tossed and turned the night before the race, but it didn't seem as though conditions were right for the record. I wasn't shaved and I wasn't tapered, because Bob had me aiming for the world championships a month later, but I had been training really well. Before the race, Bob went over some projected split times with me and he had me just under Sievinen's time. "What do you want me to do, break a world record?" I asked him. "Why not?" he said.

I dove in and was trying to hold myself back. I could hear the crowd go nuts each time I came up for air and I could feel the emotion carrying me, so I just tried to keep my form. I could tell I was swimming a PR and I thought I was breaking the record. I hit the wall, turned, saw the board, and threw my arms up. 1:57.94. That was my answer. Impossible? 1:57.94. Unproven? 1:57.94. Too difficult? 1:57.94. That bump on my shoulder was a big chip and I carried it with me for the rest of the summer each time I got on the blocks.

After the meet in Santa Clara, I came home to celebrate my 18th birthday. Imagine three causes for celebration (graduation, world record, turning 18) all within a month.

It was also an important period because I was having a difficult time with my dad. Over the past few years, we'd been having stilted conversations at his place maybe once a month and not much more. With the World Championships looming, I had two round-trip tickets to Spain available for me to give to anyone I wanted. I gave one to my mom, of course, and I decided to give the second one to Hilary, since they would enjoy traveling together and since she had been coming to most of my meets.

My dad got upset a few days after graduation because he felt that he should have the second ticket. The older I got, the more I was able to express to him how I felt about things. I was just coming out of my shell enough to confront him. At first, he confronted Mom, accusing her of making sure I didn't give him one of the tickets. Then he and Mom called me over and I told him it was my decision to give the ticket to Hilary. I didn't look at it as a choice of who shouldn't get the ticket, but rather who should get it.

"Dad, look how many meets Hilary has been to. She's always taking off work. She's always there."

"Michael, I can't believe this."

"Well, I don't know what to say. It's my decision."

I told him I was still hoping he'd get to Barcelona, but I felt Hilary deserved the ticket. Instead, he decided not to go because of the cost. Of course, he also didn't come to my meet in College Park, Maryland. It felt a little like he didn't want to support me, although he may have felt I wanted him to stay away. I thought he didn't want to be there to watch me swim, hopefully at my best. My mom was there to support me no matter what the cost was. Somehow I thought my dad didn't feel the same way. I thought he might not have wanted to put out the extra money to see his son swim. I called him one more time to talk about everything and he didn't call me back. There was no call back either after this world record just as he hadn't called after the first one I had set in Austin. There was no call back on my birthday. I don't know if he was trying to prove a point, but if you don't call your son on his birthday, it's a good indication that there isn't too much going on there.

Before I left for Worlds, I made one of those careless moves that could have jeopardized everything I'd worked for. It was 8 p.m. and my cell wasn't working inside. I made a call outside and casually started spinning my rims with my feet while I was wearing flip-flops. I went to kick at the rims and didn't pull back fast enough. The rims nailed my right big toe and the toe stayed black for some time. It wasn't a problem to get through workouts, but every time I put pressure on the toe, I was aware that I had done something dumb. The toenail started wearing away over the next six months until it finally fell off whole.

At the time, I was on the campaign trail with Mom, the I-want-a-dog campaign trail. I had been talking about getting a puppy for a while, and I sort of proposed that if I could break a world record in Barcelona that I could look into adopting one. A lab? A retriever? A terrier? So many good choices. Mom wasn't totally against the idea, but she wanted to make sure I was willing to do the necessary walking and feeding. Of course given my travel schedule, some of that responsibility would fall on her shoulders. We discussed it and agreed to discuss it again.

Actually, if you met our cat, you would think we already had a dog. Hilary brought Savannah home after her junior year of college, and she became family very quickly. I think of myself as more of a dog person, but I'm convinced that Savannah is really a dog dressed up as a cat. She will eat anything within paw's reach, and she isn't picky. She's been known to grab lettuce out of a salad and put her face into open jars. One day, she helped herself to a facefull of horseradish cheese and was still squinting her eyes and furiously licking her lips three hours later. Savannah slept under my arm at night and hopped into my lap whenever I sat at the kitchen table. She always followed me when I walked up the stairs, and if I would run up two at a time, she would sprint along right behind me. Face it, we think we adopt pets, but really they adopt us.

17

FIVE DOGS?

I knew the World Championships in Barcelona were going to be a different meet than the Olympics or my first worlds when I had only the one race. This time, I was looking at up to six events: two IMs, two butterflys, and two relays. It was a great dry run for the crowded schedule I might be looking at in Athens and each day Bob had everything figured out to the minute: when I would warm up, warm down, take my laps, get my lactate tests, have a snack between races. His paranoia and my swimming would really be put to their first big test.

After all that hassle about who would come to Barcelona to watch me swim, the answer was almost nobody. Mom and Hilary arrived at Heathrow Airport in London for their connecting flight into Spain only to learn that employees from their carrier, British Airways, had gone on strike. The walkout also stranded families of other swimmers, including Ed Moses and Diana Munz. Anthony Ervin's family was trapped at another airport. The police told everyone that if they decided to leave the airport, they would not be allowed back in. Mom and Hilary slept on the airport floor and didn't shower for two days. They finally arrived at 1 a.m. into Charles de Gaulle Airport in Paris, where security was only letting people out who had European passports. So they had to stay at that airport until 6 a.m. When they finally made it into Barcelona on the morning of the first races, they headed straight for the arena, without a shower or a proper meal.

The 200 fly the next day was my first event. We wanted a repeat of the final in Fukuoka and for the first major competition since the 2001 worlds, I had the necessary amount of butterfly training under my belt to pull it off. The best way to swim the 200 fly, we figured, was to go out fast and hold on. I did exactly what we talked about and broke the world record in the semis, lowering it to 1:53.93. I didn't quite keep to the gameplan in the final, when I trailed Ukraine's Denis Sylant'yev at the first two walls, but I took over the lead with 80 meters to go and won the race by over a second. I came back faster than I had ever done (59.08 over the last 100 meters) in that event. It was a lesson learned to listen to your coach because he knows what he's talking about. Tom finished third and it was great to get to get the title back that I had lost in Yokohama. "They used to handicap horses by adding weights to them," Tom joked after the race. "Maybe we can weight Michael."

We came back less than an hour later for the finals of the 4x200 free relay. I led off with an American record 1:46.60, and the four of us (Me, Nate Dusing, Aaron Peirsol and Klete Keller) broke the American record for the race in 7:10.26. We still finished nearly two full seconds behind the Australians, who seemed almost unbeatable in the race. Still, we were only a tenth of a second behind until the last leg when Klete just couldn't keep up with Ian Thorpe. Whatever was in Klete's head after the race, he must have realized that the Olympic final a year later would probably come down to he and Thorpe in the final 200 again.

The next evening I came back for the 200 IM semis and lowered the world record I had set in Santa Clara one month earlier to

1:57.52. The atmosphere was awesome. The pool inside the Palau Saint Jordi arena was temporary, constructed just for the championships. The building itself was originally built for gymnastics events at the Olympic Games in 1992. Swimming was held outdoors during those Games, but not this time. On the side of the arena across from the finish wall they had a huge video scoreboard. At some point, the camera operator found my mother and sister in the stands and he never quite took his eyes off them.

On the scoreboard, I could see my mom and Hilary jumping up and down and hugging. I had proposed to my mom that she should let me get a dog if I broke a world record in Barcelona, so after the race Hilary held up a handmade sign that said simply: *Dog?* Then I could see my mom put her head in her hands and start laughing, embarrassed that 10,000 people were watching her and she wasn't aware of it. She would get used to it during the week. Every time I swam, you could almost sense the crowd waiting for the mom and sister shot. Of course, they didn't know Hilary was my sister. One reporter would later ask me in the press conference if Hilary was my girlfriend. We both took a lot of flak for that one.

A day later, I had another one of those killer doubles—the semis of the 100 fly followed by the finals of the 200 IM, 50 minutes apart. I was in the ready area, waiting for my turn in the second heat of the butterfly, when Andrei Serdinov of Ukraine swam a blistering 51.76 to break the world record in heat one. I was furious. I looked up at Bob who was standing in a runway that overlooked both the pool on one side and the ready room on the other, and I just smirked at him. I was definitely feeling confident about being able to break it back.

I was so fired up that I had to tell myself not to go out too fast. The strategy I discussed with Bob was to go out in control and come home like a madman. I cruised through the first 50 meters, but I felt myself about to explode. I was dead last at the turn and I don't ever remember even winning a heat against a loaded international field from that far back. But for some reason, I felt really in control. I popped off the wall and just started picking off the field. I hit the last wall feeling as though I had just released a lot of anger, but also as though I still had a lot left. I didn't expect to see a world record (51.47) on the scoreboard. This time Hilary held up a sign that read: *2 Dogs?*

About the same time I slapped my hands against the wall and let my emotions go, a reporter was over in the mixed zone asking Serdinov what it felt like to break his first world record. Before he could answer, the public address announcer shouted out my time, 51.47 seconds. Serdinov never answered the question. His record had lasted about five minutes. I didn't feel sorry for him because his record was so short-lived; that was the nature of competition. I just didn't think I'd go through the same thing.

In between races, I got a quick massage, warmed down briefly, ate a Power Bar and had a five or ten minute shake, so I'd be ready for the IM final. I was pumped for this race, because Ian Thorpe had decided to swim the IM and I would finally get a chance to race against him in the final. Granted it wasn't a freestyle race; this was my event. You're always protective of yourself and your surroundings, and I thought, *hey, he's coming into my territory now.* So there was extra incentive to swim fast. I'm not usually very fast off the blocks, but I got a great start and actually had the fastest reaction time of anyone in the field. I had a good butterfly split (25.29 seconds) that gave me a slight lead over Ian, but I was up by almost two seconds after the backstroke. I increased it to 2.53 after the breaststroke and came home in 1:56.04. Ian took the silver in 1:59.66, two bodylengths back. I was pumping my fists, reveling in the best day of my career and the sight of the two hugging ladies displayed on the scoreboard. Afterwards, Hilary wrote up another sign and held it up. It read: *3 Dogs?* I was sensing a pattern. When I got back home later on, my friends and classmates joked with me that my mom and sister had gotten more airtime than I did, so it was also the first time the Phelpses had made a collective appearance on national TV.

I headed upstairs later for a medalists' press conference with Ian and Italy's Massi Rossalino, the bronze medalist. A reporter asked about the music I listened to on my headphones as I walked onto the pooldeck. I told them it was from Eminem. The next reporter asked Massi what he would do to try to beat me next time. "The first thing I'm going to do is buy that CD," he said. "Then I will listen to all the songs to see if one of them can make me swim that fast." Ian and I were sitting next to each other, joking around about different things when we weren't answering questions. I took a piece of paper in front of me and scribbled the words: *It's not about the CD.* After the interview broke up, several reporters made a mad dash to see what I'd written on the note. After a near pileup at the intersection of Chair and Table, a German radio reporter edged several American counterparts at the finish. Hey, guys . . . really now, it's only a note.

Nobody in our family is superstitious. Not at all. It's a coincidence that once I started swimming well in Barcelona, Hilary wore the same zebra skirt to the pool on consecutive days. She probably wasn't any more aware of it than I was that I once ate a lifetime's worth of clam chowder in a week, or that I always swing my arms back and forth when I get on the starting blocks. Well okay, so I asked her to wear the skirt again.

I think if you ask Bob, he'd admit that both of us took the next day for granted. There is a fine line between confidence, which is necessary, and cockiness, which is dangerous. And on the day of the 100-meter butterfly final, both of us crossed over it.

I was over at the practice pool, joking around with Stephen Penfold, one of the Australian freestylers, and I was way too loose. I rarely get on the blocks without some feeling of nerves or a sense that I might give less than my best effort once I hear the starter's beep. Honestly I was still riding the high from the semis and as strong as I finished, I thought, in my mind, that I could turn on the jets when I needed to. I didn't feel threatened enough or nervous enough when I jumped on the blocks in Lane 4. In the lane to my left, my teammate Ian Crocker was bouncing on the blocks, with the same sort of reserved emotion I had the night before. His PR up to that point had been the 52.21 he swam in the semis, but he was definitely an outstanding swimmer capable of a much better time.

During the race, I don't think I paid as much attention to Ian as I should have. He hit the turn in 23.99, well ahead of me at 24.61. I took the result for granted as we hit the wall. I looked up and saw my time, 51.10, which was faster than my world record from the day before. I also glanced at Ian's time, thought that I had seen a 51.98 next to his name and started pumping my fists. Only after I took off my goggles did I see that I had misread the board. If Ian had been the type to let loose with a big celebration, I might have realized it sooner, but he was smiling, shrugging and throwing his head back in disbelief. The 51.98 was actually 50.98. Not only had Ian won the race; he had broken the world record. Sure, 24 hours is longer than five minutes, but I didn't want to lose that record. "I'm going to have to look at the tape again," Ian said later. "I honestly can't believe it. I had full confidence in myself, but deep down inside you say, hey, that's Michael Phelps I'm swimming against." The point was Ian prepared for the race better than I did, he executed better and he deserved the victory and the record more than I did.

After the race, I sat by the side of the pool and Bob talked quietly in my ear for ten minutes so that nobody else could hear. "You need to think about which Michael Phelps they'll see at the press conference," he told me. "Are you going to pout or be a champion?" I was looking off into space, because I really didn't want to talk or listen to anyone at that point. I understood what he said and I knew what my mom had told me about being gracious in defeat. I would never want to embarrass her by saying something I regretted. With that in mind, I handled the press conference pretty easily. I congratulated Ian on a great race, which he deserved, and said he was a real champion, which he was. When I left, Bob lifted my spirits a bit by saying, "Better here than next summer. Remember, you get another chance at it." Honestly at that point I was still seething inside. But the thought of that other chance would drive me and push me incessantly over the next 12 months.

The next day, a local paper ran the headline *Phelps es Humano* (Phelps is Human). I was pretty mad after that race and I didn't feel like swimming the next morning. I had the 400 IM final scheduled for that evening, when I was also expecting to swim the butterfly leg of the 4x100 medley relay. But once Ian beat me in the fly final, that meant that he earned a spot in the final instead of me and I would have to swim the fly leg in the morning semi instead. I just wanted to get out of there, and the coaching staff was willing to let someone else swim the relay prelim, but Bob felt it was my responsibility to swim it as the team's number-two flier. I swam a decent fly leg and we qualified for the evening swim.

Later that afternoon, Ian Thorpe walked past me near the warm-down pool and wished me luck in the 400 IM. "What are we going to see tonight, 4:08?" Instead, I found myself toughing it out on my last drop of gas. I could feel Hungary's Laszlo Cseh running me down on the first 50 of the freestyle. *This is not good,* I told myself. I have to have more in the tank than this. I held him off by 1.7 seconds, but the result felt much closer and the race felt much tougher. I didn't have the strength to celebrate the 4:09.09 and my fifth world record. I hung on the wall and tried to catch my breath. I had never felt that tired after a big race. A 410-meter IM would probably have done me in. Afterward, Hilary took out one last sign. It read: *5 Dogs?*

For the first time since I'd arrived in Barcelona, I was able to enjoy a dinner in the hotel with everyone: Mom, Hilary, Bob, Peter, my aunt and uncle and Gerry Brewster who had made the trip to see me. As we were trying to pull away in our car, some kids were yelling at us in a combination of English and Spanish: "Por favor, please, give something, please, si." My mom was prepared. She had me sign a bunch of 5x7 cards with my picture on them before we left for Spain. As the kids came up to our car, she started passing out the cards. Mom told me that she had met Margaret Thorpe, Ian's mother, during one of the sessions, and they each said how much they admired the other's boy.

18

REACHING OUT

We had more interview requests when we came back from Barcelona. They generally came to Peter and filtered through Bob, who determined what hours I'd be available without disrupting our training. We tried to accommodate as many people as possible, but just as Bob expected a certain commitment from me, he expected reporters who came to Meadowbrook to be professional. If they weren't, they heard about it.

A few days after we returned, a local affiliate came to the pool to shoot some general footage of our swimmers in training that they could use as background material for a feature piece. They call the footage B-roll, and you see it during interviews when you hear a subject's voice, while looking at separate footage of what the subject actually does. Bob told the crew they could start filming at 9 a.m., but they actually arrived at 7 to start setting up. When he passed by their camera, he discovered that the camera was on and filming while the crew was waiting in the front hallway. Bob went up to the people and told them simply, "You're out of here. No interview. No more filming." A woman on the crew broke down in tears, but they still had to leave.

A few months later another a crew from a different TV station sent what seemed to be a drunken cameraman and a nervous intern to ask the questions. They didn't conduct themselves well and Bob called the station afterward to leave the message that they should-n't send their C team to Meadowbrook.

Bob is pretty firm when he believes in something. I pleaded with him to let me swim the 100 fly at Summer Nationals in College Park, Maryland, right after Worlds. He said no, because he wanted me to improve my range. It was the end of the summer season and I told my friends I didn't think they'd miss anything by staying away, because I couldn't see myself breaking a record. But leave it to Bob to give me an unexpected incentive. He agreed that if I could lower my world record from 1:56.04 to anything under 1:56, he would shave his head. I mean, never mind gold medals and mil-lion-dollar bonuses; this was a serious prize. This would be my 23rd race in 19 days, but maybe my legs weren't as tired as I thought.

I feed off the crowd really well and they were screaming after I touched the first wall at 50 meters. I was up by a bodylength and just kept thinking about the soon-to-be-bald eagle. I got to the final wall and saw the 1:55.96 on the board. Then I started punching the water and pointing to my head as I stared at Bob on the side of the deck. It was my seventh world record in 41 days, but when I start-ed running around the pooldeck saying, "It's gone. It's gone. It's so gone," I wasn't talking about the record. *Who has the scissors? Anybody bring scissors? Where can you get a good pair of scissors when you really need them?*

By the end of the meet I had won races in the 200 back and freestyle swims at 100, 200, and 400 meters. I become the first male swimmer to win five U.S. titles at one national championship. But even better, when I got back to Meadowbrook the next day, I could see my reflection on Bob's forehead.

After Nationals, Bob made sure I went to have my wisdom teeth removed. My dentist had told me almost a year earlier that they might eventually start pressing against the other teeth and that I would have to get them removed. We just wanted to make sure we found a window in the schedule far enough ahead of Olympic Trials to get it done so I didn't have problems with pain or infection around the most important time of the year.

I had the wisdom teeth taken out in March, and when I woke up, I waddled and stumbled around like a duck. I dozed off during the ride home from the doctor and woke up with a stiff neck from falling asleep with my face against the window. The doctor had given me Percocet to reduce the discomfort, and I was so out of it that at some point during the day, I sent messages to my mom and to Jamie telling them I needed medicine. The messages were so incoherent that they couldn't read them. When I got home, my mom gave me frozen bags of peas to sleep on. Every 20 minutes or so the bags would start to thaw and I'd have to put a new one on my pillow and give the thawed bag to my mom to put back in the freezer. I had Sony Playstation on for several days and literally never turned it off. Fortunately, I ate what I could and only lost about five or ten pounds. I only missed one day in the water and Bob was understanding when he saw how sluggish I was. Someone suggested to the oral surgeon that I could pay for the procedure by selling the Michael Phelps teeth on eBay. Okay, so now the celebrity thing is officially getting out of hand.

My contract with Speedo was set to run through 2005, but everyone wanted to extend the relationship, because it had been so positive. Peter wanted to generate some buzz with the new agreement not only for me, but also for the sport, but how could he do that when Barry Bonds was making $20 million a year and swimming doesn't usually draw the attention that some of the four major sports do in the United States? He came up with a somewhat radical proposal for Stu Isaac, who is in charge of Speedo's team of athletes. If I were to win seven gold medals at either of the next two Olympics, Speedo would pay me a $1 million bonus for equaling Mark Spitz's record for gold medals at one Olympics set in 1972.

And unlike most contractual provisions, which remain confidential, we decided to talk about this one publicly. Peter knew that this would have a significant publicity impact, but he maintained that an athlete's endorsement contract should reflect reasonable compensation for whatever value that athlete is able to bring the company. He felt I could achieve some unique things, which would generate value for Speedo, so he wanted to come up with creative and, even extraordinary, performance incentives.

Peter said the timing would be important in introducing this concept to Speedo. He waited until halfway through the meet in Barcelona and called a meeting with Speedo representatives Craig Brommers, who is in charge of Speedo's marketing, and Stu Isaac. Peter felt that by then I had achieved enough for them to acknowledge that I was at the highest level of swimming and that, with events remaining, I had potential to accomplish more than what they had encountered before.

After some initial pleasantries, Stu simply asked Peter: "So what do you want?" Peter responded: "A million dollars." Stu and Craig were silent at first, but Peter explained why he felt this approach was so important and would eventually benefit both Speedo and swimming. Stu and Craig became receptive and everybody worked to finalize the deal. It's funny, but because only the million-dollar provision was publicized, people assumed that I wouldn't be paid unless I won a million dollars, which made the story more dramatic. The contract was actually set on a graduated scale, so that I would still earn a bonus for six gold medals or five, for instance, and also for world records. Importantly, it included guaranteed money for the next few years, when I was planning to go to school, live on my own and start saving for the future. But the idea of one million dollars was new to swimming and, we figured, good for swimming. People would talk about the contract. They would mention Speedo. The buzz would give the press an extra incentive to write about swimming in advance of the Olympics, which really carries with it a narrow window out of every four years when people can promote the sport. We knew the chances of winning seven golds, against world competition as deep and balanced as it is these days, would be slim, but not impossible.

Peter and I talked about it and asked ourselves some important questions. *Are we setting ourselves up for increased pressure?* Yes. *Can we handle the pressure?* Yes. *Will it create a buzz for swimming?* Yes. *So let's do it.* I knew, at that point, that it would be almost impossible to convince the press that my goal going into the Olympics was to win one gold medal. Can't shoot for one if you publicize seven. But this was a good opportunity for me, for Speedo, and for swimming.

On November 6, Stu held a teleconference with me announcing the details. We got the sport into the headlines, which was where we wanted to see it.

The bonus even generated interest in Australia, were their dollar has a different value than ours so the bonus didn't come out to a round number. I traveled there at the end of the month for meets in Sydney and Melbourne. It was my second trip Down Under during the year, and it was the second time I had lost my training equipment.

"Bob, I can't find it."

"Well, I guess we're not here to train."

"Bob, it's not my fault if they lost it."

In fact the first time the airline sent the bag to the wrong section; this time I left it on the plane. When Bob and I have our worst arguments—really intense, serious, how-did-you-get-to-be-such-a-knucklehead arguments—they're over by the next day, sometimes by the next hour. Because we know we both want the same things and because he respects how hard I work, because I respect how much he knows, and because we both realize how much we need each other and can trust each other, we don't hesitate to use each other as an excuse to blow off steam. It's something you can only really do with close friends and family.

Of course, it's bad when you're half a world away and the guy from the baggage department recognizes you because he helped you find your suitcase the last time you lost it.

Actually I could have filled a few more bags by the time I left. A lot of these meets have sponsors who give you prizes for doing well at their meets. The event in Melbourne had a kitchen appliance manufacturer as one of its sponsors, so every time I won a race, they gave me a new blender. By the end of the meet, I had five blenders and one mixer, presented to the meet's outstanding swimmer. Ironically, one local newspaper had started the erroneous rumor that I was thinking of moving my training base to the land Down Under, or at least splitting my training time between there and Baltimore. It wasn't true, but if I had thought about it, I could have opened a nice catering business on the side.

Bob wanted to put me through some stress when we were at the Melbourne meet. He deliberately asked for the driver who was scheduled to pick us up to show up late, so I would have to spend more time waiting at the pool. He made sure a couple of the meals I ordered weren't quite right. Bob thinks of everything and he wanted me to acclimate myself to being able to react calmly when something didn't go according to plan. That way if it happened again when I was at the Olympic Trials in Long Beach or the Olympics themselves, in Athens, I would know how to work around a problem because I had dealt with it before.

Of course even Bob hadn't planned for the day that some rabid Australian fans started following me. A German swimmer helped us out by putting on my cap and switching cars with us. The fans followed the German swimmer's car as we escaped.

That wasn't the only brush with danger on the trip. Remember when Bob didn't want me to go bowling? Well, he figured I couldn't hurt myself jumping into water, even if I jumped from really high. I had been wondering for years what it would feel like to take a dive off a 10-meter platform. Jamie and I asked Bob, during the trip, if we could try it and he surprised us by saying we could. Jamie did it right. When you enter water from that high, you want to slide through it with your hands or your feet, because if you land flat, the impact feels a lot like being slapped by a door. Remember, Michael, stay vertical, as straight as a pencil and you won't get hurt. Unfortunately, just as my mind said, "Think Letter I," my body said, "Let's try Letter L." I guess I stretched out my feet as a defense mechanism, because I landed at a 90-degree angle with legs extended and butt exposed. Ouch, what a spanking! *Remember, Michael, just because you can try it doesn't mean you should do it. Remember the sledding.*

On our way back, we stopped off in Long Beach, California to do a promotional appearance for the Olympic Trials that were going to be held there the following summer in a temporary pool. I stopped off at the site where the pool was going to be built, which was still a large, empty parking lot, and used a giant piece of chalk to scribble the words: 400 IM 4:09.09. The time was the world record I hoped I would be able to break at the Trials. I signed my name underneath it.

I use whatever I can to motivate myself. Tell me I can't do something and it's like a lighted match next to a fuel tanker. I don't throw goggles anymore, but I always keep the internal tanker at the ready position. In December, *Swimming World* magazine, a very respected publication within the sport, put out an issue that contained the cover headline "Super Flyer." It was picture of Ian Crocker strumming a guitar and leaning back against his car. It also contained a two-page foldout centerfold of Ian swimming the fly. Attention all units: activate tanker. Don't get me wrong, not only do

I respect Ian as a swimmer, but I like him personally. He's about as modest and soft-spoken as any athlete who is that good and has that much to boast about. Ian also signed on with Octagon after finishing his great career under Eddie Reese at the University of Texas and he and I have become friends. That didn't stop me from ripping out the centerfold picture of him and putting it on my wall above my bed. Every morning when I woke up, I had to see the photo of Ian and it was like a double espresso and a kick in the butt put together. If I wanted to be on the next cover and have the next centerfold, I had to get up that morning and train so I wouldn't lose again.

Away from the pool, I became more aware of my increasingly higher profile in the local area and I tried to put it to use, especially to help kids. I'm a national spokesman for the Boys and Girls Clubs. I always invite the kids to my meets where my mom makes sure they receive goody bags, and I visit their center in Aberdeen.

I did some public service announcements along with Oriole catcher B.J. Surhoff and Oriole legend Cal Ripken Jr., on behalf of Pathfinders for Autism, the organization that helps those afflicted with the disease. We taped the PSAs to appear during National Autism Month in April.

But my favorite place to give back has been the Riverview Elementary School in Landsdown, Maryland. These are really good kids who have had to overcome a lot. Some of them come from broken homes or have parents who have been in jail or on drugs. For a long time, the school has had some of the lowest Maryland School Assessment test scores in Baltimore County.

Three or four times I year I go there to talk to them about what swimming has done for me and what it has meant to enjoy something so much that I'm always trying to set goals for myself and working to achieve them. I read the the story of the tortoise and the hare to the students, handed out signed poster cards and conducted a question-and-answer session. I'd go from class to class with Mick Small, the school principal, and tell the students, "My mom was a teacher and education is a very important part of my life." I try to be pretty honest with them about some of the struggles I faced as a student, myself: watching my parents separate, getting teased, not being able to focus on my work and not always being the coolest kid in school. Then I tell them just how strong they can be.

Inevitably they ask why I like swimming so much. "In some sports, you can just get by on a lot of natural talent. In swimming, it helps to be long and lean, but you can't be good at it without putting in the work. There is a direct connection between what you put into it and what you get out of it. If you have big ears or trouble focusing, but you work harder than the guy in the lane next to you, you'll beat him."

In 2003, the students began a year-long project based on my preparation for the Olympics. We figured out how many miles it took to travel from Baltimore to Athens. Then, each time the kids read a book, newspaper, or magazine article, the teachers would give them points, just like airline miles. If the students could accumulate 100,000 points, the teachers reasoned that they would have enough miles for the trip to Athens. I loved watching the kids make progress each time I visited. In late spring, Mr. Small told me that the test scores had improved and that the kids had exceeded the 100,000-point barrier. "See," I would tell the students "no goal is too high if you put your mind to it." Perhaps I was also speaking to myself.

19

I'LL FOLLOW YOU

Bob and I had a little seasonal meltdown just in time for Christmas. He wanted to push me as hard as he could over about six-week period after we came back from our trip, and nearly everything I did during that time wasn't good enough. One day I was feeling under the weather and I arrived late for practice after I overslept. A few days later, Bob thought I was loafing through an afternoon practice and told me, "If you're only going to do this much, you might as well get out." I got out of the pool and said, "Okay, I will then." Bob said, "Merry Christmas," and I was out of there. I went to Corey's house and hung out until 11 p.m., which is when I'm usually asleep. Things were rocky between Bob and me for a ten-day period. It was a game of "How much stress can you take?" and "How much can I manufacture?", and he was playing the game very hard. We both sort of knew we'd be on each other's case for a while and we also knew it was something we needed to do to be able to push each other as far as we could.

Training sessions at Meadowbrook could run about six or seven miles a day, or about 75,000 meters a week. I need extra pancakes for the days we swim our "Janet Evans sets" (distance med-leys). In the four years between the Athens and Sydney Olympics, I probably took four or five days off and none of those were holi-days. In addition to the double sessions, we also cross-train in the afternoons. Cross-training is important to swimmers, to help build strength, stamina, and flexibility.

Bob has changed my program often over the last few years, as we've discovered what works and what doesn't. I used to run two or three miles at a time, at roughly a seven-minute pace. But during sophomore year, I started feeling tight after running, and I had pain on the outside of my knees. It got so I was having trouble walking around without pain after each run.

That's when Bob had me switch to riding a stationary bike for half an hour to 45 minutes three times a week. I asked him once about experimenting with outdoor biking on dirt roads, because the stationary bike can get boring. "Absolutely not!" he told me. (If bowling was out, biking didn't stand a chance.) So boredom it is.

When we don't have meets, we exercise every day except Sunday. Apart from the bike, I do about four or five varieties of pushups, 50 to 100 at a time; several types of sit-ups and crunches, usually around 500 or more each day; and I do up to five sets of eight pull-ups, increasing the weight during each set. Bob is extremely precise about form. He says if we do our workouts the way we are supposed to, we won't get hurt.

I even have an early-morning regimen for stretching in the shower. That serves as my warm-up swim for the morning. Since I had no school in 2003-04, I'd wake up at 7 a.m. and swim until 8:30 or 9, depending on Bob's mood. The sooner I'd get out, the sooner I'd be able to eat and nap. At 3:45, we'd start up again. I'd get there at 3:15 to stretch. After swimming, we'd do between half an hour and an hour of dryland training. It helped that I didn't have to worry about messing up a test or not finishing a paper.

Apart from my scientifically balanced diet (at Pete's, that used to be one omelet in each hand), I take daily Vitamin C and a multivitamin and Bob insists that I have an instant breakfast drink after races in order to get quick carbs back into my system. I also take daily salt tablets to make sure I don't lose fluids too quickly.

We hired a physical trainer in January to start working with us, but he started destroying our legs. His program may have been good for certain types of athletes, but it didn't work for swimmers, since we have specific needs of flexibility and stamina that he didn't understand. I had never been at the point, after a workout, when I haven't been able to swim fast because I was physically too tired from the workout. We did three sessions a week with him, an additional session of dryland training and one really hard hour six days a week. After it appeared the sessions were doing more harm than good, Bob let him go after three or four months.

Bob and I were trying to iron out some technical glitches early in the year. We were trying to keep my chin down during the butterfly sessions. We were working on the roll of my hips in the freestyle events, because the longer my body was as I swam, the smoother the strokes felt. Bob also noticed that when I breathed on my right side during the freestyle races, I didn't come back far enough to my left side in order to complete the next stroke most efficiently. When I swim at my best, there are very few bubbles around my hands when I swim underwater, and Bob was trying to get me to that point. We were also trying to improve my turns because that long body that had grown to six feet, four inches wasn't good at tightening itself into a ball as I approached the wall.

We were also devoting a lot of time working on backstroke and freestyle strokes and, in essence, trying to determine which of two races I would add to my schedule during the summer. At that point, we knew I would swim my best stroke, the butterfly, twice (100 meters and 200 meters); both individual medleys that combined the four strokes (200 meters and 400 meters); and, hopefully, if the coaches decided to use me, on three relays (4x100 free relay, 4x200 free relay, 4x100 medley relay). We had a dilemma about trying more events. I had swum well in both the 200-meter backstroke and 200-meter freestyle and I knew I could conceivably try to swim either or both of those events in addition to the rest of my program. For the next few months, Bob and I would debate and discuss the merits of those two events and how they might affect my other races because of the tight schedule at both the Trials and the Olympics and the inevitable buildup of fatigue.

I had another loaded schedule at my first big meet of 2004, the Spring Nationals in Orlando. As he did at the '03 Summer Nationals, Bob entered me in five events, and for the second straight time, I won five races: the 100 freestyle, 100 butterfly, 200 IM and the two races I was thinking of adding to my Olympic program, the 200 freestyle and 200 backstroke. Of all the races, the 200 back, my first race of the meet, was also the most exciting. My Olympic teammate, Aaron Peirsol, had set the world record of 1:55.15 two years earlier in Minneapolis, and he was clearly considered the early favorite heading into the Olympics. I wanted to see how close I could swim to his time. Honestly, before that meet, Bob and I were leaning toward adding the 200 free and not the 200 back. If I were to swim a slow 200 back in Orlando, there was a chance that that might knock it off my plate for the season.

After the race began, I tried to look up at the board each time I came off one of the walls to see how far off record pace I actually was. I could see that I was a good half-second behind the pace at the 150 mark, and I needed to pick it up. I turned really well at the third wall and increased the pace as much as I could. I could tell I had a strong finish and I was hoping I had made up enough time. Nope—1:55.30. It was pretty close, but it was another hands-on-the-head moment. In the meantime, Bob was processing all of this on the pooldeck. "Hoo-wah. Yow. Ay-yaye," he said, apparently experiencing his own technical glitch in word processing. "Wow, how does he not swim it at trials after a time like that?" Bob was right. We had a success, but we also had a problem of too many options, and we weren't ready to commit to a decision about our schedule just yet.

During Nationals, Bob had spoken to Jon Urbanchek, the head coach at the University of Michigan for the previous 22 years, about the fact that Jon was planning to step down at the end of the season. Would Bob have an interest in interviewing for the upcoming vacancy, Jon wanted to know.

It was tempting. During his tenure, Jon had built the Wolverines into one of the best collegiate swim teams in the country, with 13 conference titles and an NCAA team championship in 1995, the 11th in the school's history. Jon coached great swimmers such as Mike Barrowman, Tom Dolan, and Tom Malchow, who were all Wolverines before they became world-record holders.

I had been planning to take some courses close to home, at Loyola College, while training with Bob after the Olympics. As much as the job excited him, Bob didn't want to break up our team, but he also didn't want to make a decision about a place he might stay for 20 years based on being able to coach me for another four or eight. He agreed to go to Ann Arbor for a formal interview. I was planning to go to the Bahamas to shoot a commercial for one of my sponsors, the Argent Mortgage Company. Bob had been planning to join me on the trip anyway to monitor my training, so he made a low-key detour to Michigan on March 22.

The commercial shoot for Argent was pretty memorable, because they had me swimming against a dolphin. I had never seen a dolphin up close and the people working on the set told me that dolphins are naturally people-friendly to begin with, and this one was especially used to swimming next to people. Yes, but it didn't mean I was used to swimming next to dolphins. She was bumping up beside me during the shoot and it was freaky. The dolphin would swim off, disappear for five minutes and all of a sudden she'd pop up and I'd turn and see this big, bottle-nosed dolphin sitting right in front of me. I almost freaked out when I first saw her. The skin felt kind of rubbery. I have pictures of this giant bottlenose giving me a kiss. My eyes are just bug-eyed and I'm saying, "What do I do? What do I do? I have this bottle-nosed dolphin kissing the side of my cheek."

"Relax, Michael. Whatever you do, don't panic. Just pet her. Pet her."

It was before the 1988 Olympics when Matt Biondi, the best U.S. swimmer at the time, went to swim with dolphins, not to shoot a commercial, but to learn how they move through the water so efficiently. I can see why. They are amazing creatures. They are not the best kissers.

I filmed a series of ads and promotions during the spring, trying to take advantage of the pre-Olympic window. Peter and Bob made a great team. Peter negotiated many great opportunities for me, and Bob made sure the opportunities didn't detract from my training schedule. Bob liked the idea of out-of-town trips, because they took me away from the local hype. Each time, Bob insisted that if we were going away, we would need to have a week in the other city. If we did that, he felt I could still get in good training each day; if I flew in and flew out, he figured the workouts would be unproductive and I'd end up losing training days.

I filmed a cool spot for AT&T in Colorado Springs. In the commercial, I hop out of a pool and see a guy trying to get reception on his cell phone while he's standing on the pooldeck. "Dude," I tell him, "you're going to hurt yourself. Here, try mine." Of course, it's an AT&T phone in perfect working order. As the announcer asks, "How many bars do you have?" the graphic above his head changes from one bar to a series of five raised bars that you see on a cell phone with perfect reception. It took about ten takes to get it exactly right, but I like the way it turned out.

I also went down to Miami to film a commercial for VISA. In

that ad, I swam in open water past a number of landmarks until I reached New York Harbor, near the Statue of Liberty. Then I swam to the wall, touched it, turned around and said, "One," as if I had merely completed a lap. Here are two secrets for people who have seen the commercial. First, even though I filmed the scenes in Miami, I had a body double for the scenes in New York and Atlanta. Sean Foley had joined the staff at Octagon after an accomplished career at the University of Texas. He was the swimmer in most of the scenes. People in the swimming world can probably tell the difference. Sean breathes every other stroke; I breathe every stroke. Secret number two: VISA actually filmed a second version of the commercial in which I touch a wall, take my goggles off, look up and see Bob standing in front of the Statue of Liberty with a stopwatch. Then he looks down and tells me to "pick it up on the way back." Unfortunately, they canned that version because it ran longer than the 30 seconds they had allotted, which would have cost them more money. No Bob, no royalties. Sorry, Coach.

Besides those ads, we filmed some highlights for NBC at Loyola that the network used for its pre-Olympic promotions. Power Bar ran a series of highlights from my events. And the Omega watch company came up with a deal I couldn't refuse. Not only was I going to become one of their spokespeople, but I was also going to be introduced as an Omega rep with Cindy Crawford, who was one of their other clients. Very sweet. And the watch is cool, too.

Then came the media crunch. We did cover shoots for *Sports Illustrated*, *SI Kids* and *Time*, and I gave long interviews to *The New York Times*, *Washington Post*, *Chicago Tribune* and *USA Today*. The local paper, *The Baltimore Sun*, was writing stories almost daily. Even on a day I wouldn't give interviews, there would be stories in the local papers and on the Baltimore TV stations.

All along, we had to ask, "Was the media exposure adversely affecting my training?" Peter ran everything through Bob, who had

veto power over everything. They came up with a scale of importance. Some obligations were mandatory. Before a major meet, such
as Nationals or the Olympic Trials, for example, the top swimmers
are expected to be available for a general press conference. Then if
they win a race or qualify for the Olympic team in an event, we are
supposed to make ourselves available after that race. Beyond that,
I started to get a lot of requests, especially as the Olympics drew
closer. With every photo shoot, interview request, press conference and TV appearance, Bob would ask Peter: On a scale of 1 to 10,
how much would this benefit Michael?

I also wanted to do as much as possible because it was a chance
to get swimming on the front pages, the way it is in Australia. We
did the nines and tens, tried to accommodate the sevens and eights
and had to pass on everything else. Even with the ones we accepted, Bob picked the dates and times when I'd be available. Usually
we tried to aim for 2 p.m. as a time for interviews, because I could
still have a morning practice, eat, take an afternoon nap and be
ready for a late-afternoon practice after the interview. Because I
wasn't going to school during the year, I had more hours to work
with. Even without school, I was getting a great education anyway,
a real insight into communications and into marketing.

Bob and I flew back together from the Argent shoot in the
Bahamas and he began telling me about the trip to Ann Arbor. He
was originally against the job, but he went to Ann Arbor as a courtesy to Bill Martin, the Michigan athletic director and acting U.S.
Olympic Committee president. I had competed in Ann Arbor
before and so Bob had seen the area, but when he finally saw it
through the eyes of a prospective coach, he fell in love with it. "If I
want the Michigan job, it's mine," he said. I told him I wasn't surprised and I congratulated him. That he asked the obvious question: "If I took the job, what would you do?" I answered him in
about two seconds, but I knew the question was coming and I had

my answer ready before he even asked. "Are you kidding? I would go anywhere you would be," I told him. "I like new challenges and I used to wear that Michigan cap at school."

It was more than that. No other coach could have gotten me as far as Bob. It was more than his degree in developmental psych that allowed him to plow through my attitude and get the most out of my talent; it was a brilliant mind and a great heart that he probably didn't want anybody to know about. Bob and I had always been careful not to express too much emotion toward each other because, with my dad rarely in the picture, I relied on him for the kind of counsel a father gives a son. In our moments when we weren't yelling at each other, we talked about school, friends, family, girls, music, anything. We didn't see eye to eye on a lot of it (I will NEVER like country music), but he knew and I knew that he had done more than mold me into a swimmer; he had helped me grow up, and there were days when I needed a lot of help. I like Ann Arbor and I admire Michigan's tradition, but if Bob had accepted a job in Siberia, my decision would have been the same.

20

EMOTIONAL SENDOFF

After Bob told me about the Michigan job on the plane, he also said: "You're the only one who knows about this, so please don't tell anyone yet." That was hard. Later that day, Jamie was talking about training with Bob the next year, and I had to keep my mouth shut, knowing that he would have to re-think his decision and that I couldn't speak to him about it just yet.

At Meadowbrook, we began wearing new caps that said NBAC on one side and Athens 2004 on the other. Just seeing the cap each day made me realize how close we were to the Games. I kept a calendar on my bedroom wall and I began checking off days before the start of the Trials. We had just passed T-minus 100 days, and I could feel my intensity start to pick up in practice.

Bob was planning to wait until after my next meet, the Doc Counsilman Classic in Indianapolis later that week, before making an announcement about the Michigan job. Before the competition, I went to a publicity event to promote the World Short Course Championships that were scheduled for October at a temporary pool inside the Conseco Fieldhouse, the home of the Indiana

Pacers basketball team. I knew the press would be asking a lot of questions about the quest for seven gold medals and they had more reason to do that after the publicity event. Larry Bird, an NBA legend who is now the Pacers' president of basketball operations, presented me with a team jersey that had the number seven on it. "It's Jermaine O'Neal's number," Bird said, talking about his team's best player, "but we know what it stands for."

Bob wanted to see how I would react to swimming three races in a day again. I had a winning streak of 37 straight races going into that meet. We expected that would end because I had entered the 200 breaststroke on Saturday just to tax my body a little and give me stamina in my weakest stroke of the IMP. The streak ended, but not the way I planned.

That afternoon I ate some bourbon chicken with rice in a local mall and didn't think anything of it. I'm not positive that that caused the problem, but when I went to the prelims on Friday morning, I felt really sluggish. I got through the heats of both the 200 free and 400 IMP and was the top qualifier in each. Friday night, I felt like garbage. I struggled just to finish to 200 free and finished second to South Africa's Ryk Neethling. It was my first loss since the previous July. I left the pool feeling both hot and cold, and even the towel I wrapped around my back couldn't stop me from shaking. I told Bob I didn't think I could do the IMP and he wasn't happy.

"This isn't going to give us a good indication of where we stand."

"I know, but it's not my fault. If I had known I was going to get sick off the stuff, I wouldn't have eaten it."

"Fine, I'll pull you from the race."

Bob walked away from me. I know he felt that it was beneficial to compete under stress because that prepared us for what we would face at the Olympics, but I really couldn't learn anything except how sick I was.

I went back to my room, ate some chicken soup, downed some Pepto Bismol to ease my stomach, turned the TV on and slept from 10 p.m. until noon when my mom and Bob came into the room. I didn't race the 200 fly or 200 breast on Saturday, but I did get in the water and train just enough to get my body ready for a big day on Sunday and then came back to cheer for my teammates in the night session.

In the middle of all this, reporters started approaching Bob to ask him about the Michigan job. It turned out Coach Urbanchek had mentioned his departure and Bob's hire to his swimmers, and at least one of them told somebody who ran a Wolverine website. Bob was okay answering the extra questions, but we didn't want people to think that my stomach ailments were in any way connected to the move to Michigan.

I was still a little stressed out physically and I felt pressure to bounce back after the discussion with Bob, but I felt a lot better. I won the 200 back and then the 100 free, rallying from next to last at the 50-meter turn and beating Neethling at the wall. Then I swam a 200 free by myself as an exhibition and a sort of stress test to see how I'd do with three swims in a short period of time—in this case, about 40 minutes. In between races, my lactate level was at 14, which is much higher than we ever want to see it. Right before the 200 free, it was still at 7.9, nowhere close to the 2.0 we shoot for. Still, my 200 free time was 1:48.30, much faster than the time I swam when Neethling beat me a few days earlier. More important, it gave me an idea of how I would do swimming three races in such a short period of time the way I'd have to at the Trials in Long Beach a few months away.

From there, I went right to a two-day photo shoot for Speedo at Arizona State. I was very happy with the shape I was in at that particular point. Bob usually doesn't come to photo shoots; he usually just gives me workouts and lets me swim around. But he made a big point of coming to this one so he could monitor me and make sure I was doing the right things to get ready for Trials.

We came back in time for more functions. I was excited to be invited to Ray Lewis' charity bowling event to raise money to build a park in Lakeland, Florida, his hometown. No, Bob, I didn't bowl. I picked up a football for Matt that was signed by his favorite player, Steve McNair, the Tennessee Titans' quarterback. Matt was finishing up his freshman year at Salisbury State and he let out a loud yell when I called to tell him about the football.

The following evening we had a black-tie gala inside the pool at Meadowbrook to raise money for NBAC. (Don't worry, we drained the pool.) Parents and coaches donated many items that we auctioned off, and Rowdy Gaines came in to be the master of ceremonies for the event. I donated some things, but I also wanted to get people in a bidding mood to help the club, so I also bought the first item, a weekend ski package in Jackson Hole, Wyoming for $5,000. Mom was on the opposite end of the pool when Rowdy made the announcement and said to her friends: "Did I hear that right?" Don't worry, Mom. Just look at it as a good cause.

The next day was Mothers Day and I had been looking forward to visiting my grandmother for a while. She was putting up a brave fight against pancreatic cancer, and she had been living at the Brighton Gardens assisted-living residence in Pikesville, Maryland, where many of the residents would corner her for daily reports about her grandson, the swimmer. Word was that Leoma Davisson, 85, would take the back stairs to avoid her newfound celebrity. But she had been in a hospital for two weeks after developing pneumonia. I really wanted to see her before I left for the summer, especially since her health had recently been so-so.

But as soon as I walked into the room, she turned to my mom and said, "What is he doing here?" I know my grandmother wanted to see me as much as I wanted to see her, but she was looking out for me and she didn't want me to catch any germs that she had. She insisted that I leave for my own good and I was pretty bummed about it. I've always been really close to her, and it's so fun to know that she'll say the first thing that pops into her head without filtering what she's thinking. She told Hilary once, "You know, you'd look so much better as a blonde." She told me I should never have a steady girlfriend because "Every girl needs lovin' and why should a young man be tied down? Be free. Have fun." See, when you're 85, you can say anything and nobody will tell you not to. I knew I'd be away for a few months and I wanted to make sure I saw her, because I didn't know what her condition would be when I got back.

I tried to take my mind off my grandmother's illness and the disappointment of not being able to see her. I saw two English bulldogs in the window of a pet store in Baltimore and I thought I could name them Diesel and Chief. That day I went home and asked my mom about bringing them home. It was a lost cause. "Well, Michael, if you get dogs now, you have to be able to walk them every day. You have to make sure they have their shots. You have to be able to spend enough time with them to train them to stay off the furniture. You have to find a kennel for them for the weeks you'll be away, which is a difficult thing for new dogs. You have to . . ."

"So you're telling me no."

"No, Michael, I'm not saying no; I'm just telling you that there are certain responsibilities that go with buying a dog now. If you do that and train and go to the Olympics at the same time . . ."

"Maybe I could ask them to hold the dogs."

"Michael, I think that's a good idea."

"Thanks, Mom."

Later that summer, when I left for the training camp in Palo

Alto, my mom sent me an e-mail with a picture of two dogs.

In late May, I was back in New York for a media summit put on by the U.S. Olympic Committee. They flew in Olympic hopefuls in a number of sports, so reporters would have an opportunity to talk to a lot of athletes in one place and the smaller sports would have a chance for exposure they might not otherwise have. At some point I had mentioned that I was thinking of getting another tattoo to one of the reporters, who then asked my mom about it. Okay, she was probably thinking, Michael already has the Olympic rings, what is he thinking of now? Something bigger? Something he'll regret? I know she didn't want to say no, but she also didn't want me to get it.

Peter became her representative in the no-tattoo campaign. When we were in New York, he proposed a contest. We go to the ESPN Zone restaurant where the third floor is filled with every kind of game you can imagine from foosball to air hockey to games that allow you to shoot baskets, take slapshots or drive a simulated Daytona race car. We each chose alternate challenges. "If you win," Peter told me, "I'll take you to dinner anywhere you want in New York City. If I win, I own the rights to your body art." This was serious. We each chose games we figured we could win. I picked games I could play on consoles. Peter chose mostly sports that involved more physical skills. He won when we played at the basketball hoop; I won when we played at the basketball console. He took slapshots; I shot targets. It was close, but after several hours of titanic struggle, the air hockey did me in. No tattoo. Score one for Peter. And Mom.

During one of the breaks at the media summit, Peter tried to show me that I could save time by the way I signed autographs. We talked before about the walk-and-sign trick celebrities use all the time. Don't stop going where you're going. Just keep walking as you scribble something that looks like a signature. I don't like that very much. If it's a single person, you can usually make it a more personal experience for them by asking where they're from, if they're involved in swimming, that sort of thing. If you're walking and signing for a group of people, you might end up giving a pen to the wrong person. And have you tried to write something down while you're in motion? The signature looks like a big cross-out. Peter also showed me how I could save time by coming up with a writing style so I could sign my name more quickly and accommodate more fans. You know, sign the initials and then drag the pen for a few letters worth of space. I tried it, but it looked like chicken scratch. "You want to give a kid that?" I told him. "You can't even read it. If he shows it to his friends, they won't think, 'Oh, cool, Michael Phelps'; they'll think, 'Yeah, right—Mi__ P___. Tell me another one.'" Peter agreed, so sometimes I have to teach things to him.

The next week, we went out to the West Coast for a meet at Santa Clara and it was time to learn another lesson. My first final was the 400 IMP and I was concentrating on the race as I went up to the blocks. I didn't notice the amount of water that was on my block as I jumped into the pool. Instead of diving in, I fell off the blocks and ended up swimming from a dead stop inside the pool. I still won the race, finishing two seconds ahead of Erik Vendt, but from then on I added an extra step to my prerace ritual by taking out a towel and wiping off my block before getting in the water.

The news was good and bad on the second day. I beat Ian Crocker in the 100 fly for the first time since Worlds, but I also lost to Aaron Peirsol in the 200 back, one of the wild-card races we were considering adding to the schedule for Trials. I was four seconds ahead of everyone else but still a half-second behind Aaron.

The next day I swam three finals in an hour, the 100 free, 200 IMP and 100 back, against some tough domestic competition. I wanted to leave a good impression with Eddie Reese, the Texas coach who would be our head coach in Athens and would pick the swimmers on our freestyle relay teams. Since I wasn't planning to swim the 100 free at trials, this race was a tryout of sorts for one of the 4x100 free relay spots at the Olympics. I swam well and won the race, finishing ahead of Jason Lezak in 49.26 seconds. Bob told me afterward that the result should have left no doubt in people's minds that I belonged on the squad. A half-hour later I won the IMP in 2:00.41 and then came back for the backstroke half an hour after that. The field was loaded with great swimmers, including Peirsol, Lenny Krayzelburg, Jeff Rouse, Randall Bal and Peter Marshall.   I was tired and I wasn't able to go out with Peirsol. I caught the rest of the field to finish second in 55.49, but Aaron was half a second ahead of me.

In the press conference later, Aaron said that I needed to stop playing mind games by keeping my Trials schedule a secret, but I was just going about my business. The reason we did what we did was to give us options until the last minute. If we didn't make the best decision we could, we'd have to wait four years to make a better one. A few days later Peter called to say that Aaron's agent had sent out a press release that mentioned that Aaron had beaten me twice, and included the headline: "Peirsol Beats Phelps Twice. Sun Still Comes Up on Monday." Peter used to play hockey, so he is used to sticks and pucks flying around him at high speeds. I think one of the reasons he is so good at what he does is that he always keeps his cool, even under stress, and I could hear some stress in his voice during that phone call. There are a lot of good people in our sport, and it was rare to see anyone cross a line of professionalism that badly. Hey Peter, you okay?

I came back home in time to count my blessings. Miss Janice Deamon would see to that. Miss Janice was the secretary at Towson High School, where she used to check me in every day. She liked looking after the students at Towson and hearing whatever stories they were willing to share with her, and she was as good as anyone at building up school spirit. I came by to see her one day and she had some surprises for me. First, she had cut out some cardboard from a Kleenex box and made a red, white and blue medal that she hung on her office door. Then she put holy water on my arms to bring me good luck over the summer. Talk about using your connections.

With all the visits, training and media responsibilities, I didn't realize how tired I was getting until one Sunday evening after practice. Hilary and Whitney were coming over for dinner, but I was in the middle of one of my power naps. Hilary knocked on my door and tried to wake me up. "Michael, are you hungry? We have dinner." She remembers me staring at her with a dazed look on my face and mumbling something like, "Okay, I'll be down in a minute." Three hours later, I walked downstairs and asked Mom: "Where are Hilary and Whitney? I thought they were coming for dinner." Oh well, I like leftovers.

It wasn't as if Hilary didn't have enough ammunition to tease me. There was the time I tried to buy her a nice gift for Christmas two years ago and I made a gift-buying blooper. Hilary loves Christmas; she once opened all her gifts before my mom even made it downstairs. I bought her a classy matching outfit from Ann Taylor, thinking I'd really make some sibling points with a nice gift. I would have if I hadn't bought a Size 1 pair of pants and a Size 8 shirt. I try. I really try.

Hilary looks after me so much that at times I tell her it's like having two mothers, especially the way she is taking on some of Mom's habits. Sometimes my mom drives pretty slow and enjoys the scenery. She'll point out things and places while she's driving and since she knows everybody, she always seems to stop and say hello to friends she passes on the way. Not me. If I'm going somewhere, I just want to get there as efficiently as I can. Now Hilary is

taking after Mom. Sometimes, she'll be in her car and I'll be following and after we get to where we're going, I'll say, "Hilary, the gas
pedal's on the right." She'll say, "Ah, I'm turning into my mom, I
know."

On June 30, my family took me out for dinner and then had a
19th birthday party for me at the house. With Mom's blessing, we
invited Dad to the dinner, too. He had been making an attempt to
get back into my life, which was a little unexpected.

Over the past four years, I don't think either one of us really
reached out to the other. I was so focused on going to the Olympics
that I wasn't going to change something that was working. Hanging
out with friends was different, because I could spend some time
with them and stop and go home or go to practice if I had to leave
them behind, and they always understood. If I was with my dad,
I sort of felt that there was commitment involved and that I
couldn't just up and leave without creating a "discussion." This was
really his first big attempt at trying to bring me back into his life.
The past 15 years haven't been easy on our relationship. I think it's
necessary to have a father figure in your life, even when you get
older.

He started trying to do things I like to do. He'll say, "Want to
go to lunch? Want to go to Pete's?" I'd say, "Sure, why not?" At dinner, he'd ask if I wanted to play some cards later on. He started
emailing and text messaging on my BlackBerry. When I was
younger we used to watch a lot of baseball. In high school, I
became a huge football fan. I've watched a few games on TV with
my dad lately, and I realize just how well he understands the game
because of his background in it. We'll be watching TV and he'll
look at the formations on the field and just call a play. "Michael,
this is a run play to the right." And he'll be right. It's fun to watch
the game with someone who can give you an education in it. And,
yes, it's fun for me when that person is my dad.

I've had friends ask if maybe he was making the effort then

because he doesn't want to be left out of the spotlight. I don't think that's it. My dad lost his own father when he was eight, about the age I was when he divorced my mom. He didn't have any sort of blueprint for a father-son relationship during his teenage years, years that are more complex than toddler years. It's easier, sometimes, to raise six-year-olds, when they're always hanging by your side and you just tell them *yes*, *no* and *because I said so*. It's harder when kids grow up and have to make choices. He never had his dad around to help him make those choices, so maybe he wasn't sure how to help me make mine. In my mind I haven't completely given him the benefit of the doubt; I wish he had reached out more and reached out sooner. Still, I see him trying a lot more these days. I know we won't ever be as close as we were when I was six, but I think we can do better than we have. I don't know that I'll ever forget the feelings I had at the AT&T tent in Sydney, but I also can't forget the days he took me to watch the Orioles or stood behind the blocks and told to me to *get 'em next time*. He wanted me to know then that there was a next time for me. I want him to know now that there can be a next time for him.

A few days later, I had my last chance to see some of my friends before the Olympics, and I don't think Matt and I were prepared for just how emotional that would make both of us. It wasn't as if we were never going to hang out again, but with me heading to Ann Arbor, who knew where I'd be spending my next few birthdays? Who knew how our lives were about to change?

I'm not sure if Matt and I became such good friends because he lost his father when he was three years old and neither one of us grew up with dads in our homes. We have just always seemed to understand each other in the way that best friends do. And we both had a feeling we couldn't quite put our fingers on. People move on when they get older. It probably wouldn't be the last birthday we spent together, but it might be the last time we'd all be at a place we called home for one of our birthdays. In that way, we were sharing something together for the last time.

I was busy packing my bags the next night, but I asked my mom if she wanted to watch *Miracle*. She had never seen it, so I told her I'd pop in and out while she watched and I packed. Instead I was running up and down the steps every few minutes, telling her to watch for something specific that was about to happen in the next scene. About midway through the movie I just decided to sit and watch with her. I have a bad habit of telling people what to look for in movies I've already seen. I have pretty much memorized dialogue from films like *Tommy Boy*, *Billy Madison*, *Friday*, *Scarface* and *Pulp Fiction*, and Jamie says it's impossible to watch movies with me because I'll blurt out a word before one of the characters does. Mom likes to ask if I can recite Shakespeare the way I can recite Quentin Tarantino. But *Miracle* is personal to me. I'd like to think I know what it's like to pursue a goal with that kind of dedication. It was inspiring to see the team achieve so much with so many obstacles standing in their way. They had no guarantees, just a lot of uncertainty. As I left for Long Beach, I realized I did, too.

21

TRIALS AND
DELIBERATIONS

Because there were no relays at the Trials, I had the luxury of trying to compete in six events, including the two IMs, the two flys and both the 200 free and 200 back. If I could qualify in all six, Bob and I knew I would probably have to drop either the 200 free or 200 back, but we were also trying to see if, based on what happened in Long Beach, I might think about swimming both of them in Athens.

The day before competition began, I was up at a podium giving a press conference. The first question was about how I was able to go into a meet like this with so much confidence. In fact, I was a lot more nervous than I let on. This was what all the training and sacrifice was leading to. It was one thing to go to Nationals or an invitational meet thinking about trying to break a record. Miss it and you can break it again next month. But these were the Olympic Trials and they were very different from the 2000 Trials in Indianapolis when I was an unknown. Everyone was watching me now, either expecting me to do well or hoping for me to fail.

"Michael, how many gold medals can you win?" someone

asked.

"Anything is possible," I said, "I don't think you should ever talk about things you can't do."

"Michael, what will it take to win seven gold medals?"

"Well, I have to have the best meet of my career, but I'd be happy with one gold medal."

"Michael, will people think you failed if you don't win seven gold medals?"

"I hope not. I've always dreamed of winning a gold medal . . ."

"Michael, just how many gold medals can you win?"

Finally I was feeling punchy, as if I should lose control and tell a joke, something to break the tension. "I guess I can win 15 gold medals if I want to," I said. Bob nearly went into convulsions in the back of the room. He started making the throat-slashing signal, trying to get me out of there. *Be neutral, Michael. Don't give somebody else something to put on their bulletin board, remember?* I had just given them a billboard.

It was a good thing that the 400 IM was the first event. I hated having my longest race as my last race at Worlds the previous summer. It was a long event, and it was hard to save all my emotional and physical energy for that race at the end of the meet. In Long Beach I was fresh and I was prepared, and I had one of the best swims of my life. I hit every split that Bob and I discussed and I was already up by four and a half seconds after the fly and back-stroke. I won the race by two bodylengths, lowering my world record to 4:08.41.

The 200 freestyle was the next final two days later. Of all my races, this was the one in which my times were farthest off the world record. There were half a dozen swimmers who were capable of beating me, and I was getting a fair amount of advice not to swim it, but the race also represented a chance to swim against Ian Thorpe in one of his best events, and I didn't want to miss out on that chance. I really wanted to put up a good time in Long Beach.

The day of the 200 free final, Team Phelps had lunch at Chastity Bono's Restaurant. Whitney and Hilary had bought a stuffed bulldog they showed to Mom, BJ, and Krista. When you pulled its nose, it would growl and shake; when you patted its head, it would whimper. They gave me the stuffed dog later that night, but when am I going to get the real one?

I was pretty relaxed in the afternoon, but I didn't really swim the race the way I wanted to swim it. I was simply too cautious and my turns were really slow. I won the event in 1:46.27, finishing sixth-tenths ahead of Klete Keller, but Bob and I definitely wanted to be in the 1:45s, and I left the pool that night uncertain whether I would swim it in Athens.

That was the turning point at Trials. I was angry with myself for the first time during the meet and that anger started replacing some of my nerves. I had to overdo the 200 fly the next day to sort of wake up a little more and get into the meet. I was close to world-record pace for most of the race, but again I had a poor last turn. Without anyone on my heels, I finished in 1:54.31, three-tenths off my world record, and three seconds ahead of Malchow, who finished second, to get back on the team.

Throughout the entire week, people kept asking me questions about Mark Spitz. A couple of reporters wrote stories in which they criticized me for not being very aware of Spitz's accomplishments until just before the Sydney Games. I remembered then from watching films of him during the Munich Olympics that he wore a moustache, which would have slowed him down, and no goggles, which would have affected his vision. Yet he won seven gold medals in seven events, which nodody else has managed to do. To be mentioned in the same sentence as Spitz was pretty cool. It's not every day that you're compared to one of the great Olympians of all time. I had never met him, but I knew he was in Long Beach, and I wondered if I would see him after the competition was over.

I had walked out of the warm-down pool and was talking to Bob, when I heard the public address announcer mention that the man presenting me the winner's medal would be Mark Spitz. "What!" I said. "Is he kidding?" He wasn't. Every single person in the stands was on their feet, screaming, cheering. Spitz grabbed my right wrist with his left hand, lifted it into the air in a victorious salute and pointed to me with his right forefinger. There aren't many things that can make me shake, I mean literally shake, but I could feel goose bumps all the way up and down my arms and legs. He pulled my head down to his to wish me well. "I'll be over in Athens to watch you," he said, "and I'm behind you all the way. I know what you're going through. I went through it once before. Enjoy it. Have fun with it. Go get 'em." That was amazing. I walked away and needed some time to just process the whole thing. He's the greatest icon in the sport, and it was like he was passing the torch to me. Very, very cool.

Two days later I was facing my toughest day at the trials, with four races, including evening finals in the 200 back and 200 IM followed by the semis of the 100 fly. I had been thinking specifically of this evening session since I started checking days off my calendar. The day before, Bob had read an article in one of the Sydney papers that quoted Kieren Perkins, Australia's former distance freestyle star. Perkins was criticizing me for not giving Ian Thorpe enough respect and for coming after him in a freestyle event. "The thing is, Thorpe is the champion," Perkins said. "He's competed at that level and won, and while Phelps is a great talent and he's broken lots of world records, he hasn't won at that level yet. . . . You've got an unproven athlete having a go at a proven one, and I'm sure Ian's going to smile wryly and just let it go because he knows that experience is on his side." Bob sat on the article for a day, because he wanted me to see the comments before the start of the evening session, when I had the three races.

Perkins' comments set off a bomb inside me. When I read that, I was seething. Are you kidding me? Sean Foley happened to be sitting next to me when I read those comments and I vented in his direction. *That's ridiculous. I may not beat him, but that isn't the point. The whole idea of competition is that you try to test yourself against the best. Thorpe is the greatest freestyler of all-time, and I want to swim against him when we're both at our best. We've missed a lot of chances to compete against each other. The idea that I should just sit on the side and let Ian have the event just spits in the face of meeting a challenge. Why have an Olympics if you can't chase the best? I want people to chase after me in my strongest events, because I love challenges. I hate to lose. I just . . .* "Michael, calm down," Bob told me. Actually, he planted that comment in my mind to fire me up, but it probably did more than he anticipated.

I didn't swim a very good 200 back. I fell behind Aaron in the first 50, and even as the two of us pulled away from the rest of the field, he was still nearly a bodylength better. Aaron broke his own world record, dropping it to 1:54.74. I never got close to my time in Orlando and took second in 1:55.86. Aaron was psyched. He was bouncing from lane rope to lane rope after the race, and I wasn't happy at all. I was more upset that I was over half a second off my best time (1:55.30). I always go into big races at big events looking to swim against Michael Phelps. *What has he done before? What is he capable of doing?* I didn't look at the race as a failure, because I finished second to Aaron, but I know I could have swum it faster.

Whatever happened in the 200 back, we needed to stay positive. "That wasn't a very good third turn," I said to Bob. "Let's move on to the next one," he said. Bob didn't think the IM was going to be a tough race for me, so he was pretty calm and positive before that race. But he knew the tough one would be the 100 fly at the end of the long day, so he had already planned to get in my face before the start of that race.

I had less than half an hour before getting back into the water for the 200 IM final. People overuse the phrase "staying focused," but that was what I needed to do. I needed to convince my mind that the 200 back never happened and I needed to convince my body that my legs and arms were fresher than they felt. Bob had all his speeches pre-planned, and he wanted to save his gut-check, in-your-face speech for the butterfly.

I hit my splits exactly as we wanted them. I was a half-second ahead after a 25.05 butterfly split and just stayed very even the rest of the way. My old houseguest, Kevin Clements, was third after the fly and definitely had a chance to get himself on the team with a great swim. I hit the final wall in 1:56.71, well off the world record, but very respectable with the lactate in my legs from the last race. I looked up to see the results. Ryan Lochte was second, 2.7 seconds behind me. Kevin swam well, but finished fifth.

I didn't have much chance to talk to Kevin, because I had to go back to the warm-down pool to loosen my legs a bit. I wanted to swim a competitive time in the butterfly semis, as good preparation for the final the next night. My time in the prelims had been pretty far behind Ian's, and Bob wanted me to close the gap. He gave me the in-your-face talk and told me this was not the time to hesitate or worry about fatigue. I didn't.

I went over a second faster in the semis and, at 51.89, was the second qualifier after Ian's 51.25. My most difficult day was done. If I wanted to stay with the 200 back in Athens, this was what it was going to feel like. Essentially, we felt there were three options: swim the 200 free, which would give me a chance to race against Ian but would include a deeper field. The gap between my best time and Ian Thorpe's was still three seconds, so the odds were greater that I would miss the medal stand entirely than they were that I would actually catch Ian. I could also swim just the 200 back, which would be a pretty safe race in which to get a medal. There was still a gap between Aaron at the top and me, at number two, but if I swam my race, I was also pretty far ahead of numbers three and four, so a medal looked pretty secure. The problem with swimming the 200 back was that I would have to swim three tough races in under an hour again. Even though I had done that many times in my career, these were the Olympics and much more was at stake. If I tired myself out too much by swimming the backstroke, I might still feel some of the fatigue in the 100 fly finals the next day and lose out on a chance to give it my best against Ian Crocker in a race I had a chance to win. The third option, of course, was to swim both races and simply drive my body into the ground. We still had time to decide.

After the races were finished, I felt I had just about emptied my tank. I knew this was going to be the toughest day of the trials by far and I wanted to leave the pool that day feeling that I had left all my best efforts in the pool and not held anything back, regardless of the results. Eddie Reese came up to me to tell me he had been sitting with another coach who offered to do a backflip off the stands if I could break 1:58 in the IM. Eddie assured me he was going to take him up on his offer. "Michael, that's the best night of swimming I've ever seen," he said.

What's the line David Letterman uses about different degrees of fatigue?: "I'm tired, but it's a good kind of tired." This was a really great kind of tired.

I didn't have more than a day to enjoy it. I had my last race ahead of me, the 100-meter butterfly. Ian had been swimming so well. He even qualified in the 100 free, which wasn't supposed to be his best stroke. I knew he was a great starter and would be ahead at the turn, but I had to make sure his lead wasn't too big, so I could stay with him and run him down in the last 50. Instead, Ian's start was phenomenal. I went out in 24.37, which was the second fastest time in the field, but he went out in 23.62 and virtually had the race won as he hit the first wall. I knew Ian had me with 20 meters to go, even though I actually started to close on him. My back half was actually .36 seconds faster than Ian's, but he cruised and lowered his world record to 50.76. I was second in 51.15.

After the race I went to a press conference, and some of the questions were about falling short and failing. I felt I had succeeded, and I had gotten stronger as the Trials progressed. I guess it was just a matter of people's expectations. I had just become the first person ever to qualify for a U.S. Olympic team in any sport in six individual events, yet I had been beaten twice and I had recorded a personal-best time in only one race, the 400 IM. Bob and I had set the bar very high. Now the question was how high did we want to set it for the Olympics? We had all of 24 hours to decide for sure, since USA Swimming needed to finalize its roster. We knew it was an either/or between the 200 free and 200 back. Even though the backstroke was a pretty safe medal, I told Bob for the last time that I really wanted a chance to race against Ian. Done—in with the freestyle; out with the backstroke.

The next day we saw Murray in the lobby of the hotel. He knew we had chosen to stick with the freestyle, but he thought I had a better chance for success in the backstroke.

"Michael, I want you to think about this before you do it."

"I have thought about it a lot. I've been thinking about it for a year."

22

TIME TO THINK

Bob and I still had some kinks to iron out before Athens. My starts and turns always need work, and we really emphasized those areas during the day I announced my schedule, while we were still in Long Beach.

The day after I was finished swimming at the trials, Bob enlisted Pete Malone, the coach of the Kansas City Blazers swim team, to help me with the starts. Pete gave us a few ideas, and we incorporated some aspects but left others alone. With my long body, it's hard for me to get rigid when I go into the water. Ideally I want to be locked out and straight from top to bottom, almost like a broom handle. Instead I often go in with something bent and it's usually my waist. Bob also wants me to have my head pressed against my arms so my head is not visible from the side. If you watch me dive in, my head is often drooping and you can see a space. That space creates drag and slows me down. We started working incorporating more starts into practices.

Bob and I also try to spend at least 15 minutes a session working on turns. Again, I'm tall and lean, as most swimmers are, but my

arms are also really long. I rotate too slowly into the turns, so I'm
not in a tight enough ball going into the wall, I don't change direction quickly enough and I lose momentum coming into the turns.
Bob always made sure I didn't shortchange the time we spent on
the transitions by reminding me that the Texas boys, Ian and Aaron,
usually gained ground on me at the turns.

As much work as we were putting in, I still had some time to
do some cool things before I left for Athens. A day after we
announced my schedule, I went to Hollywood to attend the ESPY
Awards, and we were almost late getting to the Kodak Theater. My
Mom noticed that my suit jacket was wrinkled, so we were franti-
cally driving around trying to find a dry cleaner who could steam
the wrinkles out of my suit jacket. My mom held the suit in the car
and we finally made it to the theater with 15 minutes to spare.

I was nominated for two awards, including best record-breaking performance, for what I did in Barcelona. It was neat that one
of my fellow nominees was Jamal Lewis, the Ravens' running back
who rushed for an NFL-record 295 yards against the Browns in
September. The winner, however, was Eric Gagne, the Dodgers'
relief pitcher who set a record of 55 consecutive saves in one season without a single blown save. I couldn't complain. I was honored just to be there. My mom sat downstairs with me and I
remember talking to NBA rookie star LeBron James and a few of
the Detroit Pistons. I sat near Priest Holmes, the Chiefs' running
back. I couldn't believe the company I was in, and just the fact that
I was there reminded me that I had already accomplished some
pretty special things.

The next day, I went to Burbank to appear on *The Tonight Show
with Jay Leno*. I was more excited than nervous. How many people
get to see *The Tonight Show*, much less be in the chair next to Jay?
And for a swimmer to have this honor? Wow, what a great chance
to talk about the sport.

Before the show, I was in the waiting area known as the Green Room with Bob, Peter, and Marissa Gagnon from Octagon. Jay walked in to shake my hand and give us a briefing of what I could expect. He was very personable and he told us about his old car collection that he keeps inside an airplane hanger. He drives himself to work each day, and we saw his old silver Cadillac that was sitting outside in the studio lot.

I called Corey and Matt from the Green Room and they were getting pretty excited to see the show. Of course they tape it in the late afternoon on the West Coast, so it was still a few hours from being on the air in Baltimore. They told me they were going over to our friend Tyler's house to play cards and wait for the show to come on. I wanted to make sure all my friends were able to watch.

I was on with actor Mark Wahlberg and singer Sarah McLachlan. I walked out and handed Jay an FS2 fullbody Speedo suit. "I wear this on TV," I told him. "You should be able to, too. This could fit you." It was a great way to break the ice and a good way to please a sponsor. I also made sure I sat with my arm draped over the chair next to mine, so people could see my Omega watch. Check number two for the sponsors. I remember I was surprised at how cold the studio was, but they need to keep it that way because of the camera equipment. I joked with Jay during the commercial break that all the 18- and 19-year-old girls were sitting in the front row. "It's like that every day," he told me. "The camera doesn't mind looking at that for an hour."

When we came back, Jay asked about how swimmers shave. Are you like monkeys? Do you shave each other? How does that work exactly? Now before anyone makes jokes about this, let me tell you they've already been made. You *cannot* come up with an original line. Basically, you shave yourself everywhere you can reach, but you can't reach your back. Jamie and I are usually each other's designated shavers. Shaving a guy's back is a little like taking cough syrup, but it has to be done.

"Mike, let's get this over with."

"Okay, go."

Two minutes later, it's finished.

I was on the set for about five minutes, but it felt like two seconds. I couldn't wait to go back.

Before we headed to Athens, we had two training camps for our team. One was in Palo Alto, at Stanford University and the next was in Mallorca, Spain. Soon after we arrived in Palo Alto, I had a chance to meet a legend. It isn't just anybody who can walk into a room and have everyone stop what they're doing, but that's what we did when we met Muhammad Ali. Everybody was in awe. He didn't tell us much. He is very soft-spoken these days because of his medical condition, but you could see a glimmer in his eye as he looked at an Olympian who was chasing a dream he once chased as an Olympian in 1960. Before people knew him as The Greatest, they got to know him as an Olympic champion, which is also pretty great.

Afterwards, I actually had a very vivid dream in which I met Ali again when I was with Matt. In the dream, Ali and I started smiling and Matt coaxed me into shadow boxing with him. Then Ali's punches started getting close and I had to walk away. The only thing I learned from that dream is that I'm glad I took up swimming.

I shared a room at Stanford with Peter Vanderkaay, a freestyler who swam for Jon Urbanchek at Michigan. Lenny came into the room a lot to play Madden Football and the games got pretty intense. Lenny won the first one, 86-68, and I, of course, suggested we play two out of three. It went down to the final game, with Lenny trailing by two touchdowns in the closing minutes. He scored twice and kicked an extra point to win the game in the last seconds. I was not happy. "Krazy, we need to play again," I said. Over the next two months, I was with Lenny at training camps, the Olympics and our post-Olympic tour. We played Madden Football a lot and I didn't let him off the hook very easily. If computer games could speak, the trash talking would be pretty intense.

There were also some important discussions going on about the selection of the relay teams. Even at the Trials, people were asking which swimmers Eddie Reese would place on the 4x100 freestyle team. The coaches can select the relay swimmers at their discretion, and the idea is simply to put the fastest four guys on the blocks who can give us a chance to be successful. That never stops the politics. I hadn't swum the race at the Trials, because we didn't want to add three more races to an already crowded program, and Bob felt that I had already made a clear case to be on the relay. Based on performances at the Trials, Jason Lezak was clearly the top-seeded swimmer for the squad. Bob felt that because I had won the Nationals in the spring and had then beaten Lezak head to head the last time I swam against him, I was at least among the top four and should be on the relay with no trouble. Some other swimmers felt that wasn't fair. Gary Hall Jr. was the most vocal. Gary is an amazing swimmer. He had won eight medals over the previous two Olympics, and he was one of the most recognizable names in the sport. He had been saying for a while that he felt I didn't deserve to be on the relay because I didn't swim the open hundred at the Trials. The order of finish there had been Lezak, Crocker, Hall, with Neil Walker fourth and two swimmer in places five and six, Nate Dusing and Gabe Woodward, who could swim in the preliminaries. Gary and I talked about the situation in Palo Alto. We agreed that we were all in this together. He said, "Gabe wants to swim fast." I told him, "Everybody wants to swim fast." After that, we both went our own ways, agreeing to disagree.

I had one last talk with Mom before the trip overseas. She stopped by not to talk about swimming, but to tell me how proud she was that I conducted myself so well over the previous year. She got pretty emotional, which is what proud moms do.

On August 1, we left Palo Alto and headed for Athens. I slept through most of the flight because—remember Bob's thorough-bred analogy—I generally travel well. It was a charter flight, so we relaxed, stretched out, and sat where we wanted. We were due to check into the athletes' village and undergo processing with the USOC at the American College of Greece, a place that was heavily fortified because of the anti-American sentiment that had been building up in the world. It was still two weeks before the start of the Games, and the village was still pretty empty at that point. After two days in Athens, we detoured to Mallorca for our week-long camp at Decallia Air Force Base, a short walk from our dorms. I acclimated quickly. Bob was happy to see that I was one of the few swimmers who jumped right into double sessions on the first day. I swam a 52.6 hundred in practice, which is as fast as I've ever gone in training.

We stayed in single rooms, and every day I'd open my blinds and look out onto the Mediterranean and watch the sun rise and set. I was more reflective than usual, and I spent some time think-ing about what it took to get me there. I wanted to break up my serious mood, so I called Matt and Corey and that really did the trick. I was pumped up to talk to them. It made me feel like I was at home. Matt told me they'd had a week of straight parties because their parents were out of town. The blow by blow was intense:

"Mike, I played poker last night and lost all my money."

"Mike, we were at Julie's house and his girl fell through an opening in the railing between houses and landed on a heating vent."

"And Bennett passed out and we took out sharpies and drew all over his face and legs."

"Then Bennett got mad and started chasing us. Corey was hid-ing behind a door and he threw a handful of flour in Bennett's face."

It was great to hear friendly voices from home, no matter what they were talking about. As I was talking to them, some of the girls on the team were tossing water balloons across the balconies. I started telling Corey how I had just nailed one of them when suddenly I felt this splash of water from an exploding balloon on my neck. Spoke too soon.

Bob and I broke the monotony of the trip by going down the hill to get some pizza. We had security with us everywhere we went. I remember one bilingual bodyguard who always walked ahead of us and entered every facility before we did. Later on, Bob did some sightseeing on his own and made sure to visit a cathedral he had read about. I started reading *Bringing Down the House*, a book about MIT students who go to Las Vegas and beat the odds by outsmarting the people running the casinos. I could either see Corey as a character in that book or on ESPN, winning The World Series of Poker.

Aside from training and sleeping, I usually found a diversion with video games on trips like these. But in Mallorca, I really had a lot of time to just sit and think. I started reviewing things that happened the summer before, about movies and phone calls and things I had tucked away in my mind for a year. I had started dating a girl named Amanda in January of 2003, our senior year, and we spent about six months together. We met through friends and fell for each other pretty fast. I loved hanging out with her, but most of all, I felt I could talk to her about anything. When my grandmother contracted pancreatic cancer, it hit me how much I would miss my grandmother if she wasn't there. It made me pretty emotional to think of how much she meant to me, and I just didn't feel comfortable sharing that with other people—or showing that to other people. But I could do it easily with Amanda. She always seemed to know when to give me space, to hang close and listen, to comfort me. Not everybody would have the patience to hear me out, but she always did.

The next three or four months were hard on her, because I traveled so much and she was at home. We basically broke up right

before Worlds. I had pretty much figured that I was going to concentrate on swimming over the next year. I was planning to take a
year off from school before heading to Loyola, and I wasn't thinking too much about dating.

I saw Amanda again at an appearance in May when Hecht's, a
local department store, was giving me a shopping spree in their
branch in Towson. It was the first time I had seen her in months.
We agreed to keep in touch and soon the text messages began flying. It was as if we hadn't stopped seeing each other at all. I wanted things to be as they were.

I started thinking about Amanda and how much I missed her.
I didn't think I could just call her and tell her that right away. I had
to think about it. I called Matt again, this time for consultation. It
was weird. We know each other so well that within seconds, he
wasn't asking how I was or what I did that day; he was asking,
"What's on your mind?" I tried to tell him "Nothing," but I guess
he sort of waited until I told him what I was thinking. As soon as I
said the name Amanda, he knew exactly where I was going.

"You know, I could see you guys being friends for a long time
and then ending up together," he said.

"Dude, I was sort of . . ."

". . . thinking the same thing?"

This wasn't your typical teenage guy talk. It's true that good
friends listen to everything you say, but best friends also hear what
you don't say. I didn't really want to be thinking too much about
anything that could distract me from swimming, but I missed
Amanda. Time for another text message. Or five.

I was still going to be well represented in Athens. My mom
was going with both of my sisters and my dad was going, too. I was
really pumped to have Whitney there, because she hadn't been to
too many meets. She had been planning to travel to Barcelona, but
she had just started a new job and it would have been hard for her

to request time off. I was psyched to have everyone there. They had always been there to help create any success I might have in my future. Now, in Athens, they'd get a chance to share in it, too.

23

BAD THIRD,
GOOD THIRD

If things seemed surprisingly quiet during the previous trip to Athens a week earlier, it didn't take long after I returned for me to realize that the Greeks were in full Games mode. I was talking to my Mom on the phone when I looked out of my window and saw a snarling policeman. "Mom, this guy in front of me has an Uzi." I guess the Games were on.

Things were also noticeably livelier when we got back to the village. The first few days at the dining hall, I ate at McDonald's. One afternoon, the people working in there asked me for pins, which are the golden currency at an Olympics. Everyone from athletes to coaches to volunteers to fans trades them. Everyone designs their own, from National Olympic Committees to Olympic teams to sponsors and media outlets. We're talking about thousands of different pins each year, so it is impossible to collect them all. Each of us on the team received a bag of about 50 pins available for trading. As soon as I got to the village, I became a two-time Olympian making a rookie mistake. I gave my bag to one of the ladies at the register. She gave me one pin and then started passing my bag back to other people working in the McDonald's. I ordered a yogurt parfait and waited for my bag to come back to me. By the time it did, there were two pins left in the bag. I had gotten the worst of the trade. From that point on, every time I walked into or even passed, a shop in the village (post office, barber shop, music store, photo shop), people always asked me for pins and didn't believe me when I told them I was already out.

The dining hall was a great equalizer for coach and swimmer. Whenever I passed Bob as he was eating, I'd tap him on one shoulder and walk off in the opposite direction. He hates that. Sometimes I'll make a sudden motion in front of him to see if he'll flinch. Bob is so wound up, he's easy prey. Every time I tap him on the shoulder, he looks in the wrong direction; every time I flinch, he flinches. If he drives me nuts for three hours in the pool, I can exact a measure of revenge in about five seconds at lunchtime.

I was rooming with Lenny on this trip and I couldn't have asked for a better roommate. In fact I did ask for him. Lenny was a team captain and a veteran who won three gold medals in Sydney. More than that, he's a very positive person and a great teammate who is all ears whenever someone needs anything. He hurt his shoulder after the last Olympics and I think some people doubted whether he'd be able to return to form. When he made the team in Long Beach, you could see the cheers shoot up not only from the stands, but especially from the athletes' section. I wanted someone around who had a very positive energy about him. Apart from our smackdown games of Madden Football, Lenny was the perfect choice.

When we needed to relax away from the pool, he and I watched DVDs. I watched the four Rocky films and recommended *Miracle*. I bought some U.S. newspapers to catch up on the exhibition football scores, but I skipped over any stories about me. I'm tired of reading about that guy.

We had a blast with rookie initiation skits. All the first-time Olympians performed imitations of someone, and some of the skits were a riot. Larsen Jensen played Richard Quick, the Stanford coach who always wore his hat a certain way. Carly Piper was Amy Van Dyken, a U.S. swimmer who was on three Olympic teams and made a few enemies by spitting in the lanes of other swimmers. Carly spent the entire skit spitting in different directions. Ryan Lochte played himself, a surfer dude, during a game of *Jeopardy*, answering some questions right and others wrong, but always answering very slowly. Scott Usher did a takeoff on my VISA commercial, when I swam across the ocean and said, "One" as if I had just completed the first round-the-world lap. The other swimmers asked Scott questions and he always had the same response:

"Michael, how many gold medals do you want to win?"

"One."

"What number is Team USA?"

"One."

Katie Hoff, who had recently turned 15, pretended to be a young Amanda Beard. At the 1996 Olympics, when she was just 14, Amanda carried a teddy bear onto the victory podium when she received her medals. Katie carried a mascot with her during the skit.

Katie reminded me a bit of myself four years earlier. She swam at one of NBAC's satellite pools, so we both represented the same club at national meets. She was also making her Olympic debut at 15, just as I had and she was a great IM swimmer whose best stroke was the butterfly. We were also similar in that we were easy targets for some razzing by older swimmers. I had often been sarcastic with Katie, teasing her about one thing or another, as many veterans did, but in Athens, I saw her at lunch and I think she was surprised when I said to her, "If you ever need anything on this trip, please ask me."

Katie wanted to stay around after the swimming to see the rest
of the Olympics. She could have had fun at the events, but I remember Bob's warning about the second week at an Olympic village,
where people who live like monks for most of the year turn into
monkeys. I told her that there would be noise, music, alcohol, and
a lot of what we could call room swapping. That isn't easy for athletes who still have to compete and are trying to get to bed by nine
or ten. And it really isn't a great environment for a 15-year-old. "I
don't want to hold you back from closing ceremonies," I said, "but
going back and getting in the water again after Sydney was the best
thing I ever did." The next day, Katie told her coach, Paul Yetter,
that she wanted to go home after she was done swimming.

My family joined me shortly before the Games opened. They
didn't get stuck at the airport for two days, but Whitney did get
married (sort of) while she, Hilary and Mom were on a cruise
before the Games began. One of the men performing Greek dances
came up to her and began doing a wedding dance. He then filled a
glass with ouzo and had her sip it, before tilting her arm back so
she chugged the drink. Then he placed a towel down on the floor,
placed her glass on top of it and spun her around on top of the glass
while she squatted down. He asked if she was married, she told
him she wasn't, so he took a string from his shoe and tied it around
her finger. Welcome to the family, sir. And what's your name?

Then on the connecting flight from Frankfurt, a German journalist, sitting next to my mom, asked her if she had any family at the
Games. "Yes," she told him cautiously.

"What sport?

"Aquatics."

"Which sport in aquatics?"

"Swimming."

"You wouldn't be Michael Phelps' mother, would you?

"Yes, I am."

After that, the man started yelling to someone in the back of the plane, "Hey, this is Michael Phelps' mother."

She grabbed his arm and tried to get him to pipe down, but she was kind of trapped at that point. It isn't the sort of place where you can step outside.

We didn't have much room, ourselves, once we arrived at the pool. We had a practice that was open to reporters, and the place was loaded with cameras. Tommy Roy, an NBC producer, pulled Bob aside and told him, "This reminds me of when Tiger Woods would do practice rounds before majors. They're following Michael's every move." Later, Bob conducted some mock interviews with me, going over talking points and making me say the answers back to him. "There is a reason," he told me, "why people can think twice as fast as they can speak." Back home, the *Baltimore Sun* began running a Phelps Fever meter with an arrow that ran from normal to delirious. And to think this was still pretty close to normal.

***

I was still on a high from my first gold medal, still leaning towards delirious on the Michael Scale when we got ready for the 4x100 free relay on the second day of competition. We had already had two meetings about the race. Gary's dad, a three-time Olympian like Gary Jr., was reported as saying that he knew who would swim on the relay a week before the race. Eddie called us together four days before to tell us that the people who would swim it would be the ones who could swim the fastest and that he hadn't determined yet who that was.

Jason was certainly going to be one of the swimmers. Ian, second at Trials, was an obvious choice for another spot. I was there based on performances during the year. But the guy who rocked in the morning was Neil Walker. He swam a 48.16, the fastest of any swimmer from any country during the prelims and faster than Gary's 48.73 on the morning anchor. Eddie was in a tough spot. He was open for criticism no matter what he did. He decided to go with Ian, me, Neil and Jason in that order. Gary was not happy to be the odd man out, but we four swimmers thought we had a chance to win. It wouldn't be easy, considering the competition. The Russians were the defending world champions and they had Alex Popov, a great veteran, anchoring their team. The Australians were the defending Olympic champions and they had Ian Thorpe anchoring their team. The Dutch had Pieter van den Hoogenband, the fastest man in the field, anchoring theirs. The South Africans had two of the fastest swimmers in race in Roland Schoeman and Ryk Neethling and were due for a great race.

We had no idea Ian Crocker was sick, that he had been fighting post-nasal drip for the past 24 hours. His first 25 looked okay, but then as he headed for the wall at the 50, it was clear he wasn't himself. In the lane next to us, Schoeman of South Africa was way ahead of the field coming off the first turn. The problem when you get off the wall behind the other swimmer, is that you end up swimming into the waves they leave behind that bounce off the wall. When Ian fell behind, he not only gave himself some ground to make up, but he also made it harder for himself to get a good push off the wall because he'd have more turbulence splashing back at him as he made the turn. As Ian headed toward me, I was still hoping we would have a chance to get a medal. We were last of the eight teams after 100 meters and our chances to win gold were pretty much gone. I swam into the waves and thought about staying positive. My first 50 was almost a second slower than I had hoped, but I rallied in the last 50. All in all, my relay leg (48.74 seconds) wasn't great, but it moved us up to sixth. Neil picked off three more teams and Jason kept us in third, behind South Africa and the Netherlands.

We took the relay loss pretty hard, staring at the water with stunned looks on our faces. Ian was talking to himself: "I'm sorry. It's my fault. It's my fault." Ian is very dedicated, but he also gets down on himself very easily. That's part of being driven to be your best, but sometimes, he doesn't give himself enough credit. "It's my fault, guys." I put my arm around him and tried to cheer him up. "Dude, this is one race," I told him. "We still have a lot of swimming to go. Remember what happened in Sydney when the Aussies beat us in the relay. Our team came back so strong. We'll bounce back." Each of us talked to Ian at some point. We're a team and we didn't want one race to affect other races. Ian is very humble and quiet. It's a testament to how hard he worked that when he was small, he couldn't get out of the guppy group with his youth club in Maine in the same way that I couldn't swim unless I was on my back. He has four guitars and knows every song Bob Dylan ever wrote. He thinks a lot, and I was hoping he wouldn't think too long about this race.

I hated standing on that third-place podium. Hated it, hated it. It wasn't the fact that we finished third that bothered us, but the fact that we could have done much better.

Third-place finishes aren't all bad. The next evening we had the finals of the 200 free, the race some people said I shouldn't try to swim. Why take on something like this with an easier option available? See, if I could be really good at other sports, I'd want to pitch to Barry Bonds, guard Michael Jordan, sidestep Ray Lewis, or stop Wayne Gretzky when they were at their best. I might not succeed, but I wouldn't want to spend my career training every day without measuring myself against the best. That's why I wanted to swim this race. I wanted to leave that pool knowing I had swum my best race against my own expectations and against someone I respect as much as Ian Thorpe. The point of competition isn't always to take the easiest way out, but to meet the biggest challenge. I love it when people tell me I can't do something, because it fires me up to prove them wrong. I wanted to race Ian in a freestyle event before either of us retired.

I hit the first turn in third place from Lane 3 with Pieter in front from Lane 4, as expected, and Ian second, in Lane 5. I figured Ian would have a better kick than Pieter, who is the fastest at 100 meters. The order was the same after 100 and 150. By then I was a second off the pace, but I could feel myself closing. As Ian passed Pieter in the last 50 meters, Klete Keller started moving on me from Lane 6. I finished the race with the fastest last hundred of the medalists, but as looked up at the board, I knew that I hadn't been able to catch Ian, in first, or Pieter, in second. My time, 1:45.32, was an American record, faster than I had ever swum it by half a second. Unlike the race in Long Beach, where I felt I could have swum faster, I left it all in the pool against a great field. I went over to Ian right away to congratulate him. He didn't have much to say, but Bob did once I got out of the pool. "You know that was a great swim," he said, half asking me and half telling me. I was more than happy to stand on the same podium that bothered me so much the night before. This challenge was personal, and I met it no matter what color my medal was. Honestly I'll remember that race with as much pride as any individual race I've ever swum.

It was hard to get back into the water an hour later to swim the semis of the 200 fly. Stephen Parry of Great Britain touched me out at the wall and was pumping his fists as he left the pool. Okay, I thought, those were the semis. See you tomorrow night.

Try telling reporters that I felt good about my performances.

"Michael how do you feel now that you can't win seven gold medals?"

"I feel great about my last race."

"Michael, why aren't you swimming that well at the Olympics?"

"I think I am swimming well at the Olympics."

"Why didn't you go fast tonight?"

"I was happy to set a PR by half a second and break the American record."

It's hard to convince people of something if they don't want to be convinced. Up in the stands, a reporter approached my mom and told her: "The world has left your son tonight." My mom was taken aback. "Excuse me?" she said. "Well, now that he won't be able to match Spitz's record, there won't be as many people around him. I mean, I'll still be there, but he won't have as many reporters to deal with. The hype is over." Of course my mom had the last word. "Well, the swimming isn't over," she said. "Michael isn't even halfway through his platform. He has a lot to show the world."

24

A TEAM EFFORT

The day after the 200 free was my only time during the Games when I had to swim two finals on the same evening: the 200 fly and the 4x200 free relay. I went back to the village that night and I was looking straight past the fly to the race our team hadn't won in eight years. I started talking to Lenny about the splits we needed, and he couldn't have been more positive. "Mike, I think we can beat these guys," he said. It was the encouraging voice of a veteran, and I was really starting to believe it.

I didn't swim in the morning prelims, so I slept in until nine. I went over to the pool, swam an easy thousand, got a massage and kept thinking about the relay.

Bob wanted to see me break the 200 fly world record, but I went out too fast. He didn't want me holding back, and he felt the only way to get beat was to let guys get ahead of me, but I was really too aggressive in the first 50. When I had broken the world record in Barcelona, I had gone out in 25.95 seconds; this time I was out in 25.55. I pushed the lead to seven-tenths of a second over Parry, with Japan's Takashi Yamamoto just behind him. By the time

I hit the third wall, both Parry and Yamamoto were starting to gain on me, and I had another bad turn at that wall. The outcome was still in doubt at 170 meters, although I never lost the lead. Over the last half lap, I finally pulled away to finish in 1:54.04, .11 seconds off my world record, but half a second ahead of Yamamoto in second.

Afterwards, I saw Tom Malchow waiting for me at the end of the pool in Lane 8. He had qualified eighth and placed eighth. Typical of Tom, win or lose, he was all class at the finish. The scene was similar to the one we had four years earlier when he told me my time would come. This time, he congratulated me and told me to go spank the Aussies in the relay. Outside the stands, my mom went over to Mr. and Mrs. Malchow to ask them to thank Tom for being a good role model for me.

Bob and I didn't say much as I rushed through the mixed zone to the warm-down area to get ready for the relay. I swam down for almost 20 minutes, but I couldn't do much more since we only had 40 minutes between races. Our order for the relay was me, Ryan Lochte, Peter Vanderkaay and Klete Keller as the anchor. I liked the order, because I like swimming from a flat start, which only the leadoff swimmer actually does. We expected the race to come down to a clash between the U.S. and the Aussies, who put together a formidable team of Grant Hackett, Michael Klim, Nick Sprenger and Ian Thorpe.

Before the race, Eddie showed us a tape of the 800 relay final at the 1984 Olympics in Los Angeles. The U.S. had led the dramatic race up until the last leg. In the last 200 meters, Germany's Michael Gross, the Olympic champ in the open 200 free, spent all his energy to catch American Bruce Hayes in the first 50 meters. At that point, everyone had assumed the race was over. Instead, Hayes stayed with Gross until the last few strokes and passed him back just at the end of the race to give the U.S. team the victory by .04 seconds, about the length of a toe. All of us knew about that race;

none of us knew how we would see a modern-day version of it happen before our eyes.

The Australians had built a seven-year winning streak in this race. Since their last defeat in 1997, they had won three straight world titles, had beaten us in the Sydney Olympics by over five seconds and had broken the world record four times.

We all started walking from the ready room to the deck as a team. As the other guys were set to walk out, I said, "Wait. Come back." We huddled. Just about everyone on our team had seen *Miracle*, some in theaters after Nationals, others on their DVD players. "I don't know if you remember the scene in *Miracle* before the Soviet game where Brooks tells the team, 'This is your time.'" I said. "Well, this is our time. I don't care what happened in the past. This is us. This is now."

To me, this really is what swimming is about. The team is always better than the sum of individuals. People remember the relays more because they're just more fun. We never had four boys from the same age bracket to make a great relay at North Baltimore, so I missed this for most of my career.

In Athens, I stood on the blocks and I had nervous energy coming out of my ears. I jumped in to swim against Grant, just as I had done a hundred times during that one trip to the Gold Coast. We practically hit the first wall together; he was ahead by a hundredth of a second. At 100 meters, I moved ahead slightly by half a tenth, and then by three-tenths at 150. My last 50 felt amazing. Just as I had in the 200 the night before, I turned it on at the end, and I could feel myself pull away from Grant. I swam the last lap in 26.78 and hit the wall in 1:46.49, giving us a 1.01-second lead on the field. As Ryan took over and maintained the lead over Klim, Massi Rosolino briefly moved the Italians into second place. The Aussies passed them back with Sprenger in the third leg, but Peter brought us through 600 in 5:21.80, and gave Klete a solid lead of 1.48 seconds ahead of Ian going into the last leg.

Standing on the side and watching your teammates swim is both elation and torture. You jump, you scream, you contort yourself into a pretzel, but you really can't do anything to make your guys go faster and hold theirs back. Almost as soon as Ian Thorpe jumped in, I wanted to throw a rope around him. Klete had him by over a bodylength, and we were hoping he could keep Ian at bay for as long as possible. Instead, Ian made up the whole deficit in the first 50 meters and pulled even with Klete before the first turn. On the pooldeck, Peter said something I can't repeat, most of the stadium was thinking: *it's over. It won't be long now before Ian shoots by him and the U.S. start fighting for second in another 800 free relay.* "He's out too fast," I told Peter. "He can't hold it." By 80 meters, Ian remained in a virtual dead heat with Klete, who was straining to hold him off. At the second wall, Ian still looked as though he could slingshot past Klete at any moment. But as the race kept progressing, Klete kept fighting off Ian's surges. He flipped first at the third wall, and as Klete headed for home, Ryan, Peter and I were just going nuts on the opposite end of the deck. I glanced at our team in the athlete viewing area and saw Erik on his feet screaming. Nearby, Jon Urbanchek was standing next to Bob and was the first one who really figured it out: "If he didn't catch him there," Jon said, "he's not catching him."

With two strokes left, Thorpe made a desperate surge. He and Klete lunged for the line and I was clenching my fists waiting for the finish. Even peering right over the wall, with the hands passing right in front of me, I had to look at the scoreboard. Show me a 1 for us. C'mon, show me a 1. We all saw it at the same time and practically left our feet in synch. U.S. 7:07.33; Australia 7:07.46. We did it. The streak was over.

I threw both of my hands into the air and yelled all the way back to Baltimore. I had been pretty outwardly restrained after the individual races, but this one I could share. Klete popped out of the water and joined the three of us for a group hug. It's the same Klete who rarely got excited about anything. "Yeah, we did it!" he said. "Yeah, we kicked their butts!" In the four years I've known him, I've never seen Klete show that much emotion. I've never seen that side of him. On our way back through the mixed zone, Klim told a reporter, "We owned that race. They stole our race."

We went to get our medals a half hour later, and I still had goose bumps over my whole body. I didn't have any hair to lose, because I had shaved down, but whatever was there was standing straight up.

Klete and Peter were done, so they went to do a *SportsCenter* interview. Ryan and I swam down, went to drug testing and went back to the village to get ready for the heats and semis of the 200 IM the next day. Typically, each night I would give my medals to Bob so he could hold on to them while I headed into drug testing. He would sometimes forget about this medal in his pocket and remember it only when he set off the metal detector (a.k.a. medal detector). This night as we walked in, I remembered to ask, "Bob, do you have something of mine?" It was ironic that the possession of a medal, the one thing that most reveals you as an Olympian, would be the thing that made security stop you and keep you from entering the village.

Back in the room, I told Lenny it was the most exciting moment of my career. I'm so glad I didn't have to swim any finals the next day, because I was too wound up. I stayed awake until 2:30 trying to sleep, getting up to play a video game, trying to sleep, firing off a dozen fresh text messages and trying to sleep. On nights when I can't get to bed, I'm usually pretty good at previewing the next day's race like a short film in my head. Instead, this film was a multi-multi-multi-feature rerun of the most incredible race of my life, the one I had just swum.

I had trouble coming down from the high the next day. My two qualifying IM swims were pretty ordinary and my breaststroke legs were horrible. Ideally I want to kick and pull with my arms

one after the other so I'm always moving through the water steadi-
ly. Instead I was doing both at the same time. Bob let me know
about it after the semis. He came over with a piece of paper and
showed me my splits with the breaststroke numbers underlined
and circled.

"Michael, your breaststroke was not good."

"I know."

"You need to work on the breaststroke."

"I know, Bob. Don't get on me now. I realize that."

Bob was worried about how I'd finish up the week. He was
clearly overreacting to my swim, but he also sensed me getting into
cruise mode and wanted to put a stop to that. I wasn't trying to
cruise. I think we both looked at my program ahead of time and figured out what I could handle physically, but we underestimated
the toll that stress from one race could have on subsequent races.
Besides, it's worse when Bob says nothing, because I know he's letting the calm build up to the storm, when he can say the things he's
been saving up and really make an impact.

"Listen, Michael," he said, "you have me for 48 more hours and
then you have freedom, so you better just deal with it." Actually it
wasn't 48, but 72 hours, according to the schedule. I had the 200 IM
finals on Thursday, the 100 fly final on Friday and, I hoped, the
4x100 medley final on Saturday, if I could qualify for it by being the
fastest American in the 100 fly. Bob may be a brilliant coach, but if
he really meant 48 hours, his crystal ball is better than I thought.

Bob could count on the cold shoulder he got from me to be
temporary. For really frosty treatment, he could go back to his
room, which came to be known as The Igloo. Bob says he likes the
room really cold at night when he goes to sleep. That's a man who
is headed to Michigan. Coach Eddie, who was Bob's roommate on
the trip, is a Texas man who is used to warm temperatures and
prefers them that way when he's trying to sleep. Because the set-
tings in their room left few options between iceberg and frying

pan, Bob kept the thermometer down. Eddie barely slept at all. "I hope you're freezing your butt off, Mr. Bowman," he'd say.

The next morning Bob got on me for coasting through the hundred fly heats. He said he had the same feeling he had about where my mind was as he did before the fly in Barcelona, when Ian beat me. Bob was on a paranoid overdrive. He went back to the village and told Eddie: "I'm so uptight about what he'll do in the 200 IM tonight."

"Bob," Eddie told him, "you have to realize a lot of times these athletes are smarter than we are about how to swim these events. Relax." In truth, Bob is so well prepared because he always imagines worst-case scenarios and tries to head them off. He probably had himself convinced I could be beaten in the 200 IM so he wouldn't loaf through his coaching—in the way he didn't want me to loaf through my swimming.

For the IM finals, I wanted to do what I did at 2001 Worlds: go out fast and make them catch me in the back hundred. In fact, I saved my best swimming for the back half of the race. I led after every leg, and each time I hit the wall, there was a different swimmer in second place. I had a slim, one-tenth lead over Brazil's Thiago Pereira after the butterfly and a two-tenths lead over Hungary's Laszlo Cseh after the backstroke. Since you can get a good look at the field during the breaststroke, I noticed that the field was still a little close for comfort, so I cranked my arms pretty hard, had one of my best breaststroke legs and built the lead to eight-tenths over George Bovell of Trinidad. I pulled away in the freestyle, came home in 1:57.14 and, for the second straight time in an IM race, I got to finish one-two with a teammate. Ryan Lochte took the silver in 1:58.78.

I had a tight turnaround of 38 minutes until the 100 fly semifinal, but first we had the medal presentation for the IM. We got on the stand and I remember that Ryan was so excited about getting his medal, he left the wreath on his head as the anthem started to play. I gave a quick whistle out of the side of my mouth and he took it off. I have to admit while we had our hands over our hearts, I spent the next two minutes thinking about one thing: how fast can I go in the butterfly? Bob had been worried about the short time between races. I only had time for an eight-minute warm-down and we didn't even bother with a lactate test.

After the presentation, I walked right into the ready room just as the first heat was going off. Ian Crocker and I were both in the second heat. Again I had an Andrei Serdinov moment. This time, I watched him swim a 51.74 to break the Olympic record and I wasn't happy about it. No sense letting that record last any longer than the world record he held in Barcelona for five minutes, is there?

Ian always goes out fast, but I had no idea what he would be able to do. Since that first night when he was ill, he had slowly been feeling better and swimming faster all week. Ian took it out fastest, hitting the first wall in 24.36. I was fifth at the time, but came back with a really strong second 50 and won the heat in 51.61, two-tenths ahead of Ian.

I was pretty happy with both of my swims. After the race I went up to Bob and said, "That didn't feel too bad." Bob showed me the splits and told me, "Nice job. That's exactly what I wanted to see you do." He said later that he had a quiet confidence about the final that he hadn't had since before the final in Barcelona, but at the time, he wanted to make sure I didn't lose my edge. "I wonder what it will take to win the hundred tomorrow," he said.

25

DREAMS FULFILLED

I swam in a race on Friday morning, only as a precaution. I was the butterfly leg of our medley relay team that advanced safely into Saturday night's final. The medley relays are always swum at the end of the meet. The U.S. teams—and most other teams—select the swimmers they use in the final based on results from the earlier races in the competition. The top American in the 100-meter backstroke, for instance, was Aaron Peirsol, who won the gold medal, so that meant Aaron had earned the right to swim the backstroke leg for us in the final. Since Brendan Hansen was our fastest 100 breaststroker, he'd swim the breaststroke leg in the final. Jason Lezak was our fastest freestyler, so he'd be our anchor. Usually, the swimmers who recorded the second-fastest times for us in each stroke would be able to swim in the qualifying heats. Only those four swimmers who swam in the final would be able to stand on the awards podium afterward and receive their medals before hearing the winning team's national anthem. But the ones who swam in the prelims would still receive medals after the fact for their team's performance.

Since the relay heats took place before the butterfly final, neither Ian nor I knew who was going to be able to swim in Saturday's
final. The one who didn't swim in the prelims could conceivably
miss out on getting a relay medal if he didn't win the butterfly.

Eddie had a few ways to handle this. Either Ian or I could have
swum the freestyle or butterfly leg of the prelim relay. That way
both of us could have been guaranteed to receive whatever color
medal the U.S. team ultimately won. Eddie and Ian decided that
Ian would sit out the heats, because he was still somewhat fatigued
from his illness. Since he had beaten me at the Worlds and the trials, he would probably be a slight favorite in the Olympic final.
I swam the fly in the prelims and was fairly confident that whomev-
er we used in the final, we'd be heavy favorites to win the event.

I slept in a bit and skipped the daily team meeting before the
fly finals, with the coaches' permission. The meetings usually only
take about 15 minutes. The coaches usually go over the day's race
lineup and show some video highlights from the day before to get
us fired up. As I warmed up before the butterfly, Bob noticed my
body language and intensity level. "Michael's going to win
tonight," he thought.

I liked my chances, not so much because of Ian's illness, but
because I really felt prepared. Ever since Malchow kicked my butt
a few years ago, I drove myself through extra fly training. Despite
our meltdowns, I had complete trust in Bob's instructions. I put off
some social things. I didn't have a girlfriend leading up to the
Olympics. All of that gave me a confidence that, win or lose, I'd be
able to say I couldn't have worked any harder to get a better result.
I was pumped.

I dove in and tried to stay within striking range of Ian. At 50
meters, I was in fifth place and Ian's lead over me, .77 seconds,
looked like too much to make up. I was down by about three-quar-
ters of a bodylength. After I hit the wall, I started kicking as hard

as I could, and I remember not wanting to look to see where Ian was. I closed quickly, but still trailed both Ian and Serdinov going into the last few strokes. It was clear that the three of us would be the medalists, but we didn't know who would place where. Bob had stopped watching the pool after the first 50, because he figured I was too far back. As he watched the race unfold on the video scoreboard, he was surprised to see how much ground I was making up, so he decided to look at the pool for the last 15 meters. "Well, second place isn't too bad," he told himself.

I reached for the wall and I knew I'd hit it just about perfectly, in other words at the full extension of my stroke rather than in the middle of a stroke. As you get to the finish, it's sometimes difficult to time it so you touch the wall with your arms fully extended as opposed to touching while you're in the middle of reaching for the wall. If you do that, you can cheat yourself out of a few hundredths of seconds. Ian didn't time his reach quite as well.

I took my goggles off first, which I hadn't done in Barcelona when I celebrated prematurely. Instead of looking at the placement numbers next to our names, I looked at our times, one by one, as if I wanted to digest the news in pieces. First I saw 51.29 for Ian. Then I saw the 51.25 for me. Serdinov was a strong third in 51.36. I couldn't quite believe it.

As it started to hit me that I'd won the race, I reached from Lane 4 into Lane 3 to console Ian. I did a quick interview with NBC after I jumped out of the pool. Afterward, I went right to the NBC truck, to look at the video with Rowdy and NBC's play-by-play announcer, Dan Hicks. Even at the last minute, I thought Ian was going to outtouch me. "How did I do that?" I said. "There's no way."

I could see how disappointed Ian was after the race. It hit me that because he hadn't swum in the morning, he was going to leave Athens without a gold medal. This didn't seem right. As much as I used my losses to Ian to motivate me over the last year, I felt an odd kinship with the guy behind the poster on my wall. He pushed me. If he hadn't been that good, he couldn't have pushed me that hard. If I didn't respect him as much, I might not have trained that hard in the butterfly. It's one thing to train your hardest, be at your best and finish second; it's another to train your hardest and have injury or illness keep you from making your best attempt. I felt that way about Whitney more than anyone, but I also felt some of that about Ian.

I started swimming down after the 100 fly. Even though confidence is good, there is a fine line between having enough confidence to believe you're going to win and having so much that you take the possibility of losing for granted. I told Bob I knew what he was doing and he shot me a look. It was as if we had been through so many mind games together and I didn't need one to focus my mind for the next race. Bob shook his head. "You know, Mr. Jimmy would be so proud to see you right now," he said. "Can you imagine how happy he'd be if he could see this?" Okay, now that got me. I had no defenses for that remark. "He's with us right now," I said, "because he's looking down at us." Bob and I nodded at each other and I put my goggles on to swim to the other side of the practice pool. When I reached the other side, I had to stop to empty out my goggles.

But actually I was feeling sympathy for Ian. Why did he have to get sick now? Was this really his best? Will he take it tougher than most? Will he be too hard on himself for something he couldn't control? Will he blame himself for not swimming well in the free relay? Will he be okay with swimming so hard and coming so close to a gold medal?

"Hey, Bob . . ." Again I had a look on my face.

"What is it now?"

"Ian needs another chance."

"What do you mean?"

"He needs another chance to show the world what he can do."

Bob took some time to think about it and asked me to take a few minutes to do the same.

I waited for my lactate to clear, then dressed for drug testing and saw Ian. "I'm glad I'm done," he said. I don't think he meant it, though. I think he had been disappointed with a couple of races and he didn't want to be disappointed again. I went over to Bob and told him, "I'm gonna do it." He didn't do anything to try to influence me one way or the other, but he told me, "Okay, but you need to tell Eddie," I found Eddie and told him I wanted to give up my spot on the relay. He asked if I had told Ian and I said I hadn't had a chance. "Michael, are you sure this is what you want?" he said. "It has to come from you."

"It is."

This set off a chain reaction of consultations. Bob passed Mark Schubert, the head women's coach and asked for his opinion. "Michael should do what's in his heart," Mark said. Eddie went over to find Everett Uchiyama, our national team director so that he could catch Ian coming out of drug testing and tell him to get back in the pool for another warm-down swim. "But why?" Ian wanted to know. "I'm done."

He swam for a while before I came over to tell him I wanted him to take my spot for the relay. Ian was surprised and humbled. He went over to Eddie and told him he didn't feel like taking a spot he felt he hadn't earned. Eventually he agreed and was too speechless to tell me much more than thank you. He seemed a little confused at first, but I could tell he was excited to have another chance.

We decided to let Eddie make the announcement after a reporter asked the first relay question at the press conference. Word then filtered to people at NBC and one of them called my mom's cell before I had a chance to tell my family. Hilary was with Mom when she picked up Mom's phone.

"He did what?"

"Hilary, what's wrong?"

"He did not."

"Did not what? Hilary, what happened to Michael?"

I was sorry for giving everyone a heart attack. It took a while for them to think it through. My mom wasn't quite ready for the fact that I had just finished my last Olympic swim.

I didn't really get a chance to speak to my family until I got to the pool the next day to watch the relay. Mom, Hilary, Whitney and Peter had talked about how they felt and came to consensus about what to say to me. When I saw them in a hallway near the seating area, everyone else just swarmed us. Whitney wanted to say something to me so she told people: "I haven't seen my brother. Can you give us 15 minutes?" Of course, people let us talk, but they hovered to try to hear what we were saying. At that point, Peter moved in and started blocking the path in front of us, so we could have a little privacy. We talked about how much we cared for each other and how we all did this together. I was especially glad to see Whitney again, just as I had been in Indianapolis four years earlier.

I got back to the athlete seating area on the deck and was psyched to watch the awesome relay team we'd put together (Aaron, Brendan, Ian and Jason). This was really our race. Since 1976, the world record had been broken on ten occasions, each time by a team from the U.S. We had set the last world record for the race, at the Barcelona worlds, in 3:31.54, but we figured with the team we had, we'd break it again unless we somehow got disqualified for a bad exchange. Our team is always really enthusiastic and really loud. Each day, different people who aren't swimming get to lead our team cheers and Diana Munz and I got to lead them for the relays.

Our relay cheer sounds like this:

U.S., U.S., U.S., relay, relay, relay
U.S., U.S., U.S., relay, relay, relay
U.S., relay, U.S., relay. Go relay, go.

Another cheer sounds like this:

When I say go, you say fight. Go. Fight. Go. Fight.
When I say win, you say tonight. Win tonight. Win tonight.
When I say boogie, you say down. Boogie down. Boogie down.
When I say go, fight, win tonight, boogie down, alright, alright.

Unfortunately, before the race, I was demoted from my head cheerleading post when I botched the boogie down section.

It was awesome being with my teammates to watch us rock the relay. Aaron led off the backstroke leg with a world-record 53.45 seconds. It's the only individual leg in which you can set a world record during the medley relay, because the other three swimmers jump into the water after a teammate hits the wall rather than at the sound of a beep the way they do in other races. Brendan had a great leg (59.37) and we were ahead of record pace. But as Brendan came to the wall, Ian jumped in very quickly. Uh-oh. I looked over at Diana, who was on one side of me, then at Lindsay Benko, who was on the other side, and I could tell we were all thinking the same thing: *I hope he didn't leave too soon. Please, no. Please, not Ian.*

We'd have to wait for official word about any disqualifications. In the meantime, Ian swam a great fly split (50.28) and built our lead to almost three seconds. All Jason had to do was swim a decent leg to get us under the world record. He finished in a strong 47.58 and we had a new record, 3:30.68.

I was slapping the railing in front of us and we were all on our feet, celebrating the world record, but we were also worried about a possible DQ. *Please,* I was thinking, *please not Ian.* Finally the results flashed on the scoreboard with the words Official Results above them. Our exchange was clean, our record stood and Ian was going to get his gold medal. I hugged just about everyone. As the swimmers on our team stood up, we each took turns walking up and down the line of teammates so we could high-five everyone. It was a sweet moment.

* * *

I finished the Olympics with six gold medals and two bronze and I had become the second athlete in Olympic history to win eight total medals. (Soviet gymnast Alexander Ditiatin won eight at the 1980 Moscow Olympics.)

Since I was no longer the 15-year-old rookie, I wanted to stay in Athens for a week after the Olympics to enjoy some sights and events. I was talking to my Mom about plans to pack up, leave the village and move on to one of the ships for the second week of the Games. She had a question:

"Michael, where are your medals?"

"In a bag under my bed."

"In a bag? Michael, you need to take care of those."

"Mom, what else can I do with them?"

I had been putting the medals in a cubbyhole under some clothes, but after we won the 800 free relay, I needed to move them to a larger place. We finally left them in Peter's hands and moved them into a safe deposit box in Athens.

It's funny, but people ask where the medals are now and what I plan to do with them, and I don't know the answer to either question. Peter has them somewhere. Eventually, I'm not sure whether I'll display them, give one or two of them to people close to me, loan them to a place where kids can see them or just tuck them away somewhere. The medals are really only important if you can

think about what it took to get them in the first place. If I hadn't
been the kid who couldn't focus, had big ears, watched his parents
split up, saw his sister struggle and couldn't go more than two minutes without arguing with his coach, the medals would still be the
same size and color, but maybe they either wouldn't be mine or
wouldn't mean as much as they do now. So the medals will find
their place. I'm not worried about them. I wouldn't have medals if
I hadn't had dreams first. The best part about waking up, after all,
is remembering how sweet the dreams actually were.

26

TOURING

Once the swimming competition was over, I was able to stay in Athens and see some other events. I watched the U.S. men's basketball team lose its semifinal game to Argentina, but I also saw women's soccer live for the first time. The game was a good one to see: the U.S. women defeated Brazil, 2-1 in overtime, to win the gold medal. After the match, I posed for pictures with the U.S. team.

I moved onto a ship and went to some rocking parties thrown by MTV, Speedo, and *Sports Illustrated*. My family got into some of the parties and when I wasn't looking, the woman shaking it on the dance floor over there was . . . Mom?

The parties were a good place for Australian journalists to pick up (or make up) stories about me. There is a friend of mine on the Australian team named Mel. We hung out together a lot. We ate together in the dining hall, we rode with each other to the pool most days and she came with my family to the *Sports Illustrated* party. The day after one of the parties, an Australian publication reported that I had asked Mel out on a date and she rejected me. So, let's make up *every* aspect of a story. By the way, I don't believe in the so-called *Sports Illustrated* curse. I made the cover twice and I didn't feel jinxed . . . unless the jinx extends to Aussie reporters at *SI* parties.

Greetings and interview requests were coming in from everywhere. In the second week, I had over 500 text messages. One day, Peter had to borrow my phone battery after using up his own, except that he used up mine, too. From the ship, I did a cool segment for the *Today Show* in which I raced against Matt Lauer.

Almost as soon as I got back from Greece, I went on a tour with Ian Crocker and Lenny Krayzelburg that required an amazing team effort from a lot of people and really showcased swimming in a fun and inclusive way. Disney got behind it and so we called it the Disney Swim with the Stars Tour. The tour began in Disney World in Orlando, Florida, at the end of August, criss-crossed the country for a month and ended at Disneyland in Anaheim, California. In between we stopped in places such as Atlanta, New York, Baltimore, Chicago, Dallas, Denver, Salt Lake City, Sacramento, and San Francisco.

We traveled on this amazing bus that slept 12 and used to belong to David Copperfield, the magician. The bus had a huge video screen in the front, next to tables and a microwave. In the back there was another large video screen where we often played either Madden Football or Tiger Woods golf.

We visited schools and then conducted shows at local pools that usually seated one or two thousand people. We began each show at places that had video boards with a series of video clips from the Olympics. The three of us gave swimming stroke demonstrations and raced against each other in different strokes from show to show. (Who knew Lenny was such an intense breaststroker?) We conducted question-and-answer sessions, and then the three of us took our turns as anchors on relays of local kids.

Sometimes if the kids weren't very good swimmers, we'd jump in and have them ride on our backs. After each show, Lenny, Ian, and I would get back on the bus and discuss what worked and what didn't with Shaun Jordan, who was the MC for the events, and the tireless Octagon staff (Peter, Marissa Gagnon, Morgan Boys, and Sean Foley). Along the way, we shortened the stroke demonstration part of the show, frequently searched for appropriate background music and tried to come up with better ways to sell merchandise. Ian, Lenny, and I were practically signing as many hats, shirts, and posters as we could fit on the bus.

It was honestly like being in an advanced event marketing class. It's early to be talking about my post-swimming career, but I've picked up on a lot of business and marketing-related things because I've been able to live some of them. I've been able to be a part of contracts, appearances, photoshoots, and this tour. I've lived what people teach, and I'm very lucky.

We had great sponsor support on the tour from Disney, Speedo, PowerBar, AT&T Wireless, USA Swimming, W Hotels, and VISA. We sold most of our tickets for around $25, which was pretty reasonable for families, but we also sold a handful of VIP seats for $100. The VIP would get seats on the pool deck and have a dedicated autograph session with us at the end of each show. Of course we always signed for the other spectators, too. Disney even constructed a pool on Main Street in Disneyland just for the event there. Peter pointed out afterward that there is a model now for the type of tour that didn't exist before. Other swimmers will be able to do this after future Olympics in the way figure skaters have post-Olympic tours.

The most amazing response was definitely in the Baltimore area, where county leaders gave me their first honorary key to the county and then organized a parade for me they called the Phelpstival. Local politicians named a street in my honor on Cedar

Avenue, near Towson High School. Two rival politicians, Democratic mayor Martin O'Malley and Republican governor Robert Ehrlich, got onto a stage at Courthouse Plaza to welcome me home.

The Baltimore Sun held a contest to choose a nickname for me. Entries included: Phast Phish, Phlash, The Phin, Physique, the Phantom of the Aqua and Greece Lightning.

One afternoon, I was heading for an hour-long autograph session at one of the AT&T centers in the area, and I couldn't find the entrance because a large group of people were blocking the storefronts near a multiplex cinema. "What's playing here?" I said. "It's doesn't even get this crowded at night." Only when I saw one of the teenage girls waiting in line did I realize the line was for me. The shirt on her back that read "Marry me, Michael" was a dead giveaway.

The session passed the two-hour mark and the line was still around the corner, but we needed to get to the show in time. I apologized for leaving and we headed out along the Interstate. From the rooftop of a car in the lane to my right, out popped two girls holding up Wheaties boxes with my picture and screaming my name. I was laughing pretty hard about that. After a van that was in front of us moved up, I sped up so my car could be alongside theirs. In stop-and-go traffic, the girls' mother passed the boxes through the passenger-seat window and eventually to me. I signed three boxes, passed them back and then pointed ahead to remind the mother that she was in a moving car on a road and the effusive thank yous weren't necessary.

Things got a little crazy in Baltimore, where people would show up at our door to pick through our trash and even the local funeral home had a sign at its entrance saying: *Congratulations, Michael Phelps.*

Peter saw to it that I had a plainclothes security guard with me whenever I went out in public on the trip. After each event, we would walk through a line of screaming kids outside our bus and the security guard often led the way. He was a cool guy named Ricky Frazier, a former New York cop who once fought Roy Jones for the light heavyweight title. We would often find girls' phone numbers taped to the outsides of the doors. It was pretty overwhelming. I'm not sure how I ended up in this movie.

At different stops on the tour I also appeared on *Good Morning America*, *Regis & Kelly*, and made a second appearance on *The Tonight Show*. On September 16, I broke off the tour for a day and flew to Michigan where I helped open The Ryder Cup golf tournament and met Donald Trump, who gave me his business card and told me to call the next time I came to New York.

We made a stop at Penn State, where I fielded some questions from the audience. The first guy was a swimmer who asked about pre-meet meals. I told him I usually favored carbs over protein just before I raced, because I needed the energy. A girl asked the second question. "Hi, Michael," she said, as muffled laughter spread through the crowd in anticipation of her question. After a long pause, she asked, "Are you single?" The crowd broke out in laughter. I replied that I was, and for a minute I thought somebody had turned a mouse loose in the room. Whoa, this is getting out of hand.

When the tour stopped in New York, I made an appearance on MTV's popular TV show *Total Request Live*. The host who brought me on started joking about the way all athletes my age had huge egos. Then I walked out and surprised the audience. They asked about my choice of music (hip hop, of course) and one of the hosts, Vanessa Minnillo, convinced me to lift up my shirt partway to show my abs.

I really liked what we accomplished for the sport during the year. USA Swimming usually gets about a four percent jump in membership after an Olympic year, but this year the increase was around eight percent. There is a lot of credit to go around for that, but I'd like to think that what we did in Athens and what we did afterward, including the swim tour, was a big factor. After the Games, the Wolverine program held swim camps for almost a thousand kids. Families flew in from places like El Salvador and Thailand so their kids could attend the camps. The sport was enjoying a great upward swing in momentum.

I really appreciated that swing after a surprise conversation that took place at a party in New York for ESPN's 25th anniversary. I met a number of sports legends there, including Joe Theismann, Franco Harris, Ozzie Smith, and Jackie Joyner-Kersee. But one man I'll never forget came up to tell me, "You know, you really did the country proud and it was so much fun to watch you." It was Mike Eruzione, the captain of the 1980 hockey team whose miracle story became my favorite movie and a source of inspiration.

Unfortunately, during the tour, I felt a twinge in my back during an exhibition stop in Portland. I suppose the hours sitting and sleeping on the rocky bus didn't help. I completed the tour, but still felt some discomfort during easy swims. It was time to pull off the throttle, but we had world short-course championships coming up in Indianapolis. It's the sort of meet a tight back might have made me skip in other years, but this was in front of a home crowd, and one of my sponsors, Argent Mortgage, was behind the meet, so I didn't want to disappoint. Scott Heinlein flew to Indianapolis to look at my back, and I decided to go ahead and race.

I swam in one race and won the 200 free in 1:43.59. Then my back started to tighten up again the next morning. I really didn't want to drop out of the meet, but it was clearly the right thing to do. I went back home the next day to be looked at by doctors Lee Riley and Peter Rowe at John's Hopkins, one of the best hospitals in the country. They gave me a bone scan and an MRI, which revealed a pars fracture, a malady of the lower back that involves repeated bending and stretching of the spine. It's something I may have had since I was a little kid. Nobody wanted me to undergo back surgery, because that would have kept me out of the pool for months. The doctors decided I would wear a removable brace and stay out of the pool for six weeks. If the back didn't improve during that time, then they would need to surgically fuse the vertebrae. I was worried about it because of what had happened to Whitney. I tried not to think that my career might end prematurely, as hers did, but of course it entered my mind.

27

A BAD MISTAKE

I didn't drink in high school. Some of my classmates may have experimented or tried to be cool by showing they could handle alcohol, but I really was focused on swimming. I didn't stay out late and I skipped a lot of parties, another choice I don't regret because it allowed me to reach my potential as a swimmer. When I did go out, I was often a designated driver, and my mom got used to calls from me that I'd be a few minutes late because I had to drop off one of my friends.

After my swimming was finished in Athens, I had a drink to celebrate. The minimum age in Greece is 18, so it was legal there. Up until my last race in Athens, I was focused on the job I had to do and I wasn't going to jeopardize all the work I had put in to get to that position.

That changed in early November. I was antsy upon my return to Baltimore, nervous about the future and unable to get back into the water. Dating back to the Olympics, it had been several months since I'd been in my normal routine. Still, that was no excuse for making a terrible choice. This isn't easy to write about. In fact I hate talking about it, but I know it was an important lesson for me and that sort of lesson can be important for other people, too. One night I went to visit a friend who was studying at Salisbury University nearby. I hung out with him for a while at a party before we split up and I started talking to other friends and people I didn't know as well. I also made a terrible choice to drink at the party before driving home. I say choice, because even as I have tried to rationalize what happened, the fact is it wasn't something anyone did to me; it was something I did to myself. The responsibility and consequences for my actions rest squarely on my shoulders, and I was lucky I didn't get in a wreck. When I was pulled over by police after driving through a stop sign, I was as scared as I have ever been. What had I done? As I realized what was happening, my initial reaction was, "I screwed up. I ruined everything. Why did I do this?" I understood right away that this wasn't something trivial. I would have to be held accountable for doing something very wrong.

I called Peter first, mainly because I didn't know how I was going to tell my mom and Bob. I had never been away from both of them for prolonged periods, but I shouldn't have had to rely on them to avoid losing my self-discipline altogether.

First I had to face the people who mattered to me. Bob was at a meet in Wisconsin when I called him. He was supportive, but he also let me have it over the phone: "Michael, just because you want to blow off some steam doesn't mean you can be an idiot." Facing my mom—literally just looking her in the eye—was a killer. I was so sorry for what I had done that I almost didn't know how to say I was sorry.

Peter, Bob, my mom, and I sort of had a team meeting to talk about the situation, which didn't become public right away. I kept some public appearances over the next few days, but we decided that it was best for people to learn what had happened from me as opposed to someone else. I called friends and extended family, but I also called reporters I had come to know over the years to tell them straight out that I had messed up and was willing to take responsibility. It was a long, uncomfortable process, but I had to do it. The best way to atone for screwing up is to start by acknowledging you screwed up.

Over the next few days, reporters wrote about what impact my misbehavior would have on my public reputation, what my sponsors would do, and so on. I never even had time to think about any of that. All I knew was that I had let down my mom. Other people around me, good people, knew me as a swimmer. She was the person who would always look at me as her son, regardless of whether I ever jumped into a pool again. She didn't care about raising a gold medalist; she wanted to raise a son who did the right thing. This was one time, more than any other in my life, when I had let her down. I didn't fear facing the cameras, facing my friends, even facing Bob, because he had seen so many different sides of me already. But the day I had to face my mom after making such a bad decision and setting such a bad example was one of the worst days of my life. Of course, she was forgiving and understanding; but she also hurt—not for herself, but for me. More than anything, I hated putting her in that position.

Over the next few weeks, I was amazed at how many people provided support, everyone from sponsors and influential people within the swim community to friends and fans who offered support privately. For the first time, USA Swimming held an awards presentation in New York called the Golden Goggles. It was a great affair held in a ballroom near Madison Square Garden. Every swimmer on the Olympic team attended. The guys dressed in tuxedos; the women wore nice dresses and gowns. NBC's great Olympic anchor Bob Costas emceed the event. There were speeches and highlight videos all evening. I was honored with the swimmer of the year award and had a chance to thank everyone who stood by me. I had prepared some notes, but when I got to the part about my grandmother, I started to choke up and had to ad lib my way through the speech. I also got pretty emotional when NBC Sports Chairman Dick Ebersol, the man who runs the network's Olympics coverage, got up to speak and started to talk about my character. As I said, it's easy for people to stand by you when they can only see good things. Mr. Ebersol's comments were a great example of the way people looked past a time I messed up to remember the good things, and I'm very grateful for that.

Pretty soon I started going around and talking to people, especially kids, about what I had done. I went to the Boys and Girls Clubs in Aberdeen. These were kids who made me feel so at ease over the years, because I knew they looked up to me, and I knew anytime I said something to them I was having an impact on their lives. At the least, I could make them feel better about their day. Maybe I was even inspiring someone to strive for goals. It always feels good to do something good for someone else. I almost don't know how to explain it, but as great as it feels to win medals and set records, I really appreciate what I've accomplished more when I see kids stand a little taller just because I've gone in to see them. Now I wondered what it would feel like to see them. Most of them had heard about the DUI. Would they still look at me the same way? I didn't know.

I was a little more nervous than usual speaking to the kids this time, but I was as honest as I could be about what happened and that seemed to make it easier. I talked about making good decisions. The kids seemed to understand both the message and how hard it was for me to give it. Some of them came up to me afterward and told me about mistakes they had made, too. I think this session especially was as helpful for me as it was for them. Each day, I began to understand more and more that the people who stood by me when I wasn't famous were going to support me through tough times, too.

The next day, I gave another speech at a local health and fitness expo. The age range in the audience was bigger, but the butterflies in my stomach were about the same. I started to feel more at ease when I went back to another high school and was able to talk to students who were really at a stage of life I understood. "I've been in your shoes," I told them. "Some of you are looking forward to prom. I know you can have it all and lose it all. It isn't worth it to take a stupid risk. It's a part of my life that will stay with me as much as the swimming medals. The one thing I can do is not to make the same mistake again."

It was obviously a difficult time in my life, but that fall, a trip with my family helped me keep things in balance. I went to New York with my mom and sisters for a special tour of Ground Zero. We started by visiting the offices of NYC2012, the organization leading the bid to bring the Olympics to New York. The window from their conference room directly overlooked the area known as The Pit, where the buildings collapsed and the rescue workers pulled out the last remaining survivors from the rubble. Since three years had passed since the tragedy, the area looked a lot like a regular construction site, but you could get a vivid perspective of what had happened from where we were standing. It seemed like we were extremely high up and yet we were only a third of the way to where the tops of the World Trade Center buildings reached.

As we were looking at the site, a surprise visitor arrived. Jason Read was one of the first people on the scene that day. At 26, he wasn't much older than me, but he had been elected chief of the Amwell Valley Rescue Squad in New Jersey for seven straight years, making him the youngest chief in the Tri-State area of New York, New Jersey, and Connecticut. Jason spoke to our family about the early morning call he received that day, about rushing to the site with the smoke, the smells, and the reality of what had taken place. Like most of the rescue workers, he pretty much worked around the clock, eating in a makeshift mess hall, sleeping in a gutted booth of an adjacent restaurant with inches of soot and ashes all over the place. He was there when the rescue workers found the last survivor among the debris.

The one thing we didn't realize about Jason was that in addition to his great work in the community, he was also a gold medalist in Athens. Jason was a member of the rowing team that won the men's eights event in Greece. I have no idea how he managed to keep such an important job while training for the Games.

Afterward, he took us down to St. Paul's church, which was already famous because George Washington had worshipped there. In the days after September 11, it was a sanctuary for the volunteers, who received refreshments and could read cards from families around the country thanking them for their work. It was great that so many people pulled together and pitched in during that time, but sad that it took such a terrible event to get people to think about helping. It was really a visit that put a lot of things in perspective, like the highs of Athens and the lows of my DUI. Some events in life are just bigger than all of that.

28

OFF TO ANN ARBOR

Before I settled in at Michigan, I spent time looking for a home in Ann Arbor, near the campus and the Canham Natatorium where I'd be training. While I was looking, I moved in with Bob in his new place, and those were the longest weeks of both of our lives. It wasn't a lack of physical room, but rather a lack of space, if you know what I mean. You don't really have freedom to do much when you have a roommate. When that roommate is your coach who drives your butt into the ground half the time, well, I'm not sure we could have lasted another week. I wanted to come and go. He was still stuck in watch-over-Michael mode, especially after the fallout from the DUI. Little things set us off. Even by our standards of random bickering, it was a combustible time.

Bob was getting after me pretty hard one day when I told him I was out of there. "Okay," he told me, "don't let the door hit you on the way out." Of course I didn't expect him to beg me to come back, but the fact that he was so unfazed by what he said set me off even more. "I'm going back to Baltimore," I told him. I barely had enough time to throw things in the car when I was back on the road. A few minutes later I called my mom to tell her I was heading home, and as always with Debbie Phelps, calm soon trumped panic. "Now Michael, what are the advantages of coming home? Of course you can come back, but would you train here?"

She had a point.

"Are you going to find a new coach?" she continued. "What about school?"

Okay, time to turn the car around. Mom is the ultimate steam defuser. I was back at Bob's a few hours later, still grouchy, but still there.

My mom and Hilary helped a lot by scouring real estate ads, looking for apartments and houses. I kind of liked the idea of a house, but my mom pointed out the advantages of an apartment, including security. Score another point for Mom logic. Hilary actually found the place I bought. It had more space than I needed, room for a large TV and all the essentials a young man needs to become domestically capable without having his mom there to cook, wash dishes, wash clothes, pay bills, dust, vacuum, and figure out where the keys are hiding at a moment's notice.

Once my mom left for Baltimore, it was time for Domestic Ace to show his colors. I woke up one morning ready to start my day. I had bought both milk and cereal, so what else do you need to have a bowl of cereal? Maybe a bowl? The house didn't come with any, so it was time to improvise. I had a Gatorade canister, which was going to have to do. I poured some milk and some cereal into the canister and sort of drank my breakfast.

Once I actually had dishes, I didn't want them to pile up and get dirty, so I put them into the dishwasher and tried to follow the directions exactly—with just one small change that shouldn't really make any difference, should it? I put liquid hand soap in the dishwasher instead of the dishwasher soap I was supposed to use. This worked just fine for the first five minutes. Then I spent the next few hours trying to get the bubble bath out of my kitchen.

I had been at the apartment for a while when I first tried to make steak the way my mom used to cook it: seasoned just right. I figured I could do the same, except that the steak came out like shoe leather. So I had to order out. At least I had cooked myself a good pair of jogging shoes. I was having a conversation with some-one about it, and he gave me a few tips: put the salt and pepper on the outside before you start and make sure the pan or grill is really hot so you get a nice sear on the outside of the meat. That keeps the juices from getting out. Then let the meat rest for a few minutes before slicing into it, so the juices have time to settle and don't run and make the meat fatty and chewy. Good, I could use the advice, except, well, the guy giving it to me was a vegetarian. Am I really hurting that bad in the kitchen?

At least I took care of the important priorities. I found a place close by that had a satellite dish where I could watch the Ravens. And even though I wasn't a huge college football fan before I went to Michigan, I started enjoying Wolverines games. It's hard not to when the stadium seats 100,000 fans. We rarely compete in places that seat more than 10,000. A few weeks earlier I had watched the Wolverines beat Michigan State in triple overtime and it took me a few hours just to wind down. By the way, sorry Mom, but you know those Olympic rings I had tattooed on my left hip in the name of team spirit? Well, there's this, um, Wolverine "M" on the other hip.

Because of my schedule, I began college life just taking courses in public speaking and sports marketing. I have some experience in both areas and I think once I retire from competitive swimming I might be doing things that involve one or the other. We had a lab of sorts in the speaking class that I enjoyed. Each student wrote down a random topic on a piece of paper, which was placed in a bag. Then each of us reached into the bag and pulled out a slip with a topic we had to discuss ourselves. My topic turned out to be sleep, something I know a lot about. I started by saying that as an athlete, rest was very important to my preparation. I never trained well if I didn't have the right amount of food or the right amount of sleep. A lot of people might not look at proper sleep as an important part of a training program, but without it, I wouldn't be able to do what I do nearly as well. See, sleeping in class is bad, but talking about sleep in class? Not so bad.

The tradition and training atmosphere at Michigan are great. Just look around. NCAA and Big Ten banners line the upper level at Canham. The Wolverines had won 11 NCAA team championships and 156 NCAA individual titles before Bob took over. Since the 1924-25 season, the men's team has had a winning record in dual meets every year except one (1955-56). If you go through a back entrance to the pool, you pass a series of glass-enclosed cases holding caps from all the countries represented by Michigan swimmers at the Olympics over the years. Each cap (72 from 11 countries) has the name and flag of a Wolverine Olympian. On the side of the complex near the diving tower, there is a large clock located below large Olympic rings. The clock doesn't have the current time. Instead, it counts down the time until the opening ceremonies in Beijing. The second fractions are extended to eight decimal places.

The culture of swimming is everywhere. Bob was in local deli a week after starting his job when a father and son noticed his USA Swimming jacket and started to chat him up. After wrapping Bob's turkey sandwich, the student behind the counter pointed at him and added, "and you swam at Florida State."

29

THE **WAKEUP** CALL

I could come up with a lot of excuses from the bad back to the DUI to the move to Michigan, but the fact is I was about to have a very unsatisfying year in the pool. It wasn't a total failure, but I always want to be able to build on the previous year, and by the winter of 2005-06, I really didn't feel I had improved in any one area since the Olympics. Bob and I had talked about trying to incorporate more weights into my training program after Athens, but we didn't dare try it in 2005, because we were worried about what that might do to my back. I still did a lot of cross-training strength and core work, like push-ups, pull-ups, sit-ups and work on the medicine ball. Barbells would have to wait.

I think Bob was looking for a way to keep my energy level up during the post-Olympic year. Especially with the bad back, he wanted me to train and recover with the right amount of caution without having to think cautiously all the time. It was a good year to experiment, so looking ahead to World Championships over the summer in Montreal, he decided I would swim two new events, the 100 and 400 freestyles, while dropping two familiar ones: the

200 fly and 400 IM. I would still swim those periodically during the year, but not during the season's big meet. If we decided afterward that we wanted to go back to the old program, there was still plenty of time to do that before the next Olympics.

The competitive year kicked off in March at the American Short-Course Championships in Austin. Bob entered me in six races over three days, both to test my back and get ready for World trials in Indianapolis a month later. This was home to a lot of the guys on our national team: Brendan, Aaron, Neil, and Ian. The Reeses, Eddie and Randy, have really done a great job in keeping the college and post-collegiate programs strong down there. My first day went okay. I broke Matt Biondi's old American record, winning the 200-yard freestyle in 1:32.08, won a 400 IM in 3:42.74, and swam a leadoff leg for our Club Wolverine against the Longhorn guys from Texas, which we lost. I wasn't happy with my times, but at least my back felt okay. The next day, I swam a 200-yard breast, missing my personal record (PR) by a second and finishing third behind Brendan. I won two more races on the last day and felt as though I could go through a long meet without worrying about tweaks and aches.

Next I went to Indianapolis for our World trials, not knowing what to expect in my new events. I swam the 400 free on the first day and by the end of the night I was in as much pain as I had experienced in a race. None of the top swimmers were in my morning heat, so I reacted to the lead I had and almost didn't qualify for finals. Unfortunately, I overreacted at night and did the opposite. I didn't mean to take it out as fast as I did, but I was ahead of world-record pace at 50, 100, and 150. That was too fast. It felt like knives were digging into my arms on the last lap. I finished in 3:55.70 and qualified for Worlds, but I was whupped.

The next night I won the more familiar 200 free in 1:46.44 at a much more comfortable pace. Bob said he was happy with it because I hadn't been able to train at a hundred percent after the Olympics, but I wasn't satisfied with being a second off my PR. I was warming down when I heard that Aaron had lowered his world record in the 100 back from 53.45 to 53.17. I gave him a high-five and realized how far away I felt from being able to break them myself.

On the third day, I raced Ian again in the 100 fly final. It started out as a typical contest between the two of us. Ian took a strong lead at the first wall and I came back on him at the end. Either of us could have won the race easily if we had hit the wall right, but we both jammed at the finish, causing us to lose time. I barely out-touched him in 51.34. I still didn't have a PR in Indy, but it was the first time since I returned to racing that I didn't think about my back injury.

I was feeling more like myself, really gunning for a best time in one of my last few races. On Day 4, I finally got it in the 100 free, holding off Jason Lezak at the wall in 49.00. To be fair, Jason had been away from training, too, for most of the winter and wasn't in shape to challenge his American record, 48.17, but even a PR of .05 for me felt like a mile. I came back an hour later and won the 200 IM in 1:57.44. The time was okay, but I felt I could have gone faster. Afterward, Bob told me he thought I should drop the 200 back on the last night. I sort of felt I wanted to swim it because things were starting to go well again, but with the 100 and 400 frees on the program, we felt I'd be better off skipping it.

Sometimes I get invited to strange events: pool parties, birthdays, bar mitzvahs, Eagle Scout ceremonies, even a Halloween party at the Playboy Mansion (I didn't go). But in 2005 I was invited to be a judge at the Miss USA pageant at the Hippodrome Theater in Baltimore. Well, let's see, April 11? I just happened to be free on that day. The judging panel included fashion designer Pamela Dennis; model Ksenia Maksimova; beauty expert Frederic Fekkai; fellow Olympian Sugar Ray Leonard, host of *The Contender*;

Brody Hutzler from *Days of Our Lives*; supermodel Molly Sims; and Raj Bhakta, a contestant on *The Apprentice*. We judged the contestants in three categories: evening gown, interview, and swimsuit, with the winner going on to the Miss Universe pageant in Bangkok. When you swim every day, it usually gets pretty routine hanging out with people in swimsuits, but, well, this wasn't so bad. I gave my highest marks to North Carolina's Chelsea Cooley, who ended up winning the contest. She came off as very composed and confident and I felt better after the announcement, because many of the other judges knew this world better than I did. So I was relieved that I wasn't alone in my selection. We weren't allowed to talk to the women before the competition, but I did meet a few of them afterward and have stayed in touch with one of them. (No rumors, please. We're just email pals.)

I was back in Indianapolis in early June for six events in three days at the Counsilman Classic. I was six-for-six in two frees (100 and 200), two IMs, and two butterflys, but I really wasn't satisfied. Then in late June, I won six races at the Santa Clara Grand Prix meet. I got smoked by both Jason and Canada's Brent Hayden in the 100 free and didn't feel good about the lead-in to the World Championships in Montreal. I was feeling more tired at the ends of races and meets, I wasn't turning any better than I was the years earlier, and I went through another multi-race meet without a best time. My biggest meet of the season was just a month away.

In the meantime, I was fortunate enough to win an ESPY Award for Best Male Olympic Performance. I love going to the ESPYs, even if only to mingle. One year I met Shaquille O'Neal at the ESPYs and I have never felt so short in my life. It's been a long time since I stood next to someone nearly a foot taller. I also remember the year LaDainian Tomlinson, the great Chargers running back, told me, "Seriously, dude, I can't even swim."

Of all the other athletes I've met in other sports, I don't think I've ever talked to anyone more down to Earth than Peyton

Manning, the Indianapolis Colts' quarterback. We talked for 90 minutes about everything from our sports to our families. Years before Peyton led the Colts to a Super Bowl championship, the team used to play in Baltimore. So we talked about some of the old Colts players and about some of the current Ravens. He told me the Ravens have one of the toughest defenses to play against. "I do nothing but watch tape for a week before we play you guys," he told me.

At the World Championships, I was looking forward to facing Ian Thorpe and Grant Hackett in the longer freestyles. Ian was still the man in the 400 free, but I was convinced I could do another best time in the 200 and test myself against the best again. I was disappointed to find out that Ian was planning to skip the meet and take the year off. Not only that, but Pieter van den Hoogenband, who finished second to Ian, had to miss the meet because he was recovering from hernia surgery. The 200 free in Athens was a very satisfying race for me, even though I didn't win it. I managed to swim a best time and I really think having Ian and Pieter there to pull the rest of the field through helped me get that best time.

Then again it was pretty clear from the first day that I wasn't prepared for the 400 free. I was able to fight through that race at trials, but not in Montreal. I had never failed to make the final of an individual race since I had started swimming at the elite level, but I fell apart at the end of the qualifying heat. I wasn't in pain, so much as I just wasn't moving. My back was fine, but I wasn't sure about my brain. I had never just shut down the jets at the end of a race, so this might have been the worst race of my career. Bob stared at me after I got out of the pool. He didn't say much—"Well, that wasn't too good, was it?"—probably because he knew I had to swim a leg in the 4x100 free final later that evening.

Between sessions, I went over to wish Grant well in the final, which I figured he'd win. He wished me luck in the relay, but joked that his "mates" would need it more. By that he meant that he knew

I'd be pretty fired up for the next race. Sure enough, the relay went much better. We got some revenge from our third-place showing at the Olympics. I led off, followed by Neil Walker, Nate Dusing, and Jason Lezak. We ended up winning pretty easily with Canada nearly three seconds behind in second. Without Ian to swim a great anchor like he had in Sydney, the Australians finished another second back in third place.

The newspapers let me have it the next day. One headline read: "Phelps Flop." David Stubbs, a columnist for the *Montreal Gazette*, swung the hardest. "Visitors to the World Aquatics Championships the past week have been wondering why the city of Montreal has lifeguards posted around the pool," he said. "Any chance you saw Michael Phelps struggle home over the final two laps of his 400-meter freestyle heat yesterday? The U.S. superstar was breathtaking in the worst way imaginable, failing to make the eight-man final, while looking like a weary age-grouper."

Of course, when I started winning races later in the week, I was either out of the headlines or the headlines were smaller, but that's how the media business works sometimes. It's news when somebody who isn't expected to win does, and it's news when someone who is expected to win doesn't. You get more credit for being on the way up and near the top than you do for actually staying at the top if people expect to see you there. It's like you get extra credit for being the underdog.

I wanted to get back to swimming finals right away, but that day I had only the semis of the 200 free and posted the fastest time. I was really proud of the way Katie bounced back and handled her second big meet. A year earlier, she came to Athens with big expectations, missed the 400 IM final (and got sick after the race), and finished seventh in the 200 IM. This time, she swam an almost perfect 200 IM, leading wire-to-wire and breaking an American record. You could tell Katie had learned from her experience in Athens.

Katie has really become one of my better friends on the team, almost like a little sister, and, well, who can you pick on if you can't pick on your little sister? We like to play what we call the dollar game. One of us will challenge the other about some random fact and if that person can't answer, we'll say, okay, cough up a buck. The question I ask if I want to stump her is an odd one. I'll wait until she sits down, then ask her what the color of the wall behind her is. Works every time.

We actually first met when she was 10 and I was 14. I had just swum a national qualifying time and she came up to ask for an autograph, "because you'll be the best." I was kind of stunned, so I scribbled MIKE PHELPS on a program and told her, "You too, someday." We have a lot in common besides our backgrounds at NBAC. We both made our first Olympic teams at 15 and we both swim the IMs and butterflys. She was once afraid of the water just as I was, so much that her mother even washed her hair as little as possible. Katie's mom had been a great basketball player at Stanford and maybe that's where she picked up that critical ingredient to success: a total disdain for losing. There's a good story about the time Katie hosted a party for some teammates. Afterward, Paul Yetter, Katie's coach who's done a great job with her, asked a general question about the party. She said the party had gone horribly wrong, because she had lost at cards all night. Never mind that the rest of the party was fine. Katie just didn't like to lose.

Neither did I. The next day, Dave Salo, our team's head coach, was using a poker analogy to help me forget about the 400. Just think about having an ace-king in Texas Hold 'Em and losing to a guy who has an eight-three. For those not familiar with the game, a player with an ace-king has a huge advantage over a player with an eight-three. But the night of the 200 free final, I swear I didn't see anyone or hear anything. The phrase "tunnel vision" is way overused, especially in sports, but I was concentrating so clearly on what I had to do. I still made mistakes in the race. My start wasn't great and I jammed my last turn, as usual, but I was ahead of world-record pace at 100 meters and I finished first in a PR 1:45.20, a second ahead of Grant.

I had a tough double a day later, with finals in both the 100 free and 200 IM. I wanted to get my freestyle under 49 seconds, but I knew I'd have to be a lot faster to be anywhere near the lead. If I could just get off to a good start, I felt I could stay out of the wake of the other swimmers and not eat their splashes that came off the wall. So much for Plan A. I got out too slow and was last at the turn. I came back okay, but passed only one guy. Italy's Filippo Magnini won the race in 48.12 seconds. I finished seventh in 48.99.

In the ready room afterward, Ryan was pumping me up for the IM by saying, "let's go one-two, just like Athens." I didn't get out as well as I wanted. Laszlo Cseh was slightly ahead of me at the hundred. I swam a good breaststroke, which is not one of Laszlo's strengths and grabbed the lead heading into the freestyle. If I could point to one area that had improved during the year, it was definitely the free, and I was able to extend my lead into the final wall, winning the race in 1:56.68. I pumped my fist after the race, but it was as much from relief as elation. I was still seven-tenths off my record. Laszlo was a second back, just touching out Ryan for silver.

I had another quick turnaround the next day, with just 30 minutes between the semis of the hundred fly and the final of the 800 free relay. My fly time (52.02) was second best in the field, but it was almost a full second behind Ian (51.08), who looked like he was heading for another world record. We had the exact four guys on the relay who rocked the house in Athens (me, Ryan, Peter, and Klete) and it was our first chance to swim together since the Olympics. Even with our victory in Athens, the Aussies had owned this event for many years, winning every world title since 1982; so I really wanted to take it on my shoulders to get us off to a good start. My leadoff split was 1:45.51 and kept us ahead of the field. Ryan and Peter kept us ahead of record pace and Klete shook off the rust from his layoff to bring us home in 7:06.58. It wasn't a world record, but it was three seconds faster than the Canadians, four seconds faster than the Australians, and a satisfying way to end a long day. I slept during the whole ride back to the hotel.

Of course when I woke up, I was already thinking about racing Ian in the fly the next day. He was swimming so well, in top form, and I should have known this wouldn't be like the final in Athens. Ian killed it, just nailed it. He swam a 50.40 and beat me by more than a second. Typical of Ian, he didn't react much after he hit the wall. Then again, the rest of us were still busy swimming. I knew this was Ian's best race, but the improvements he made during the year really highlighted to me the improvements I hadn't made. I tried to be positive when I talked to the press after the race, but when I saw Bob afterward, I told him, "I want to put a bag over my head." Bob then looked at me and said: "Me, too." It was a wake-up call, a slap in the face. I had a lot of work to do. Ian was on another planet in the fly, Ryan was getting better every day in the IM, my two new races turned up two bad results, and I honestly felt that after setting records every year, I had practically stood still for 12 months.

I came back the last morning to swim in a prelim for the evening's medley relay. Because I swam in the heats and because we won the final, I received a fifth gold medal for the meet. But watching the team win felt nothing like watching in Athens. I felt like my mind was in quicksand, along with my swimming. In my head, I kept replaying the meet and everything that had happened since Athens. It was far from a highlight reel. I needed something to take my mind away and, fortunately, that's where family comes in.

30 | NEW FAMILY, NEW PLACES

I hadn't seen much of my mom during the week, because, as usual, my focus remained on the pool. She and Hilary were acting a little strange and I knew it wasn't just my fatigue that was making me think so. It turned out Whitney had gotten engaged and the wedding wasn't far off. There is a pattern here of me learning about engagements and weddings right after major swim meets. Anyway, this news made me feel much better than the bombshell in Sydney. Whitney was marrying Bob, a manager with Enterprise Rent-a-Car and a great guy who I could talk football with. Bob, repeat after me: "Go Ravens." Okay, welcome to the family.

For several months leading up to Worlds, cameras followed the Phelps and Crocker camps intensely for a DVD about our rivalry called *Unfiltered*. The DVD looked at both of our lives in and out of the pool. You see Ian fixing cars and playing Bob Dylan songs on his guitar and you see me playing a lot of video games. You see the somewhat neglected pool where Ian first started swimming, and grow to appreciate the dedication it took for him to get to where he is now. There are even interviews with my sisters, my mom, my prom date, and my dad, who gets emotional about the way our relationship dissolved over the years. The film appeared at a special screening in Montreal before the championships and later at the Tribeca Film Festival in New York. It was weird looking up at the screen in a big theater and seeing . . . myself.

We had our summer nationals in Irvine a week after Worlds and I really wanted to salvage the year by breaking a world record. I pretty much knew the 400 free was history—at least at a future Worlds or Olympics—and I was eager to get back to swimming the 200 fly. I was on record pace until the last 30 meters, then faded at the end. My time, 1:55.26, was second-fastest in the world in 2005, but to me it was just another effort that fell short, this time by more than a second. I took off my cap, flung it in front of me, turned around, and slapped the wall in disgust. I don't usually do that and it isn't something Bob approves of, but I was ticked. I remember thinking: Bob is going to drop a bomb on me. He's going to put a hurt on me in training. I wasn't looking forward to it, but I knew I needed it. I was still only 20 and I refused to believe that my best wasn't still ahead of me.

With the Beijing Games still three years away, I went on my first trip to China with the Octagon team in September. I had signed a contract with Matsunichi, a Hong Kong–based electronics company that was gaining momentum in the marketplace by coming up with a lot of cool products like cameras and MP3 players that could probably keep me occupied for a week straight without sleep. I went to the Olympic city and also made a detour to Hong Kong during the visit. I definitely wasn't prepared for the initial reception. Almost as soon as I left the plane, people presented me with flowers and gifts. It was extremely hot, but very dry. I felt as if I should be sweating, but I couldn't because of the dry air. In Hong Kong, I got out of a taxi and saw this giant billboard featuring me in an ad for Omega.

We were welcomed at a reception dinner with the chairman of Matsunichi. The menu went a little beyond franks and burgers: heads of jellyfish, gills of eel, soup of bamboo shoots, and a salad made of flower petals. You know the familiar feeling of facing unfamiliar food? This was new territory, although I have to say I could have eaten about six helpings of Peking duck.

I will also never forget jogging with Peter on the Great Wall. We looked to our left and right and for miles we saw nothing but The Wall. We celebrated afterward by going to McDonald's and practically buying the place out of burgers. David Schwab was the surprise appetite champ of the meal, downing three Big Macs. I wonder if that was a PR?

When I got back to the States, we did a cool commercial for Matsunichi in which I jumped into a pool, swam a lap and then, with the help of some special effects, kept swimming right through the wall at the end of the pool, actually swimming my way up until I stepped onto a roof. Then, as you see me listening to my MP3 player, you hear me say: "The power of music by Matsunichi."

In the lead-up to Beijing, I filmed spots for other companies and TV networks. ESPN produces some of the most clever commercials around. Since I'm a SportsCenter junkie, it was a lot of fun for me to be in a commercial of my own. In my spot, I walk into the ESPN offices and ask Stuart Scott, one of the network anchors, if I can borrow his computer. I'm wearing a wet bathing suit and after I start to work, sparks start flying and the computer shorts out because of the moisture that drips into the keyboard. In a second commercial, I have my cap, goggles, and medals with me in their office. Jay Harris, another one of the announcers, grabs one of the medals and uses it as a coaster for his cup of coffee. After I stare at him, he looks back at me and says, "It's only a bronze."

In October, I officially gained a brother-in-law. After the wedding, I remember looking at some old pictures of Whitney and me together. It was hard to believe the older sister who used to make me breakfast was actually getting married.

Back in Michigan, I was taking just a psychology class, keeping my course load light, and I joked afterward that if nothing else, the class helped me figure out Bob a little better. He and I started making some needed changes to my training. It was probably a good decision to be careful with my back all year, but it was no fun being stuck in what felt like competitive quicksand.

I started running again. Although just a couple of miles, it was enough to confirm that my legs were still better suited for water. I also began incorporating weight training into my program, something we'd put off because of my poor back. Lifting weights didn't really work earlier in my career when my bones were still developing, but now my body was stronger. I had grown another inch since Athens to 6'4" and I wanted to do everything I could to be stronger at the ends of races. I started with some basics like bench presses and machines rather than free weights. We still did dry land training, medicine ball work, and plyometrics, gradually building up to three hours a week. It would take me a good year to really understand what I was doing, but I really enjoyed it. The workouts were good breaks from the laps in the pool. I could also feel how they made my muscles burn afterward and, more importantly, how the training was impacting my swimming. I wish I had been able to do this earlier. I was ready for a better 2006.

Unfortunately, more bad news was in my future: my grandmother passed away. Gran was a fighter who did things on her own terms, including her fight against cancer. I can almost hear the doctor telling her she had so many months to live, and then Gran's response: "The disease will have to wait until I'm good and ready."

I went back for my grandmother's funeral in Western Maryland. Seeing so many people who knew her brought back random memories of Gran. We used to play cards together, usually Kings and Rummy, and I could never seem to beat her. Maybe that's why I've taken to Texas Hold 'Em. It isn't Gran's game, which, therefore, makes it a game I have a chance to win. I made sure to leave two cards with her at the cemetery.

As soon as she was diagnosed with pancreatic cancer, she made it a priority to follow every event I entered. Doctors gave her six months max, but she beat that max by a multiple of seven and was able to watch my Olympic races from home. That was Gran. She went out the way she lived: on her own terms. I think about her every day. She was very sharp, but she often used her age to her advantage, because she would always say whatever she wanted as if she couldn't be held responsible for her words. She used to brag about me to her friends in the nursing home, and she would show off the full-sized poster of me wearing a Speedo on the pool deck. Before Pan-Pacs, I promised I would break a world record for her at some time during the year.

Although we knew Gran's time was short, nobody expected the tragic news that hit the Michigan swim family in January. Eric Namesnik had gone from being a great Wolverine swimmer to an Olympian to a member of the Michigan coaching staff. One morning, we got word he had been in a nasty car accident on an icy stretch of road on his way to practice. Doctors induced a coma to reduce swelling around his brain, but unfortunately he never woke up and died four days after the accident. He was only 35 years old. I first met Eric when I was 11 and remember him giving me a hard time about my limp handshake, something my dad told me to avoid. He had a great wife, Kirsten, who also swam at Michigan, and two kids, Austin and Madison, who will no doubt be hearing stories about how awesome their dad was for many years. Snik had friends everywhere.

Snik's favorite saying tells his story: "Dream no small dreams, for they have power to move the hearts of men."

31

REBUILDING

After a disappointing year, Bob wanted me to take time to build myself up. I didn't compete again until February, at a low-key, short-course, world cup meet in East Meadow, Long Island, outside of New York City. I won four races over two days, saving the best test—a 200 free in which I trailed Italy's Filippo Magnini until the last 30 meters—for last.

Soon after, I went to Torino with my mom to see the Winter Olympics for the first time. I really enjoyed going to watch Apolo Ohno skate in person. Short track skating is cool, a little like roller derby. You have to pass the other skaters while keeping the tightest turns possible. Collisions happen all the time. Of course the next night my mom dragged me out to see ice dancing. I'm sure there's more to it than I realize, but, Mom, you're on your own next time. It was actually a trip of superlatives even without the sports events. I saw the biggest snowflakes I'd ever seen and I went for one of the best meals of my life at a local restaurant. Just how many antipasti can one swimmer eat?

I got a huge boost in April, when Erik Vendt joined our group in Michigan. Erik is awesome to train with. If I'm not pushing every day, he'll kick my butt in practice. Erik doesn't fit the proto- type of a great swimmer. Most elites are supposed to be tall, with long wingspans that shoot us through the water like rockets. Erik is listed at 5'11", which seems a bit generous. The man makes up for any size shortcomings with an amazing work ethic. Somewhere along the line, someone must have suggested he wouldn't be as good as he is, because he trains with a healthy chip on his shoulder.

We also got word that Kaitlin Sandeno would be joining us in May. Kaitlin has four medals over the last two Olympics and we were excited about adding another Olympian to our pool. I wasn't in full competition mode yet for the season, but already I was start- ing to feel that I was leaving 2005 behind.

Because of Bob's travel schedule and his obligations to both the college and club swimmers, he couldn't always be with me for each meet and training session. Still, he'd always find clever ways to keep me motivated, even when he wasn't there to watch. One day, he left behind some notes for a workout he called the Tour de FRIM (short for freestyle IM), a takeoff on the Tour de France bike race. We assumed this would be a pretty dull session, but it became pretty spirited because of the way he structured it. To begin with, a FRIM is a freestyle individual medley in which we swim IMs, but replace the butterfly strokes with additional freestyle strokes. Bob broke the day into six stages, the way they do in France. Erik won the first 1,600-meter stage and we started to get competitive. At one point we looked around for a yellow cap to be worn by the leader, just as the Tour de France leader gets to wear a yellow jersey as long as he keeps his lead. I outlasted Klete on the final stage to win the unofficial Canham "Bowman is Nuts" Tour de FRIM title. It was a proud moment.

Bob upped my competition schedule as we drew closer to Nationals in Irvine, California, and Pan Pacs in Victoria, B.C., the big meets during the season, and each one made me feel stronger. In May we had a meet in Ann Arbor to honor Eric Namesnik. I swam six races there, but the most meaningful were the 400 IM, which was Eric's event, and an 800 free relay, which I asked Bob if we could arrange with Peter and Klete, the Wolverines who won the relay with me in Athens. We hadn't planned it, but Bob understood we all wanted to do it for Snik, and the crowd reaction was pretty tremendous.

I continued to make progress at events in Charlotte and Santa Clara. I was right where I wanted to be, with world-leading times in both IMs, an improved freestyle, and a lot more stamina than I had at the same time a year earlier. I was also making significant strides with my weakest stroke, the breaststroke. Now I was keeping my shoulders up closer to my ears, holding my hands flat when I shot forward, and putting my fingertips up once I shot forward.

All the extra work was starting to make me feel the way I did in Athens, where I thought I was ready for anything. Of course, that wasn't the case outside the pool. A week before we left for Nationals, I had another household incident when my smoke detector started blaring. Fire? Where's the fire? I'm not cooking. There are no matches around. The stove is off. What could possibly be on fire? I called Bob, the answer man, for answers.

"Michael, when was the last time you changed the battery in that thing?" he asked.

"Oh, um, you need to do that?"

"Well, if you don't want the Ann Arbor Fire Department camped out in front of your place, you might look into it."

Considering all the times Bob lit a fire under my butt at practice, this was pretty ironic.

I went to Nationals in Irvine hoping I'd be able to break my first record since 2004, so I was a little disappointed to come away without one. Still, my three wins did give me a piece of history. I entered the night tied with Adolph Keifer, a swimmer during the

1930s and '40s, with 28 national titles, the most by a U.S. male swimmer. I knew of Keifer, who was still alive at age 88, because he manufactured a lot of swimming equipment we use. I never swam in his nylon tank suit he designed 50 years ago, but I still use his kickboards.

The next night I had another showdown against Ian. He always seems to bring out the best in me. Neither one of us swam our best in Irvine, but I managed to pull ahead with 25 meters to go and barely edge him at the finish. We knew we'd see each other again at Pan-Pacs. I came back to win the 200 IM, barely holding off Ryan, who had blossomed into a versatile swimmer. Afterward, a reporter asked me what it felt like to have a young gun going after me. Okay, I thought, but Ryan is actually a year older than I am.

I still had a bad taste in my mouth from the bad turns at Nationals. I hadn't set a world record in two years and the 1:53.93 I swam for the 200 fly in Barcelona was still standing. I wasn't looking at it as a world record anymore; I was thinking that this was supposed to be one of my best events—maybe my very best event—and I hadn't set a personal best in three years. The lack of improvement at this stage in my career worried me. I also wanted to break a world record for Gran.

I was disappointed that Ian Thorpe wouldn't be competing in Victoria, since I really wanted to face him in the 200 free. Without Ian, Bob and I agreed that on the first night I would skip the 200 free to be completely fresh and go after the record in the 200 fly final an hour later. I felt good when I jumped in and was .16 ahead of record pace at the 50. Then I lost pace a little bit, partly by design, so I could really come back strong at the end. At 150, I was behind Japan's Ryuichi Shibata, but I knew I had a lot left. After finally nailing the last turn, I passed Shibata and started to hear the crowd get louder. I had a good feeling as I touched the last wall. It had seemed like forever since my last record and I almost didn't want to look up to see my time. Okay, so I looked. The scoreboard read 1:53.80. "Yeah!" I screamed, holding up my arm and tossing my head back. That's what I'm talking about. I felt the burden and frustration lift off my shoulders.

I felt great about the result, but even more than that I felt psyched about how hungry and passionate I was in the days and hours leading up to the race. If the post-Olympic 18 months had been a giant wake-up call, I was finally awake—and still hungry. It took a while for me to get through interviews and drug testing.

I won two more gold medals the next night, in the 400 IM and 800-free relay with Ryan, Peter, and Klete. This wasn't anything like the relay in Athens. Our team led wire-to-wire, beating Canada and Australia by more than seven seconds. Our final time, 7:05.28, was just off the Australians' world record. We were nowhere near that record a few years ago. We were just trying to find a way to give the Aussies a race, since they had kind of taken over the event. But a relay record wasn't far off.

In fact, the next night was definitely a record night. First I had to swim the 200 back against Aaron. When he's on his game, Aaron may be the best ever at this event. Even though Bob didn't assign me an experiment as bold as the 400 free this year, the 200 back isn't one of my better events. It's a good challenge and a way to improve the backstroke part of my medley swims. Aaron's technique is just about perfect and it looks like he could swim the back in his sleep. This was one of those nights. Aaron led from the first wall and broke his own world record. I was more than two seconds back. When Aaron saw the results, he reached into my lane and slapped me on the back, but I was already thinking ahead to our 400 free relay half an hour later. I was leading off with Neil, Cullen, and Jason to follow. I gave us a lead and we pretty much stayed ahead of pace the whole race. Jason swam a great anchor, touching the wall in 3:12.46, seven-tenths ahead of the mark the South Africans set when they stunned us in Athens.

The last big race in Victoria was the confrontation with Ryan in the 200 IM. Ryan really pushes me every time we compete, and this was a great race. I was under world-record pace after the fly when I really wanted to make a statement. Ryan didn't back down and he took over the lead, under record pace, after the breast-stroke, leaving me with the freestyle leg to catch him. We both looked at one another as we came up to breathe and I definitely felt that one of us was going to break the record. I caught a glimpse of Ryan four strokes before the finish, enough to feel scared I was going to swim a great race and still lose. When I touched I thought I'd won and broken my record, 1:55.94, but I had to look up to be sure: 1:55.84. I put up two index fingers and went over to hug Ryan, who finished in 1:56.11. I really have to thank Ryan for that record. The fear of losing is worth an extra tenth when I need it most.

Afterward, I choked up when I told people I had dedicated the race to Gran. "She's definitely watching down," I said. I'm guessing it was the kind of day when she was winning at cards, too.

After no world records for almost two years, I had two individual and one relay record in a week. Yet the best part of the whole week was the feeling at the end that there was more work to do.

32

OPTIMISM ABOUNDS

The same week I finished with Pan Pacs, my mom opened a new chapter in her life as principal of the Windsor Mill Middle School, a school she helped get off the ground. The student body at Windsor, about 500 in all, is more than 95 percent African-American. Many schools in the Baltimore area were overcrowded and this was the first middle school the county had built in 22 years. My mom really put a lot of effort into making students feel comfortable at Windsor. The hallways are bright, the windows are big, the walkways are large. It feels like a great place to learn without a stuffy school feeling. If I can gain energy, passion, and inspiration as I get older in a similar fashion as my mom, then I may swim for another seven or eight Olympics.

I had another surprise waiting for me when I got back to Ann Arbor. After years of talk, anticipation, signs in the stands in Barcelona . . . this needs a drum roll . . . I got a dog! After some consultation with Mom, Peter Carlisle gave me a great gift, an English bulldog, exactly the breed I wanted. His name is Herman. He has black and white patches randomly spotted all over his body, and when they adopted him, they must have left his energy in the shop. Herman is allergic to anything strenuous. Most dogs like to run around and tug at their leashes, like they want to explore the world, or at least take over the neighborhood. Herman stands at the corner, looks up at me and pokes his nose in the direction of the front door. Sometimes he'll try to pick up a stick, and when he can't get the stick in his mouth, he'll look up at me as if to say, "Hey Mike, little help!"

I may be a good sleeper, but Herman is the champ. When he's in the zone, or I guess, when he's out of it, a bulldozer can't wake him. There seems to be some sort of magnetic attraction between Herman and my couch. Sometimes I look at him and think, Herman, why don't you just get up and move a little? But that involves the two things he hates the most: getting up and moving. Doctors say sleep is good for a long life, so Herman should be good for a few hundred in dog years.

Herman even got to be a star in a pre-Olympic ad for NBC. They interviewed me in my home in Ann Arbor and at one point showed a graphic that read: "Herman. No medals." Then they had footage of him lying on the couch with me and separate footage of him doing what he does best: snoring. I never met Herman's parents, but I'm sure he'd make them proud.

In March, Whitney gave birth to a daughter named Taylor. How does Uncle Michael sound? Taylor is adorable. Whatever issues I used to have with random people asking me to hold their babies for pictures don't apply to my niece. I feel completely comfortable as an uncle. Taylor is really ticklish. If you nuzzle her cheek, it's hard for her to stop laughing. She also does some very creative things with her food, which only occasionally finds its way into her mouth. I guess I'm easily amused, but she gets this look when she tosses a piece of cheese onto the floor that just cracks me up. It's a very different look from the one Whitney has that seems to say, "Michael, stop encouraging her." Sorry, but I just can't help myself.

It's impossible to keep a poker face around Taylor. I've had practice. Poker has kind of become my downtime game of choice. Maybe someday when I'm done swimming I'll play in the World Series of Poker. First I have to work on my poker face. If I just study Herman long enough. . . .

I'm trying to understand more about investments, and I have a financial advisor who handles a lot of my money. One morning, my advisor gave me a chart with my investments, gains, losses, and taxes for the year. I didn't understand all of it, so I brought it to practice and Bob's eyes got really big. It was either good news or bad news.

"Well, is it good?" I asked.

"Ah, yeah," he said. "You made 23 percent."

I should have waited until after practice. Bob was on my butt all day. No problem, Coach. I'll teach you about portfolios.

Bob started racing one of his horses, a two-year-old he named Vanderkaay. I needed clarification about the name. Our conversation went something like this:

"Hey, Bob, I've been with you longer than Pete. How come you didn't name a horse after me?"

"Michael, that's a lot of pressure to put on a horse. That's a lot to live up to."

"Bob, it's a horse. Think he knows the difference?"

"Well, it's a polite, obedient, well-behaved horse. When I find one who bites me, I'll call him Phelps."

"Thanks, Bob."

The fall wasn't exactly vacation time, but it was time away from competitions when Bob and I could work on things for the pre-Olympic year. I usually show up just grouchy enough so Bob won't speak to me for a good half hour. It's our answer to library time and, believe me, that silence is golden.

I got some disappointing news in November when Ian Thorpe announced his retirement from swimming. I had to be happy for Ian if he was at peace with the decision, but I'll always regret not having a chance to race him after Athens. He was the champ in the 200 free and I owed him a debt of thanks for being so good in that race and pushing me by setting a standard of exceptional freestyle swimming. When I won that race in Montreal, it wasn't the same without him and I hoped I'd get to race him on his home soil in Australia.

In order to get ready for the early World Championships in March, we started with competitions in December. I started the season with a thud at the U.S. Open outside Indianapolis. On the first night, I was disqualified for a false start in the 200 back and two days later Club Wolverine's 400 free relay was DQ'd for the same thing. Two DQs in one meet!

The day after Christmas, we left for an altitude camp in La Loma, Mexico, an isolated place ideal for training. We had breathtaking sunsets and ate eggs at so many meals, I never wanted to see a hen again. With Melbourne Worlds only two months away, Bob wanted me to test my endurance and challenge myself as much as possible. We did that with a new twist at the Southern California Grand Prix, a three-day meet in Long Beach, where the races were contested in yards. The first couple days were fairly standard. On Saturday, I won the 100- and 500-yard freestyles. The next night I won a 400-yard IM and lost to Brendan in a 200 breast, which is definitely his race and a good test for me to see how close I can stay to him. But on Monday, Bob was on brainstorm overdrive, trying to toughen me up as we got ready for Worlds. The meet schedule included 100-meter finals in the butterfly, backstroke, and breaststroke, all within 41 minutes, with world record holders in each event scheduled to swim. That's three races against a murderer's row of Crocker, Peirsol, and Hansen, with barely enough time to get out of the pool, get a lactate test and jump back in. "So," says Bob, "why not race all three of them?" This was an easy call for Bob, since he was easily accessible from Ann Arbor by Blackberry, but not by flung tomatoes or slung torpedoes at poolside.

At 5:45 that night, I jumped in for the fly, finishing in 46.05, well behind Ian, who took it out fast and had me put away at the turn. Then at 6:26, I finished second to Brendan in my worst stroke. Even though the races were in yards, which I don't swim as often as meters, I still swam best times in the events I didn't win. Afterward, my legs felt more tired than my arms, but I was happy about the experiment because I knew I felt fit. I called Bob to tell him what happened. He could hear a good energy in my voice, but I still had to give him a little bit of a hard time.

After we discussed race details, he asked, "So, did you miss me over there?"

"Um, no, not really," I told him. "Stay home anytime."

Bob was away again for the first part of the Missouri Grand Prix in February, my last meet before Worlds. Jon Urbanchek was there and was doing his best Bowman, firing me up before my first race, the 200 fly. Jon was watching other swimmers lower their PRs and told me it was my turn. I reminded Jon that we still hadn't started our taper and world records would probably have to wait until next month at Worlds. I was even wearing a goatee and had some long hair sticking out of my cap. "Okay," he said, "but why not get one tonight anyway?" You can't argue with Jon. He is as nonconfrontational as Bob can be exacting, combative, a pain in . . . well, if you ask Jon why he is the way he is, he'll start talking about butterflies. "Chasing happiness is like chasing a butterfly," he'll say. "If you go after it, it will get away from you, but if you wait for it calmly and patiently, it will land on your shoulder." Of course if you ask Jon about Bob, he'll tell you, "Bob is the one person who can reach out and snatch the butterfly anyway." You know, I've never heard Bob use a butterfly analogy.

Anyway, Jon was right. I broke the 200 fly world record for the fifth time, lowering the mark to 1:53.71. At first I actually misread the clock and couldn't understand why the crowd was making so much noise over a 1:57. Then I took a second look and started to celebrate. I was feeling strong and ready to have a great meet in Melbourne. All the weight work, the patience Bob preached about my back, the heavy race load, the great training at Michigan, and the bad taste in my mouth from the last World Championship had me feeling as well prepared for any meet I had ever swum.

And now, I was able to share that feeling as never before. In February, a group of us from the swim community started a cool website called Swimroom. Anyone can join and communicate with each other or some of their favorite swimmers. There are videos, podcasts, forums, places to buy souvenirs, event listings, and regular blogs from a lot of us on the national team. And it isn't limited to swimmers. Laura Wilkinson, the 10-meter diving gold medalist from Sydney, has a regular blog, too. It's another great way to help grow the sport and get people psyched up about swimming.

33

ON TOP OF
THE WORLDS

I felt great coming into Worlds, knowing that since the last ones in Montreal, I had accomplished the little things I needed to do to get better. As if I needed more motivation, Australian coach Don Talbot, who usually has the words to provide some, told a Melbourne newspaper that Ian Thorpe's accomplishments still outranked mine. "Thorpe's still number one in my opinion," Talbot said. "Phelps doesn't outdo him yet."

On the first day of the championships, I led off for our 400 free relay. At most championships I was ready to be shot out of a cannon. I swam an easy leg of 48.42 that gave us a good lead. Neil, Cullen, and Jason, the same three I'd swum with at Pan Pacs, brought us in ahead of the Aussies for our first gold. The result tied me with Ian for most world golds in a career with 11, but I was just happy to get off to a better start than I had in Montreal. At least I swam in a final on the first day this time.

Talbot had more to say: "The Americans want to claim they invented Jesus Christ before he came, and the same with Phelps. They were saying he was the greatest in the world when Thorpey was the thing." I mean what is up with this guy? I know you want to stick up for your swimmer, but could you say some of these things a little more diplomatically?

My next final was the 200 free, a race in which I had hoped to compete against Ian, because he had won it with such a great swim in Athens. Bob and I had spent a lot of time studying Ian's technique. We worked on a really effective underwater dolphin kick, which Bob says is a good thing because the more time I spend underwater at practice, the less he has to listen to me. He also spent time correcting what he called "a little gallop" in my technique, which was essentially wasted up-and-down energy. Now was the time to put that extra work to the test.

Pieter van den Hoogenband was in lane four because he had swum the fastest time in the semis and I wanted to get a jump on him. I turned first at 24.17 and 51 flat at the first two walls and each time I could see from lane five that Pieter was barely off my shoulder. I started to open up the lead to four-tenths by the third wall and could sort of hear the crowd start to buzz. On the scoreboard in Melbourne, a superimposed red line followed the race along at world-record pace, so fans could see how close the leader was to breaking the existing mark. The crowd obviously sensed that I was close to Ian's 1:44.06 mark he had set at the 2001 worlds in Fukuoka, where he and I appeared in the same headlines for the first time.

I had a good turn and lost sight of Pieter, who started to fade on the last lap. I took my goggles off as I hit the wall, looked up to see the time and let out a safari sound effect. There it was: 1:43.86. I knew I had a chance to set records in other races and I felt I could swim a best time in this one, but this was the sweetest individual record I had ever set. As we were waiting for our medals, Pieter told me on the stand he was sure the record would last for a decade and asked me what my PR had been. When I told him 1:45, he rolled his eyes. I had never felt this sharp.

Coming off that race, I was more confident about setting another record in the 200 fly the next night. The funny thing was I had a lousy warm-up. My arms felt sore and I only swam for four laps before jumping out of the warm-up pool. I was hoping I just needed some time to get loose, so I moved around more than usual in the ready room. Maybe it was just nervous energy, but I let it out in the pool. I was about a second ahead at 100 and almost two seconds at 150. Unlike the 200 free, this felt like a record pretty early in the race. I touched in 1:52.09, three seconds ahead of China's Wu Peng in second and 1.7 seconds better than my race in Victoria.

Wow! 1.7 seconds. I felt giddy. It felt like I was 12 years old, lopping whole seconds off my best times. Back then my safari yells were more like screeches. Even Bob came by and just smiled at me. That's how good the race was: I shut Bob up. Afterward, Grant Hackett mentioned that I had beaten the red line with my feet. The *Herald Sun*, Australia's largest newspaper, ran my picture across the front page with the headline: "Greatest."

The ease was gone by the next night. I swam the 200 IM against Ryan and Hungary's Laszlo Cseh, who always gives me a good race. I was half a second ahead of Ryan going into the last leg, the freestyle, when my goggles started sliding off my eyes. I couldn't see Ryan or Laszlo at all during the freestyle, because my eyes were full of water. Some people thought I was angry because of the way I ripped off my goggles at the finish, but I really just wanted to see the time. It was 1:54.98, .86 seconds better than my time at Pan Pacs. New records, new goggles.

The next day, Bob and I watched a video on the scoreboard of me setting a world record back at the 2001 Worlds. "Wow, how old was I, like 12?" I asked. "More like 10," Bob answered. I really did a double take looking up and seeing that kid on the screen. At those same championships in Japan, the Aussie 800 free relay team set a world record, 7:04.66, that was still standing. Ryan, Klete, Peter, and I had talked about wanting to wipe it off the books. Our relay selections had been pretty consistent over the past few years, so we had a good feel for competing together, pulling for one another, psyching each other up in ready rooms, getting good exchanges at the turns. We felt confident another record could fall.

We didn't want to take anything for granted, but with Ian Thorpe retired and Grant Hackett sitting out the final, we were thinking more about that record than about the other teams. I led off and gave us a lead. Ryan and Klete kept just ahead of the red line and Peter started to pull away from the line on the overhead scoreboard. It's odd to look at that thing, because when you're in the pool, you can go by feel or the sound of the crowd. Sometimes you hear the announcer call out splits, but you can't actually see the line. Still, as one of the early legs of the relay, I was able to follow it throughout Peter's swim. As the line fell past his shoulders, past his back, down to his legs, we started to celebrate. Relays are the best. You don't have to search for someone to hug and high-five; your teammates are right there. Peter came in at 7:03.24 and we had our world record.

One of the best things about watching TV in my hotel room was the international sports coverage that included programming from ESPN. They may have Australian rules football down under, but I could still get some off-season info on the Ravens, even in Melbourne.

One morning I was watching *Around the Horn*, an ESPN show in which writers from different parts of the country debate a topic and a moderator awards each of them points based on the strength of their arguments. It's pretty scripted, since the guys never agree and they pretty much choose opposing viewpoints in order to be controversial and entertaining; but writers can't score points with the moderators without valid opinions.

On the morning I watched, the topic was actually, well, me. J.A. Adande, one of ESPN's correspondents, took a favorable stand for me and for the sport of swimming. His opinions started racking

up more points than the other writers. I loved where the commen-
tators' discussion was headed: *Were my performances a big deal because
of the world records, or did people just not care because swimming wasn't as
popular with the sporting mainstream as baseball, football, or basketball?
Could I be as big as Tiger Woods?*

It wasn't so much that they were talking about me, but that they
were debating the future of swimming. When I think about chang-
ing the sport of swimming, I think about employees standing
around the water cooler at work arguing about whether Phelps will
beat Crocker or Crocker will beat Phelps. I think about people
comparing Spitz to Evans and guessing which world record will
fall next. I think about swimming getting mentioned in newscasts,
comedy skits, movies, variety shows. I think about it going where
it doesn't normally go. Swimming is huge in Australia, and that's
how I'd like it to be in the U.S.

The big news in the Australian swim world was just hitting.
Ian Thorpe had apparently failed a doping test in 2006, when his
test showed an elevated level of testosterone. It didn't make sense.
Ian was always very outspoken against doping. He held a press
conference to deny wrongdoing. With the respect I had and still
have for him and his place in the sport, I could only support him.

I really looked forward to the next showdown against Ian
Crocker in the fly. With the Australian Ian retired from swimming,
I appreciated having someone to battle in a tough race who could
kick my butt if I wasn't at my best. I swam the semifinal conserva-
tively, but I didn't like qualifying with only the fourth-fastest time
and having to swim in lane six. Ian got out fast, as usual, building a
sizeable lead at the turn. Since he was two lanes over, I couldn't
really tell that his 23.56 was that far ahead of me. Way over in lane
one, Serbia's Milorad Cavic was second in 23.61. At 23.99, I was at
the head of a tightly bunched trail pack, with fourth through seventh less than a tenth behind me. Because of my 200 fly, I usually
finish well in the hundred. I knew I had gained on the field as we

came to the finish, but I had no idea if I'd touched before Ian until I looked at the board. I had to look twice before seeing Phelps at 50.77 and Crocker at 50.82. Unlike my other races, this one didn't send me into a big celebration. Ian and I are such good friends that when he rocks the pool, I want to congratulate him before I deal with my own disappointment. When I do beat him, I respect his disappointment. We patted each other on the head and slowly swam out of the pool.

Afterward, reporters were asking me about making history. With two final swims left on the last night, I had a chance to win eight gold medals. Since the 400 IM was one of my better events and since our medley relay team would be enormous favorites, they talked as if it was in the bag. But I didn't believe that. I never believe there is something I can't do if I work at it, but I also don't take anything for granted. I used the familiar poker analogy that if you're holding pocket aces, the guy next to you can outdraw you with his seven-deuce. I knew anything could happen the next evening. I didn't realize that something would actually happen before the late session started.

With the two finals at night, I wasn't swimming the relay in the morning heats, when our guys just needed to get a qualifying time for the evening final. I won my heat of the 400 IM and thought about the double at night. The guys who had the second-fastest times from our country in the open hundreds of their strokes were set to swim the medley prelims soon after.

Ryan started by giving us a solid 54.07 in the backstroke. Scott Usher jumped in next and gave us an equally good 1:00.84 breaststroke. Ian and Neil followed, getting us what appeared to be the fastest qualifying time. Bob had talked to everyone about getting safe starts, so we wouldn't risk disqualification, and it seemed like everything had gone according to plan, because the team's winning time was posted on the board. "No controversy," Bob remembers saying. "Just the way I like it." We found out later that Ian had taken off four-hundredths before Scott touched the wall. Rules allow for a gap of three-hundredths, so we were disqualified from the evening final. Everyone felt bad for Ian. Mark Schubert, one of our coaches, went over to console him, because he was pretty down. It could have happened anytime to anyone. What can you say except that we'd get it back in Beijing?

A few hours later, I couldn't let myself think about the race I wasn't going to swim. Matt had sent me a text message earlier from home predicting I'd swim the IM in 4:06.40. That was pretty bold, considering it was two full seconds faster than my best time. I had been thinking about the race all week, because, coming at the end of a long week, it was going to be the most physically demanding race, and because I often swim it first rather than last.

Ryan and I basically traded best strokes. I took the lead after the fly and he passed me briefly after the back. We were both under record pace. My breaststroke is probably my most improved stroke, so I slowly started to pull ahead of Ryan. Then came the furious freestyle, my last few strokes when there was no sense thinking about holding back or being sore. I wasn't sure if I was still on pace, but on the last lap, I saw a rare sight soon after I turned: a random spectator jumping and cheering. Was I beating the line—and my best time—again? I got to wall and saw Ryan still swimming in. That stunned me, but not as much as the 4:06.22 on the board.

So I had won my seventh gold medal. Even if I hadn't done it at the Olympics, I had climbed a huge mountain. The Olympics were 16 months away and they couldn't get here fast enough for me.

34

BEIJING BECKONS

It was only appropriate that we stopped in China on the way back from Australia. It was actually one of two trips I had made there during the year. On the first trip, we attended a VISA Friendship Lanes tour to promote swimming and the Special Olympics. I met some amazing kids at some schools in Shanghai. I'm not sure if they knew who I was and whether they really cared, but someone who didn't quite understand what they said was paying attention to them and trying to make friends. That they certainly understood, even without a translator.

We attended a runaway media event in Beijing as part of the tour. I say that because as we were outside our tour bus one day, we were swarmed by over a hundred people with pads, picture cameras, and video cameras. It wasn't so much the numbers of people, but rather the way they fought one another for positioning as we were trying to make our way through the crowd. People shouted, elbowed, and plowed one another over. If only the Ravens were here to take some lessons. Katie was on the tour and started to freak out because of all the congestion. We managed to call in the local police who appeared in force and cleared everyone out in seconds. I guess when the police tell you to disperse in China, you don't question them.

We went out for karaoke one night on the second trip and I'm pretty sure *American Idol* won't be calling for the video. I sang "Sweet Caroline" in a moment that will not be repeated for public viewing again. Peter and Drew each tried their hands at Madonna. The performance was, um, borderline.

Ian, Katie, and I have since started to learn the language using the Rosetta Stone program. Chinese is a lot harder for Americans to try to understand than Spanish or French, which have some similar words you can sort of pick out. I remember *ni-hao*, which means hello. The rest I'm still figuring out.

While I was away, I had friends look after Herman, who didn't seem to miss me as much as I missed him. He was so inspired by my return that he thought about running a few laps around the block, but instead he rolled over and took a nap. Even if Herman didn't care much, it felt good to be among familiar distractions (and new ones). Besides poker and my usual array of video games, I can get pretty caught up in whatever challenge someone puts in front of me. Whoever thought up the Nintendo Wii is a genius. You swing a remote control the way you would a tennis racquet or a golf club and a ball on a video screen reacts to your swing. I played the Tiger Woods golf game the first day I had it for about two hours. The next day at practice, Bob couldn't figure out why my right shoulder was sore. By the end of the day he had banished Wii to the same fate as bowling. Okay, I told Bob, maybe I can try the Wii version of bowling. We're negotiating.

Sadly, a little over a year after losing Gran, I got more bad news about one of my inspirations. Soon after Worlds, I got word that Stevie Hanson's health was failing. I traveled back to see him, but Stevie had already stopped responding when I went to visit him in the hospital. I sat with Stevie's family and one by one, we all talked to him, hoping there was some way he could hear us. I held his hand at his bedside and started talking about the time we played basketball at his house and the day we went to the Baltimore Blast soccer game. "Remember that, Stevie?" I said half out loud. "Remember how much fun we had?" I'm sure he did.

I read a poem at his funeral, but I wished I could tell him how much I admired his strength and spirit in the face of challenges. As I neared the home stretch to the Beijing Games, when I was in need of a role model to inspire me to overcome smaller obstacles with a sense of purpose, I could think of Stevie, who overcame bigger obstacles every day. He believed great things were possible and he helped me believe it, too.

I know I'll carry Stevie's optimism with me to China, no matter how bold the challenge. When reporters asked Mark Spitz what it would be like if I won seven gold medals in Beijing, he told them: "Second man on the moon." When they asked what it would be like if I won eight, he responded, "First man on Mars."

But of course leave it to Bob to grab the article that would set me off like a rocket. Bob was scheming, knowing that somehow he can always count on the Australians to fire me up. He read an article in an Australian paper and was determined not just to show it to me, but to let it get to me. He neatly underlined all the relevant parts of the story he thought I could use for motivation. The article quotes Ian Thorpe, who was asked about my prospects for winning seven or eight gold medals in Beijing. "I don't think he'll do it, but I'd love to see it," Ian says. "There's a thing called competition. There won't just be one athlete competing and in a lot of events he has strong competition."

I then took the article and taped it to my locker. Whenever I look inside the locker each morning after arriving at the pool, the underlined story is the very first thing I see.

If I'm dragging trying to accomplish what I need to do, I think about Gran, about Stevie, and about Ian's words. Then I train a little harder. I'm grateful for the doubters and believers, and I'm especially grateful for the wonderful family, friends, and supporters of an amazing sport who have given me a chance to turn doubters into believers.